Boxes and Bullets: Personal and Persuasive Essays

Lucy Calkins, Kelly Boland Hohne, and Cory Gillette

Photography by Peter Cunningham

HEINEMANN ◆ PORTSMOUTH, NH

This book is dedicated to Patrick. Without you none of this would be possible. —Kelly

This book is dedicated to Mary Ann, my lifesaver. —Lucy

This book is dedicated to Joanie Gillette. I miss you every day, but your voice in my head is always there. —Cory

*first*hand
An imprint of Heinemann
361 Hanover Street
Portsmouth, NH 03801–3912
www.heinemann.com

Offices and agents throughout the world

© 2013 by Lucy Calkins and Kelly Boland Hohne

Cataloging-in-Publication data is on file with the Library of Congress.

ISBN-13: 978-0-325-04737-9
ISBN-10: 0-325-04737-5

Production: Elizabeth Valway, David Stirling, and Abigail Heim
Cover and interior designs: Jenny Jensen Greenleaf
Series includes photographs by Peter Cunningham, Nadine Baldasare, and Elizabeth Dunford
Composition: Publishers' Design and Production Services, Inc.
Manufacturing: Steve Bernier

Printed in the United States of America on acid-free paper
17 16 15 14 13 VP 2 3 4 5

Acknowledgments

FIRST AND FOREMOST, we are grateful to Kate Montgomery, who spent time with us to develop the storyline of this unit. She was our sounding board, and her ability to see the forest for the trees helped us to create a unit that is clear and straight.

We are grateful, also, to all of the teachers who piloted versions of this unit—the hundreds of classrooms where teachers tried out new work, the leadership groups and think tanks and advanced summer institute sections that have convened around essay writing over the past few years—thank you for your feedback and ideas. This book stands on the shoulders of the teaching and learning we have done together. We thank especially Liz Ryan, Robyn Scher, and Stephanie Parsons.

A project such as this requires enormous behind-the-scenes work, and there are a few people who we want to thank in particular. This book brims with the photography of Peter Cunningham, who so beautifully can capture moments in time and childhood, and we thank him for his art. We are grateful to Teva Blair for her thoughtful editing and advice and to Abby Heim for her meticulous production design. Sarah Fournier handled all of the student work and art, and we thank her for helping us to show the journey of this unit. We are grateful, also, to all of those at Heinemann who spent tireless hours bringing this book into the world.

As with all the units in this series, the class described in this unit is a composite class, with children and partnerships of children gleaned from classrooms in very different contexts, then put together here. We wrote the units this way to bring you both a wide array of wonderful, quirky, various children and also to illustrate for you the predictable (and unpredictable) situations and responses this unit has created in classrooms across the nation and world.

From Cory: I am particularly grateful to Lucy and Kathleen, my professional mentors, who raised me in this work and taught me how to be a leader. Thank you both for always seeing more in me than I saw in myself. I am who I am today as a teacher and learner because of all the amazing people I have had the opportunity to work with through TCRWP over the years. I have to add a special thank you to Brooke, my other professional half, who has been my faithful companion in the daily ups and downs of this work, and to Stephanie and Jenny, my constant colleagues. I was so lucky to embark on this project with writer extraordinaire Kelly Boland. I could not have asked for a better partner.

I also want to thank Jack and Joanie Gillette, my parents, my first and most influential teachers, and Jeremy and Jasmine, who bring joy to me even on the stormiest of days. Thanks for cheering me on, dancing in the living room, and making me laugh 'til I cry.

From Kelly: I want to thank my former coteacher, Carla Miragliotta, for exploring the teaching of essay writing with me for all those years, helping me to try out new ideas and revise my thinking. She never failed to push me to be better.

I want to thank my coauthors, first for their original book and second for all their help and support through the process of revision. I was so lucky to have their expert guidance. I thank Cory Gillette, for always being willing to plan and talk things through and for teaching and leading in ways that I so admire. I thank Lucy Calkins for pushing me to do more than I thought I could, for her critical eye, and her ability to always see what is best for children. The community of practice that she has created within the Teachers College Reading and Writing Project has been my source of inspiration from the start.

Contents

BEND III Personal to Persuasive

Welcome to the Unit

THIS UNIT OF STUDY is designed to help students with the difficult and exhilarating work of learning to write well within an expository structure. This unit stands on the shoulders of a book from the former Units of Study for Teaching Writing, Grades 3–5 series, *Breathing Life into Essays*. That unit has been revised here to match the demands of the Common Core State Standards, to better develop an approach to essay writing that can transfer across the curriculum, and to help students write on-demand, structured, thesis-driven essays when necessary, including on standardized tests. More than this, the unit has been revised to reflect our teaching of it for eight years in hundreds more classrooms. In addition, while the unit has always supported transference and application of learning and raising the cognitive demand put on students, that emphasis has been brought out and articulated more explicitly in this iteration. Students are held more accountable than before for accumulating and drawing upon prior learning, and they are charged with developing even greater independence.

The unit aligns with and exceeds the Common Core's expectations for fourth-grade opinion writing. In the third-grade opinion writing unit, your students learned to introduce topics clearly and to provide facts and details to support their thinking (W.4.1a,b). Now, in this unit, you will help them learn a variety of more sophisticated strategies for introducing their topics, and you'll teach them to provide reasons to support their opinions, as well as facts and details to elaborate on these reasons.

One of the major shifts in opinion writing from fourth to fifth grade is in the area of logic and organization (W.5.1). Fifth-graders must create pieces that are organized logically as well as provide logically ordered reasons. By sixth grade, students will be writing arguments—in which the logic, relevance, and sufficiency of the evidence matters. Although this is a fourth-grade unit,

you take a big step toward teaching some of this critical work now, showing students different ways they can arrange their reasons and evidence.

This unit does not attempt to take on the job of teaching students everything about essay writing, but rather it focuses on teaching a few key qualities of that kind of writing. For now, in this unit, you teach children to collect evidence, but it isn't yet research evidence and it does not yet involve quotations from texts. Those skills are instead taught in the literary essay unit later this year and in the fifth-grade research-based argument essay. Instead, this unit places an emphasis on the more foundational aspects of this kind of writing: structure and elaboration. The need to write a well-organized piece is stressed from Day One. In addition, as students develop their essays, they learn to include and elaborate on a variety of evidence. Later, once the form of essay writing is well in hand, students will take up writing about more generalized topics for which they will need to gather outside evidence and to consider how both the content and form of their piece supports their point.

Some people—especially writing workshop purists—may question the rationale for teaching students to write within a traditional thesis-driven essay structure. They may say, "But Thoreau and Wadsworth and E.B. White didn't write within a thesis-driven structure. Their essays didn't have a claim and supports." It is true that many published essays do not follow a template like this and that they are more like ruminations.

Still, supporting students to work within a more traditional essay structure is important. If we simply show children rich, complex, finished publications and say, "Have at it! Write like this!" some children will progress with remarkable success and many, many others will not. We believe that by reducing some of the complexity of finished essays, by showing students moves that are well within their reach, we can invite youngsters to explore this important work. Just as we ask beginning readers to point underneath words as they read and only later tell them that, actually, pointing under the words is not necessary or even forever helpful, so too, we can teach children to write explicit thesis statements and topic sentences and only later point out that, actually, essayists often write toward main ideas that are implied but not explicitly stated.

Another reason for teaching children to write traditional thesis-driven essays is that this is a structure that real-world writers do rely on often. Chapters in nonfiction books, in professional development books for teachers, for example, often pose an idea and then elaborate on that idea in parallel categories, each introduced by a subhead. Many speeches, grant applications, persuasive letters, and editorials rely upon this fundamental structure.

Then, too, when children learn that they can, if they so choose, think and write according to what we call a "boxes-and-bullets" format, this helps them construct a mental model comprised of main ideas and support information as they read expository texts and as they take notes on books and class lectures. Finally, in middle school and high school and on standardized tests, this is the form of writing that children will rely upon most. They will need to write in this form with speed and finesse while also carrying a heavy cargo of disciplinary ideas and information. In most secondary schools, students receive very little instruction in this challenging kind of writing before they are assigned to write an expository essay on a book or topic. Secondary school teachers, often responsible for well over a hundred students, assign and grade this kind of writing but rarely teach it.

The unit aligns with and exceeds the Common Core's expectations for fourth-grade opinion writing. The work of the unit builds directly on the work of the third-grade opinion writing unit, in which students learned to introduce topics clearly and began to provide facts and details to support their thinking—fourth-grade expectations for opinion writing (W.4.1a,b). Now, in this unit, they will continue to introduce their topics clearly to readers through a variety of more sophisticated strategies, and they will provide reasons to support their opinions and facts and details to elaborate on these reasons. They will also learn to create pieces that are more cohesive by incorporating more sophisticated transition words. And they will learn strategies to conclude their pieces in ways that follow from the pieces themselves. Across the unit students will engage in writing pieces quickly, in on-demand situations,

and will develop longer pieces across a sustained amount of time, work that pushes them to meet the range-of-writing standard in fourth grade (4.10). And they will learn strategies for each part of the writing process to help them to strengthen their writing with guidance from adults and peers, work that is expected by standard W.4.5.

Yet this unit exceeds the expectations for fourth-grade opinion writing. One of the major shifts in opinion writing from fourth to fifth grade is in the area of logic and organization (W.5.1). Fifth-graders must create pieces that are organized logically as well as provide logically ordered reasons. This expectation pushes fifth-graders to take the first step toward writing arguments, when the logic, relevancy, and sufficiency of the evidence is what matters. This unit directly tackles this critical work, showing students multiple ways to arrange their reasons and evidence and supporting them in seeing that deliberate intention in organization is key to a successful argument.

Boxes and Bullets also works to support students in meeting several key Common Core State Standards in Language for fourth-graders. In addition to supporting multiple conventions of language through editing lessons, the unit also is focused on a key Knowledge of Language Standard, Standard 4.3a, which expects that students will choose words and phrases to convey ideas precisely. This is a standard that the authors of the Common Core have designated as being particularly challenging and one that may require being taught across grades. You will see that this unit repeatedly returns to pushing students to do the work of conveying their ideas precisely. In addition, the unit is focused on supporting students in spelling grade-appropriate words correctly, another key language standard in fourth grade (4.2d), and correcting spelling fragments and run-on sentences (4.1f).

OVERVIEW OF THE UNIT

This unit, like a number of other units in this series, begins with a quick intense immersion into the whole process of writing this new kind of text. The goal for "essay boot camp," as the opening days of the unit are called, is to help students develop a sense for what it feels like to write a whole essay. The students first work together as a class to construct a simple class essay by "writing-in-the-air" together, and then they go off to flash-draft the spoken essay onto paper.

Then, students will spend the next few days gathering entries in their notebooks, writing long about ideas about people, objects, events, and so on. To raise the level of this work, students will engage in an inquiry into what makes for strong freewriting and will look at mentor examples of this. They will also look back at their previous writing and reflect on ideas lying between the lines and create new writing from this reflection. As the bend ends, students will use what they've written in their notebooks to develop thesis statements, and they will build plans for their essays.

In the next bend, or part, of the unit—"Raising the Level of Essay Writing"—students will write out the evidence to support the reasons for their opinion. One option for organizing this evidence is for students to set up folders in which to collect evidence for two of their reasons. They will collect mini-stories to support reasons as well as lists and then organize this evidence by selecting the most powerful and revising it to angle all information to support their reasons. They will construct a draft of these two sections of their essay, using transition words and phrases to create cohesion. Students can then decide on the system that is best for them to develop their third reason. As they take themselves through the process of constructing the third section of their essay, they will also learn to use the introduction of a piece to orient and engage the reader and the conclusion to provide final related thinking. They will self-assess to determine how much they have grown from their on-demand and will revise with goals in mind. Students will correct for clarity, such as finding and correcting run-on sentences and sentence fragments, and share their work in a mini-celebration.

Bend III of the unit, "Personal to Persuasive," is about transference and raising the quality of work. Students will develop persuasive opinions that are more generalized and develop a plan for a persuasive essay. They will then be charged with taking themselves through the process of developing and drafting this essay with greater independence, transferring and applying all they have learned and all the resources, tools, charts, and so on at hand. They will learn to include a greater variety of evidence, such as outside evidence, and revise not only this current piece but all of their essays by elaborating on how that evidence connects to their reason and opinion. They will again self-assess, reflecting on their growth across the unit and setting future goals. Students will edit using all they have learned about conventions and, in particular, ensure that all grade-appropriate words are spelled correctly. They will publish their pieces in a final celebration.

ASSESSMENT

Prior to launching the unit, you will want to assess your students' grasp of opinion writing. One way to do so is to ask students to write in response to an opinion prompt. We recommend the following prompt, found in the *Writing Pathways: Performance Assessments and Learning Progressions, K–5* book:

"Think of a topic or issue that you know and care about, an issue around which you have strong feelings. Tomorrow, you will have forty-five minutes to write an opinion or argument text in which you will write your opinion or claim and tell reasons why you feel that way. When you do this, draw on everything you know about essays, persuasive letters, and reviews. If you want to find and use information from a book or another outside source, you may bring that with you tomorrow. Please keep in mind that you'll have forty-five minutes to complete this, so you will need to plan, draft, revise, and edit in one sitting. In your writing, make sure you:
- Write an introduction
- State your opinion or claim
- Give reasons and evidence
- Organize your writing·
- Acknowledge counterclaims
- Use transition words
- Write a conclusion"

This on-demand task will give you vital information about students' current strengths in terms of their knowledge of persuasive writing as a genre—its purpose, craft, and structure. You and your students will be able to assess these on-demand pieces against a checklist, or students can lay them out and describe to each other what they already know how to do as writers that they'll carry into this unit. The Opinion/Argument Writing Learning Progression can guide your assessment of this work. You can look at the rubric for fourth grade, noting which students meet grade level expectations (a level 4 on the rubric) and which students fall below (levels 3 and 2) or exceed (level 5) expectations.

We suggest gathering with your grade team, each of you bringing pieces of writing that represent the levels found in your classrooms. Then, as a grade level team, you can create a set of pieces representative of each level. Assigning an exact level for each student is not as important as the conversations you have about the work, which will enable you to align your vision as a grade. With this anchor set of papers, you can then go back to quickly assess the rest of your students' work. All of this information will help you plan predictable small groups for your advanced writers as well as those who need extra support.

In addition, the Opinion/Argument Writing Learning Progression can offer next steps for teaching, and the checklists that align to the progression can help your students to self-assess, set goals, and develop action plans. You will see that across the unit, there are opportunities for students to check their own progress, holding their pieces against the checklist, asking, "How am I getting better? What can I do to push myself to get even stronger?"

You will see that this unit essentially teaches students two types of writing—the analytical freewriting that is the work of the first bend and then the more formal essays. Because of this, the Opinion/Argument Writing Learning Progression is not incorporated as much in the first bend as it is in the first bends of other units of study. Asking students to assess their freewriting by looking for qualities of effective opinion writing would not be helpful to them because freewriting is not expected to have these qualities! Instead, you will see that the third session supports students in doing an inquiry into what makes for effective freewriting, which is itself an assessment because they will take what they are noticing and apply it to their work.

Once the students have developed a draft, they will assess this draft with the Opinion/Argument Writing Checklist. Students will be asked to write quick essays for homework at a few points across the unit and to assess these as well as their longer published pieces. We have noted places where this homework is particularly important because students will spend the first part of the next day assessing this work in class.

The checklists students will use have two columns—one for grade 4 expectations and one for grade 5 expectations. This checklist is meant to be a tool to hold them accountable, not to teach them new work, so you will see that many lessons teach toward meeting fifth-grade standards. Another reason for the double-column checklist is that you may have students who are already meeting some expectations for fifth grade, and by giving them this checklist, you are helping to meet the needs of the range of learners in your room. (Of course, this means that some of your learners may also need to revisit the checklist for third-grade opinion writing, but you won't want to settle for that level of work!) All of this information will help you plan predictable small groups for your advanced writers as well as those who need extra support.

At the end of the unit, you'll probably give the performance assessment again. You can give the same task on a different topic with a different text set. We've found, though, that there is something very powerful for children in doing it again, with the same texts, and then laying their two pieces alongside each other and marking them up, annotating them, and showing off their new skills. It's easier to see the new work when the research was the same.

GETTING READY

Getting ready for this unit mainly involves gathering your own demonstration writing. Across this unit we have provided samples of demonstration writing that you could use, but your teaching will be more effective if students see you engaged in this process alongside them. Thus, before the unit starts, we highly encourage you to sit with your grade team, one of you taking the role of teacher, and work through the teaching points of the lessons quickly, doing your own writing. The writing you gather can thread through all of your lessons, but more importantly, you will get a sense of the work of the unit, including the challenges of the unit and how you can better support your students through these. To be responsive on the spot to what students need, as models of teacher effectiveness are calling for, each teacher needs a sense of the pathway of learning. Doing your own writing can help provide that sense of the pathway and will allow you to make choices about how to help all of your learners along that pathway.

Essay Structure Boot Camp

IN THIS SESSION, you'll teach children that writers use an essay frame to help structure their writing. You will give writers a vision for what they are working to create by the end of the unit.

THE OBJECTIVE

GETTING READY

✔ A sample student essay written by your previous students or other students over the years to show as a model of an exemplar essay (see Figures A, B, and C on the CD)

✔ Your own thesis statement, "I love ice cream," written on chart paper, in a box, with three bullets underneath (see Teaching)

✔ Three possible reasons to support the thesis statement "I love ice cream" in mind to help you as you guide and support students

✔ Essay frame outline written on chart paper (see Teaching)

✔ A pack of loose-leaf paper, enough for everyone in the class to write a quick essay or "flash draft"

✔ Enough sharpened pencils or pens that there will be no excuse for your students to stop writing

✔ The Opinion Writing Checklist, Grades 3 and 4 written on chart paper (see Share)

✔ Copies of the Opinion Writing Checklist, Grades 3 and 4 for your students to use to assess their on-demands

✔ Copies of the students' on-demand pieces for them to self-assess and revise

✔ Loose-leaf paper for writers to use to write brand-new revisions drafts of their on-demand pieces

COMMON CORE STATE STANDARDS: W.4.1, W.4.4, W.4.5, W.4.10, RI.4.1, RI.4.2, SL.4.1, SL.4.3, L.4.1, L.4.2, L.4.3

A VERSION OF THIS UNIT was written five years ago and published as *Breathing Life into Essays* from the Units of Study for Teaching Writing, Grades 3–5. Since then, literally thousands and thousands of teachers have taught the unit, using that edition as a guide. This new edition stands on the shoulders not only of the former one, but also of all the subsequent teaching yet it is different in substantial ways. Today's minilesson is entirely new and reflects the realization that for children who are new to writing essays, structuring expository texts is more complicated than one could imagine. And in an essay, without structure, one has nothing.

So this lesson is a down-and-dirty, brass-tacks attempt to provide all students with what I have tended to call "essay boot camp." There is nothing fancy or artsy about the work of today. This won't be a day when you teach students to live like writers, carrying their notebooks with them everywhere, seeing the world as brim full of potential essays. That lesson and others like it will come soon—but for now, your goal will be to teach students strategies that will help them structure their essay writing, a Common Core State Standard expectation for all fourth- and fifth-grade opinion writing. The lesson begins with an assigned topic and then puts the students through the routine of learning a disciplined way of writing a very basic essay. The topic is a relatively mindless one, and that isn't a mistake. Because this work is challenging and rigorous (fitting our thinking into boxes and bullets is not easy), every possible complication has been reduced to focus students' attention—and yours—on the fundamental infrastructure that undergirds the simplest, most accessible sort of essays.

You may be thinking that true essayists don't write in such a formulaic fashion, nor do they write bland, voiceless texts. I agree. However, I also know from experience that learning this basic structure of essay writing is an important skill for communicating clearly and serves as a foundation for students to build on as they write increasingly sophisticated essays. It took years of trying to teach a fancier kind of essay to come to grips with the fact that many youngsters need to follow the advice of Julie Andrews, when teaching the von Trapp family to sing, to start at the very beginning, which, as she assured them, is a very good place to start!

This session is unusual not just because you have all kids writing on one topic and in a rather prescriptive way, but also

---

"This lesson is a down-and-dirty, brass-tacks attempt to provide all students with what we call 'essay boot camp.'"

because the minilesson does not follow the usual architecture. You do not demonstrate something and then send youngsters off to use what they have learned with independence as they work on their own important writing projects. Instead, today's minilesson "keeps youngsters on the rug" for a long time, engaged in a whole-class piece of shared writing. Much of

your teaching happens through "voiceovers" as you call out prompts and suggestions while your students work. This is teaching through guided practice, not teaching through demonstration. Your students likely experienced a mini-version of the boot camp last year as similar work begins the third-grade unit in opinion writing, *Changing the World*. Those who are familiar with that unit will recall how it starts with a shared experience writing a persuasive speech. Students gain a sense of writing for a real-world audience as well as a sense of how to create an organizational structure that lists reasons as they create speeches about changes they want to see in their school, such as more magazines for the school library. Essay boot camp stands on the shoulders of that previous work, but ramps up the level of expectation.

The work of today's session is somewhat freestanding. It immerses kids in an experience, works on one set of muscles, and then draws a line in the sand, leaving this work behind until Session 6, where writers take their opinions and craft them into a plan for an essay. You may decide to skip this boot camp and alter Session 6 a bit to incorporate some of this instruction into that minilesson. But I think you won't want to do that, and that later, you'll say, "I thank my lucky stars that you suggested we start the unit with 'I love ice cream.'"

Essay Structure Boot Camp

CONNECTION

Support your children's identities as writers by exclaiming over their stories and rallying them into this very grown-up unit on writing essays.

"Writers, when you read aloud your fiction writing at our publishing party, I was amazed at the way your writing took me away to new places—to a grandmother's kitchen, to a playground. Your writing was like a magic carpet, bringing me to new places. Congratulations. Give yourselves a pat on the back." Grinning, the students patted their backs.

"I think you are ready to graduate to some new and very grown-up challenges. In this next unit of study, you'll be writing essays. Do any of you have older brothers and sisters? (Thumbs up if you do.) I'm pretty sure you will have heard about your brother or sister working on essays—because this is a kind of writing that people do a lot when they are in middle school and high school and especially when they are in college.

"If you learn to write essays well, that skill will give *you* a magic carpet, helping you get into great colleges and get scholarships. An ability to write essays well will give *you* a magic carpet that will take you places in life.

"The entries you've collected and the stories you've developed are wonderful—but writers don't just write stories. For the next few weeks, instead of writing *stories*, you will write *essays*. Instead of writing about *small moments* or *scenes*, you will write about *big ideas*."

Show writers an example of a finished essay, helping them to see this with the eyes of soon-to-be essayists.

"This is new work for you, writers. Before anyone starts a new project, it helps to see an example of what they're going to make. When you want to learn to dive, it helps to watch someone else doing the dive you aim to do. You notice the way the diver points her toes as she leaps off the board and the angle with which she hits the water. You watch, thinking, 'I'm going to try to dive in just that way.'

"It is no different when you want to write a new kind of text, a new genre. It helps to study the work of someone who has written that sort of text. So listen and look as I read you an essay written by a writer just your age. As you listen, you'll be thinking, 'I'm going to write in just that kind of a way.' Pay careful attention to the moves this writer makes (see Figure 1–1)."

◆ COACHING

You'll find your own ways to talk about the work your children did in the preceding unit and the effect their published writing had on you and others. Recall times in your own life when your hard work was recognized, and remember the way in which this recognition spurred you to work harder. Your children will work harder for you if you can help them feel that their efforts are recognized. You might be thinking: "Are my students really going to want to pat their own backs?" Try it. You might find that a chance to pat their own backs, give themselves mental high fives, or engage in a quick silent cheer is just the thing your students need to get them engaged and rallied up for the work ahead.

I like beginning a unit by conveying a sense that we're entering a new chapter in children's writing lives. And I do believe that essays are fundamentally different from stories.

Notice that rather than sharing a published essay, I share a child's writing. I'm hoping to show respect for all children by elevating one child in this way. Also, the essays by authors like E. B. White and John McPhee are far more complex than those that children can write, while this essay resembles those I'll ask children to write.

① A True Friend

No other relationship is like my greatgrandmothers relationship with me. I really understand her, I could tell her anything, and everytime I saw her I felt happy.

The first reason my greatgrandmother Evelyne was special to me is because I felt like I was the only one who really understood her. An example of that is when, one day I went to her house. Everyone was getting ready for dinner. I noticed my greatgrandmother Evelyne, just sitting alone at the dinner table. I sat down next to her. My aunt came over. She asked grandma,

"What... do... you... want... to... eat... for... din...ner?"

Why is she talking like that to greatgrandma? Just because she is old doesn't mean that she is stupid, I thought to myself. My grandma didn't reply. This time I asked her, but now I would ask anyone.

"Grandma what do you want to eat for dinner?"

② "Whatever you are eating Sophie". She said softly. I felt that if only everyone talked to her like that, maybe she would feel normal. She could tell that I really understood her.

I really understood her because we talked to eachother. I really understood her because we listened to eachother. I really understood her because we spent time with eachother, sometimes you can get to know somebody without words.

Not only did I understand her, but I knew I could tell her anything. An example of that is when, one day at school I wasn't happy. Someone was bullying me. So I went to my greatgrandmothers house, I sat down next to her. I put my hand on her hand. I told her what had happened. When she answered, she always made me feel like I was right. She never said, "Just stay away from him" or "Just ignore him he'll stop". She always listened carefully, and she would say,

③ "You're right sophie you're doing the right thing." When she told me that I forgot about why I was angry.

I could tell her anything because we didn't tell eachothers secrets. I could tell her anything because we understood eachothers problems. I could tell her anything because we didn't judge eachother. Everyone should have somebody in their life they can tell anything to.

Perhaps the most important reason why she was special was because when I saw her I felt happy. I felt happy when I saw her on Chanaka. It was a time when everyone was together. I felt happy when I saw her on thanksgiving because when we said our thanks she always prayed for me. I felt happy when I saw her on her birthday because everyone was there and peacefull.

An example of how she makes me feel happy is, one day I just woke up on the wrong side of the bed. I was very cranky that day. I went

④ to my greatgrandmothers house. I slumped on the couch. I heard my great grandmothers voice, "Sophie" she said "Why the long face?" She sat down next to me.

"I'm just tired that's all!" I said.

"Okay do you want something" she said, "I'm okay!" I said to her. I put my head on her sholder. I could tell that she was trying to make me feel better. I smiled, I realized that because of my greatgrandmother I was feeling good. I am always happy when I see my greatgrandmother Evelyne. Every minute of the world is special when you have somebody to comfort

Although I can't spend time with her anymore, the memories I have of times we spent together are so precious. Just because she isn't actually here, doesn't mean I don't feel her with me. As Martin Luther King Jr. said "Love is the key to the problems of the world." I know that the

⑤ love that we shared help solve our problems. I will meet many other people in my life but nobody will ever take her place.

FIG. 1–1 Sophie's A True Friend is one possibility for an essay that can serve as a model for what your students will create.

Establish the reason for today's lesson: Writers need the chance to practice unfamiliar writing structures.

"Writers, today, we are not going to have a typical minilesson where I teach you something, you try it, and then you go off to work independently. Because I want to give you a feeling in your bones for what it's like to write an essay, instead of a typical minilesson, we'll do some shared writing-in-the-air, working together to write a flash-draft essay that you'll then each write onto paper. Last year you probably worked to write a shared speech to make a change in the school, arguing for a cause such as getting more magazines for the school library. This time, instead of a shared speech, we're all going to work together to write a shared essay. As we do this, I especially want you to learn about how writers structure, or organize, essays."

❖ **Name the teaching point.** *This is the target.*

"Today, I want to teach you that when writers write essays about their opinions, they structure their essays so that they communicate their thesis statement—their idea—and their reasons for their thesis statement. Sometimes writers refer to this as 'boxes and bullets.'"

TEACHING

Teach through guided practice. Take children through multiple cycles: channel them to plan with a partner, then to write-in-the-air while you coach, then elicit their work while you add comments, then repeat the cycle, with children now working from the growing shared draft.

Give children a thesis statement and channel them to generate reasons.

"Usually when writers write essays, they start by making opinions of their own, but for today, we're all going to work with an opinion that I hope most of us share: I love ice cream." I revealed chart paper on which I'd written the thesis statement inside a box. Adding bullets under the box, I said, "Right now, think of reasons to support this thesis statement. To do this, what many writers do is they say the claim to themselves like this: 'I love ice cream because . . . A. I love ice cream because . . . B. And most of all, I love ice cream because . . . C.' What will reason A be? B? C? What's one reason you love ice cream?" For a minute, the room was quiet. "Thumbs up if you have a reason."

David pitched in, "It's fun to add different toppings?"

Nodding, I repeated, "I love ice cream because you can add different toppings." Then I said, "Everyone, we'll use David's reason as our first bullet." I added it below the box and touched the additional bullets as if nudging children to add their own reasons alongside them. "With your partner, repeat the thesis statement and write-in-the-air your three reasons. Start by saying, 'I love ice cream because . . .' and take David's reason as your own."

Here you'll notice we're harkening back to the work described in the third-grade opinion writing unit, Changing the World. *Whenever possible we want to remind students of the work they have already done so as to make it easier and more likely for them to not only transfer and apply that work but to build on it.*

You may be thinking that "I love ice cream" cannot be called a thesis statement. And eventually, of course, we want students to move toward writing more complex thesis statements that do not just state an opinion but that can be argued for, anticipating counterclaims and counterevidence. But, just as we call a child's first attempt at writing poetry—with just a couple lines of text—a poem, so too do we want to call initial atttempts at thesis writing a thesis statement. We want to instill in children a sense of what they are working toward. Soon they will be asked to write thesis statements and to develop them with strong reasons and evidence. Therefore, we think it is prudent to start using the language of essay writing today, when the stakes are low.

Coach with lean prompts that raise the level of what individuals do. Then convene the class, collect suggestions for the next portion of the shared essay, and synthesize them into the frame for a shared essay.

As the room erupted into talk, I listened and coached, "You can use your fingers to help you." I illustrated by reading off one child's work, raising a finger each time I cited another reason.

After a bit, I reconvened the class. "We will use the bullets the way some of us use fingers—to list reasons." Pointing to the second bullet, I said, "What are some other reasons why you love ice cream?"

Stella dictated, "I love ice cream because there are so many flavors?" her intonation suggesting she was unsure. In response, I jotted alongside the next bullet: "I love ice cream because there are so many flavors." Before long, we'd also written a third bullet:

FIG. 1–2

> I love ice cream

- I love ice cream because you can add different toppings.
- I love ice cream because there are so many flavors.
- I love ice cream because it's refreshing on a hot day.

Set members of the class up to use what will now be a shared box and bullets to write-in-the-air their own version of the essay's first paragraph.

"Okay, we have a thesis statement and reasons—box and bullets. We have our plan. Now let's write-in-the-air one body paragraph that supports our first reason. Think of some details or evidence—at least three—you can use to support the first reason: 'I love ice cream because you can add different toppings.'" After a moment of silence, I said, "Thumbs up if you have thought of at least three details." When children so signaled, I said, "Start at the beginning of the essay, repeating the thesis statement." I pointed to the box. "And the three reasons." I pointed to the bullets. "Then proceed to the first body paragraph, which will start . . ." I pointed to where I'd outlined the general frame for an essay.

> (Thesis statement) because (reason 1), (reason 2), and most of all, because (reason 3).

- One reason that (thesis statement) is that (reason 1). For example, (evidence a), (evidence b), and (evidence c).

- Another reason that (thesis statement) is that (reason 2). For example, (evidence a), (evidence b), and (evidence c).

- Although (thesis statement) because (reason 1) and because (reason 2), especially (thesis statement) because (reason 3). For example, (evidence a), (evidence b), and (evidence c).

When we ask writers to say to a partner the exact words they might write, we call this writing-in-the-air. You'll ask your students to do this often, so it's worth checking to be sure children actually do say the words they could write instead of simply talking about their ideas. If their conversations do not sound to you as if they are dictating the words they could write, stop and clarify the direction. Then hold children to following these directions even if this requires you to stop them midstream yet again.

Listen in, interjecting lean prompts that raise the level of what individuals do. Then convene the class and elicit from students the first part of a shared essay. Coach into the writing to raise the level.

I listened as children recited essays to each other, many of which went like this:

> I love ice cream because you can add different toppings, because there are so many flavors, and because it is refreshing on a hot day.

> One reason that I love ice cream is because you can add different toppings. For example, you can add chocolate sauce or butterscotch sauce. You can also add chocolate chips, nuts, sprinkles.

"I love that you are using words like *also*, *in addition*, and *another example*," I voiced over. After a bit, I reconvened the class, and this time, Abby dictated her essay to us. After reading the introductory paragraph, her first body paragraph went:

> The first reason I love ice cream is because you can add different toppings. There are at least sixteen kinds of candy to put on ice cream, maybe more. There's also stuff like shredded coconut. In addition, there are a lot of sauces to go on top, too.

I interjected, "Now close your paragraph by referring back to key words from your thesis and your reason: 'The toppings are a reason why I love ice cream,'" and Abby repeated my words.

Debrief. Show the class what the writer did that you are hoping all writers have learned to do and then set them up to practice writing-in-the-air with partners again.

"Writers, did you see the way Abby started by repeating the thesis statement," I pointed to the box, "and the three reasons? Then, in a first body paragraph, she repeated the thesis (the box) and the first reason. Then she gave a few details to support the reason and closed her paragraph by referring back to the thesis and reason. She's ready to start a second body paragraph by saying something like, 'Another reason why I love ice cream is . . .' or 'I also love ice cream because . . .'"

ACTIVE ENGAGEMENT

Channel children to write-in-the-air and to then flash-draft the essay each has just written in the air.

"Right now, with your partner, write-in-the-air the whole essay, taking Abby's paragraph as your own (or use yours) and then adding on the next two reasons with details to support each." The room erupted into talk. Before long, after hearing some more and some less successful leads, I called out, "You've got it!" and I dictated the start to the essay.

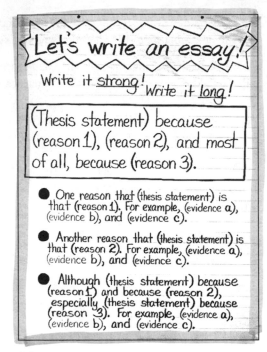

FIG. 1–3

I love ice cream because you can add different toppings, there are many different flavors, and it is refreshing on a hot day.

The first reason I love ice cream is because you can add different toppings. There are at least sixteen kinds of candy to put on ice cream, maybe more. There's also stuff like shredded coconut. In addition, there are a lot of sauces to go on top, too. The toppings are a reason why I love ice cream.

Another reason I love ice cream is because there are so many different flavors. For example, at the ice cream shop near me, you can choose . . .

I then gave children some time to use my dictated lead in their oral version of an essay.

LINK

Restates the teaching point.
–Send them off to write right away. Don't go over rules...

Send writers off to finish flash-drafting the shared essay.

"Writers, you are speaking like essayists. Now take everything we just did and go off—fast, all of you—and flash-draft this essay. On a piece of loose-leaf paper, write the whole essay. I'm giving you ten minutes, only, so write up a storm. You might even be finished sooner because you already know what you are going to write. Okay, go!"

Notice the use of the term "flash-draft." When I ask writers to flash-draft a piece of writing, I am differentiating that writing from a draft—a piece of writing which is the product of much time and effort and possibly multiple revisions. Flash-drafting implies fast and furious writing and helps to give the impression that the piece of writing will not be perfect and thus sets the stage for later revisions.

Voiceover and Coaching to Ratchet Up the Level of Student Work

BECAUSE THE MINILESSON was an unusual one, involving extended guided practice, there will be less writing time than usual and therefore less conferring time as well. Then, too, children only have ten minutes to write entire essays so you can't talk to them for long, and you likely will not want to disrupt them with a mid-workshop interruption. But you absolutely will want to be involved in the work that children are doing. The best way to do this will be to observe their work and either interject small comments, almost whispering in as an individual writer works, or call out voiceovers that relate to the whole class. Either way, your coaching will aim to ratchet up the level of students' writing by reminding them of moves that are integral to writing within an essay structure and by nudging them to write "long and strong."

At the start of the very brief writing time, nudge writers to get themselves started writing without delay. In this world of high-stakes testing, it is important for students to grow up understanding that there are times when they need to write with great dispatch. After all, on SAT and ACT tests, students are given less than half an hour to read the prompt, plan, and write an essay, and a study conducted by MIT professor Dr. Les Perelman and cited in the *New York Times* (Winerip 2005) found that students' scores on the essay portion of those tests are directly correlated with the length of their essays. Those students who produced an essay that spanned two sides of a page almost always scored far better than students who wrote just a page. In this instance, the content and wording of the essay are already established, so this is a perfect occasion for students to leave the starting block right away. Note students who have started quickly, especially complimenting children who have not traditionally excelled in narrative writing; this unit and new genre can give those children a place to shine.

Compliment and push writers purposefully. "Fabulous, you've gotten half a page written," you might say to one writer. "That whole page will be filled in three minutes." If you raise your voice a bit when prompting individuals, others will overhear you, and that will help your cause. "Don't stop mid-sentence," you will tell another writer. "Just keep going. Keep your hand moving down that page."

Once children have gotten themselves started, you'll want to shift your prompts to remind them to incorporate the transitional phrases in the frame on chart paper at the front of the room. Chances are good that many of them will need reminders to indent when they come to new body paragraphs. Paragraphing is a very big deal when writing an essay, so you will want to make a fuss about this. Of course, once students are within their body paragraphs, you can coach them to write more than one example, to "unpack" or discuss the example in relation to the thesis statement and to recap what they have said at the end of each paragraph. Don't worry that any of this be done perfectly—consider it, instead, an "exercise text."

Remember that the charge you issued was for every writer to write a complete essay—with a thesis statement, several body paragraphs, and a closing—all within ten minutes. You may extend that window of time (quietly) just a bit if you need to do so, but this is what you need to know: your students can do this.

Okay, it may take them twelve minutes, not ten, and the work won't be perfect. But in classrooms across even the high-needs schools of New York City, every child has written an essay within this little window of time, and your students can do this work as well. And your confidence is nine tenths of this. "You can do this," you will convey to your writers through every word and action. And they can.

Although every writer will not completely finish the draft today, every writer will have experienced the essay structure. Toward the end of this unit, you will invite students to do some large-scale revision on these early pieces. By then, their abilities to plan and structure an essay (as well as their stamina) should have developed to the point where they will each be able to write a full flash-draft essay, all on their own, within ten or fifteen minutes. As students become adept at writing within the familiar structure of the five-paragraph essay, you will be amazed at how easily they can produce quick little flash-draft essays—and that skill will be incredibly useful across all the content areas.

Pushing Students to Meet and Exceed Goals from the Start

Convene writers and ask them to remind themselves and discuss what they already have learned about opinion writing in previous units and years.

"Writers, can I have your eyes and attention? One of the reasons to do the sort of work we've been trying out today is to make sure the writing you do after this is a higher level right from the start. But you can always go back to improve previous work, too. One way to improve previous work is to make sure it shows all that you have already learned to do. So I bet that as you've been doing this work, you are likely thinking back to opinion writing work you did in earlier grades. If you are remembering persuasive speeches, letters, petitions, reviews, and realizing the work you are doing now is a lot like that, you should be very proud of yourself. Give yourself a little mental high five. So right now, will you remind yourself of some things you already know about opinion writing? Thumbs up when you have thought of at least one thing you've learned already." Across the rug, thumbs popped up. "Okay, turn and talk with your partner about things you already know about opinion writing." The room buzzed with talk.

"List reasons and give evidence," Isabel said.

"Yeah, like quotes and examples," Stella added.

"And hook the reader," Isabel added.

After giving the writers a quick minute to discuss what they already knew, I pulled them back together. "So writers, whenever you are doing new work, you should always be thinking about work that you have already learned to do and make sure that your new work shows all that you have *already* learned. And you can also always push yourself to ask, 'How can I do more? How can I make this work even better?'"

When we ask children to talk in pairs, then listen in on their conversations and report back some of what we hear, we can design our reports in ways that provide the class with clear guidelines. To report back on a conversation overheard during turn-and-talk, you essentially use the same muscles you use when you notice what a child has done and turn that observation into a mid-workshop teaching. You use a case-in-point to teach the entire class something that your quick assessment tells you is needed.

Put up some selected items from the third- or fourth-grade Opinion Writing Checklist, ones you are fairly confident your students were taught the year before.

"Right now I'm going to put up a chart with some goals. You've seen a chart like this before in the fiction unit and also you most likely saw charts like this last year." I uncovered the chart. (A complete, full-size, reproducible version of the Opinion Writing Checklist for students can be found on the CD-ROM.) "So I hear a lot of you saying these goals seem very familiar and you're right. These are goals you likely worked to meet last year. Right now, each one of you is going to spend some time making sure that our writing shows every-thing that we have *already* learned to do."

Involve writers in assessing their on-demands and setting goals using the goal chart.

"Let's try this out with some writing you did right at the start of the unit. In a minute I'm going to give you back your on-demand writing piece. I have read them all, taken notes on them, and made copies of them. I'll give you a chance to study your writing against this goal chart and circle the goals that your writing is meeting. Push yourself to not circle a goal unless you see evidence in your writing that you are meeting that goal. Okay, do that work now."

Opinion Writing Checklist

	Grade 3	NOT YET	STARTING TO	YES!	Grade 4	NOT YET	STARTING TO	YES!
	Structure				**Structure**			
Overall	I told readers my opinion and ideas on a text or a topic and helped them understand my reasons.	☐	☐	☐	I made a claim about a topic or a text and tried to support my reasons.	☐	☐	☐
Lead	I wrote a beginning in which I not only set readers up to expect that this would be a piece of opinion writing, but also tried to hook them into caring about my opinion.	☐	☐	☐	I wrote a few sentences to hook my readers, perhaps by asking a question, explaining why the topic mattered, telling a surprising fact, or giving background information.	☐	☐	☐
					I stated my claim.	☐	☐	☐
Transitions	I connected my ideas and reasons with my examples using words such as *for example* and *because*. I connected one reason or example using words such as *also* and *another*.	☐	☐	☐	I used words and phrases to glue parts of my piece together. I used phrases such as *for example*, *another example*, *one time*, and *for instance* to show when I was shifting from saying reasons to giving evidence and *in addition to*, *also*, and *another* to show when I wanted to make a new point.	☐	☐	☐
Ending	I worked on an ending, perhaps a thought or comment related to my opinion.	☐	☐	☐	I wrote an ending for my piece in which I restated and reflected on my claim, perhaps suggesting an action or response based on what I had written.	☐	☐	☐
Organization	I wrote several reasons or examples of why readers should agree with my opinion and wrote at least several sentences about each reason.	☐	☐	☐	I separated sections of information using paragraphs.	☐	☐	☐
	I organized my information so that each part of my writing was mostly about one thing.	☐	☐	☐				

As the writers bent over their writing and began to circle goals they had met, I crouched among them, coaching into this work, and asking questions such as: "Where in the piece do you see evidence of your meeting that goal?" "You won't want to check it off if you just barely did something once—is there real evidence of mastery?" "Can you find some next steps for yourself? Cool!"

After a minute, I called out, "Writers, I hear some of you saying that you don't see evidence in your piece of everything you have already learned. That is an *emergency*. Your work should always reflect all you know and have learned. The good news is that now that you are aware of what goals your piece is or is not meeting, you can start setting some goals for yourself. The best news would be if you are locating the next steps you can take to get better. How many of you have found goals for yourself? Thumbs up!"

It's usually more reasonable to reach for a set of related next steps than to try to isolate just one. For example, a child learning to ride a bike can't easily zoom in on only the goal of balancing the bike, later progressing to pedaling!

After a bit, I said, "You may not be finished assessing which goals you are meeting but you can do more of that work tonight and tomorrow. Right now, decide which of the goals you have located so far that you want to set as personal goals for yourself. They might be goals that you are just starting to meet or ones that you have not really thought about yet. Star those goals like crazy or draw fireworks or a happy face around them. In a minute, I'll ask you to turn and tell a partner your goals and how you plan to meet those goals. Okay, turn and talk now." The room erupted with talk.

Get writers started in revising their on-demands using their personal goals.

"Writers, I'm hearing you all talk about how you plan to make your next writing piece stronger and that is totally wonderful. I want you to know you can always go back and make your old writing pieces stronger. But I have something else very important to tell you. Writers, each time you write a piece, that piece should show *all* that you have learned. We carry all of our learning with us and transfer and apply it to each new piece. So right now, each one of you is going to take that on-demand piece and revise it to try to make it even better. And yes, you will also push yourself to see if you can make your piece meet all the goals that you learned as well as some of your new goals. In a minute, you'll get started rewriting your on-demand by working right here in the meeting area and then you can continue so you finish for homework. Instead of just fixing one or two places, I'm going to give you another piece of loose-leaf paper and tell you to make a whole brand-new second draft that is way better than the first. I'll have a bulletin board ready to go tomorrow and we'll put up your first on-demand and your second piece for everyone to admire and learn from. And we'll put up a big sign that says, 'We are Working to Meet and Exceed our Goals from the Start.' I'll hand out loose leaf and you get started writing a brand-new, revised, *way better* on-demand. Let's start this unit out right! Go."

This is a lot of talk. You'll tighten this and talk quickly so it's not as ponderous in real life as it looks on this page!

ESSAY STRUCTURE BOOT CAMP

Revising and Redrafting to Meet Personal Goals

Writers, tonight I'd like to see you spending more time with your goals chart. Continue working on your revision of your on-demand piece and making sure that it shows how you are trying to meet your personal goals. Be ready to talk tomorrow between your two pieces and explain how you made sure that your second piece was way better than the first. So you might even reread your piece after you finish your new draft and star places that you especially want to talk about with a partner, to show your partner what you tried out to meet your goals. Or you might want to firework a section that was tough for you and show your partner that section tomorrow to get some help. Be ready to explain not only what goals you set, but what plan you made to try to reach them.

Collecting Ideas as Essayists

IN THIS SESSION, you'll teach children that writers use several strategies for growing insightful ideas including using important people, places, and objects as inspiration.

GETTING READY

✔ Your own example of a person who is important to you so you can demonstrate coming up with ideas about the person and starting to freewrite an entry about the person (see Teaching)

✔ Your own example of a place and/or object that are important to you so you can demonstrate generating ideas for entries (see Mid-Workshop Teaching)

✔ Your own example of a scene from memory that stands out in your mind about which you could model having thoughts (see Share)

✔ Blank chart paper to write on in front of your students

✔ Writing materials and writing tools for students

✔ "Strategies for Generating Essay Entries" list on chart paper with the strategies you are teaching today (see Share)

COMMON CORE STATE STANDARDS: W.4.1, W.4.3, RI.4.2, SL.4.1, SL.4.3, SL.4.4, L.4.1, L.4.2, L.4.3

WHEN YOU LAUNCH CHILDREN into a new kind of writing, one of the best ways to induct them into that new work is to teach them a small handful of strategies for generating whatever that new kind of writing might be. Usually, minilessons on strategies for generating the new kind of writing double as opportunities to immerse students in the sound and feel of the new genre. For example, in the third-grade opinion-writing unit *Changing the World,* students begin by collecting many mini–persuasive speeches in their notebooks before developing a claim and beginning to gather evidence to support that claim. In this unit, however, writers do not begin the process of writing essays by collecting a notebook full of rough underdeveloped mini-essays. Instead, the process of generating an essay begins with writers writing in ways that foster new insight and new ideas, and that writing rarely takes the formal shape of an essay. Instead, that writing is more apt to be "freewriting." To help children get started on this kind of writing and thinking, then, you need to consider, "Where *do* ideas for essays come from?" "What is the life work of being an essayist?"

This question is dear to my heart because the keynote speeches and book chapters I write are essays of a sort. So for me, the question is a very personal one. How do I grow the ideas that eventually become themes in my own nonfiction writing?

I find that to develop ideas that feel new and significant, it is best for me to approach the page expecting that new ideas will surface as I write. All of us have a shelf of ready-made, prepackaged ideas that we could, at any point, heat up and use in a new essay, but the ideas that will work best to take readers on a journey of thought are almost always ideas that also take the writer on a journey of thought. The famous poet William Stafford captures the power of writing to generate new ideas when he says, "It is like fishing." Stafford says that he sits, waiting for an idea to surface, ready to follow those impulses. He explains that he must be receptive and "willing to fail. If I am to keep writing, I cannot bother to insist on high standards. . . . I am following a process that leads so wildly and originally into new territory . . . I am headlong to discover" ("A Way of Writing," *Field,* Spring, 1970, 10).

There are several strategies that I especially use to grow new ideas (rather than simply restating old, clichéd ideas), and the various sections of today's whole-class teaching illuminate several different ways of writing to develop ideas.

For example, ideas often come as I study stuff—objects, prior writing, the interactions in a particular place—expecting new thoughts to surface. For example, I might start by putting

---

"When I teach children to write essays, I first teach them to pay attention. I teach them to collect bits of life—and then I teach them to take a leap of faith, declaring those bits to be precious, and surrounding them with the thoughts and responses that make them significant."

---

myself into the hubbub of real life—for me, into classrooms and conversations about teaching—and then try to observe and listen keenly, pushing myself to have some thoughts in response.

This is how many writers grow ideas. When Newbery Award–winning author Katherine Paterson was asked about her writing process, she answered by telling the story of her son David, out in the backyard. He called, "Mom, come quickly! He's about to shed his skin!" Together, Paterson and her son watched closely as a tiny slit emerged in a cicada's back, then gradually extended, as though the bug had a waist-length zipper. They then saw hints of color through the slit: first green, then yellow, aqua, cream, and flecks of gold, appearing like jewelry on its head. Next the wings emerged, first crumpled ribbons, then glossy and smooth. As they watched, the cicada swung like an acrobat onto a twig and eventually flew off, "oblivious to the wake of wonder it left behind." Paterson wrote, "As I let the wonder wash over me, I realized that this was the gift I really wanted to give my children, for what good are straight teeth and trumpet lessons to a person who cannot see the grandeur that the world is charged with?" (*Raising Lifelong Learners* 1998, 77). That insight came to Paterson as she watched the cicada tumble away, yes, and also as she wrote.

Malcolm Cowley edited a series, Writers at Work, in which he interviewed dozens of our most famous writers. At the end of that experience, he was asked what he learned about the processes writers use. He answered that above all, he learned that every writer is idiosyncratic, that there is no one shared process all writers experience. But then he added that most writers begin with a precious particle—an observation, an image, a phrase, a bit of data—and grow their writing from that particle.

When I teach children to write essays, I first teach them to pay attention. I teach them to collect bits of life, and then I teach them to take a leap of faith, declaring those bits to be precious, and surrounding them with the thoughts and responses that make them significant.

Collecting Ideas as Essayists

CONNECTION

Use a metaphor, such as a beautifully designed cake, to stress the value of content as well as form in essays.

"Writers, I want to tell you a story about a TV show that I like. It's a show where people compete to see who can make the best cake. Give me a nod if you have seen a show like that. Well, as you know the bakers get judged in two ways—how the cake looks and how the cake tastes. So, last night, this man on the show made a beautiful cake, five tiers tall. But when the judges tasted it, they made faces. Even though his cake was definitely the best in form, in the outward design, the man lost because the contents of the cake didn't work.

"It may seem strange that I'm telling you about cakes during writing workshop, but I started thinking about essay writing while I was watching the show. I started thinking about how essay writing is sort of like making a big, beautiful cake. When you're making a cake, the form—the shape—matters a lot, but so does the actual batter, the contents of the cake. In the same way, when you are writing an essay, the form or shape matters, but so do the contents."

Point out that the entries essayists collect are not usually miniature essays. The goal in these entries is to grow new, insightful ideas, and often the entries are lists or freewriting.

"Remember that earlier I told you that essays are a grown-up kind of writing? That means it will be challenging but rewarding work. You will have a steep learning curve. So here is the first thing I need to tell you.

"Collecting entries for essays is not like collecting ideas for narratives. When you collect entries in a narrative unit, those entries are little stories. The entries look similar to the final products. But this week, and for the rest of your life, when you collect entries to get yourself started in essay writing, those entries will not be little essays. Instead you will collect entries for one reason only: to come up with ideas. Those entries can be lists or a jumble of ideas or chains of thought or marginal notes or stories with notes all over them, or they can be fast-draft essays. When essayists carry notebooks, the only goal is for those notebooks to be seed beds for new and insightful ideas. Today I'll show you how to collect entries that can grow new and insightful ideas."

I often reach for a metaphor to make abstract work seem more concrete to students. In this instance, a cake serves as a concrete representation of the work the students will need to do—create products which are strong in both form and content. Watch as I return to this metaphor throughout the unit. Of course, you may be thinking of your own metaphor, and I encourage you to use those metaphors of which you are especially fond to make your teaching powerful and accessible. Know that you will want to lean on one that can thread through multiple sessions.

Those of you who know the original version of this unit might find it interesting to contrast the minilessons in this edition with those in the previous edition. You'll note that our connections are much more to the point. We realized that sometimes the long, detailed stories or metaphors in the original version were enthralling to kids, but drew their focus away from writing to the subject at hand. Here, we make an analogy quickly, and waste no time showing how our point relates to writing.

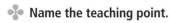

❖ Name the teaching point.

"Today, I want to teach you a strategy essayists use to gather essay entries. One strategy that works is to think of a person who matters to you, and then list specific ideas about that person. Then take one of those ideas and write an entry in which you think about that idea." (See Figure 2–1.)

Bro

- My brother can be annoying.
- My brother can have anger and whining issues.
- My brother can have mixed feelings.
- My brother can be nice and mean at the same time.
- My brother can say the wrong and right things at times.

My brother can say the wrong and right things at different times. Like one time I had a drawing and I showed it to him and he said, "Did you really draw that? It looks like a three-year-old drew it." And it hurt me a lot. But another time when I was playing a game he said, "Wow, you're really good!" And it made me feel really good!

TEACHING

Demonstrate the step-by-step process of thinking of a person who matters to you, listing ideas, choosing one, and beginning an entry about it. Deliberately model the work of making and fixing mistakes.

"Let's try this strategy together so you'll each have one strategy that can get you started writing today. We'll think of a person who matters to us, list ideas about that person, and then choose one and write an entry exploring that one idea. So, first we each need to think of someone who matters to us.

"Now, I'm not going to list just any person, like my mail carrier or a neighbor I don't see all that much. I am going to pick someone who matters to me. I could write about my dad or my mother or my friend. Hmm, . . . I think since my dad popped into my head right away, I'll try writing about him first.

"Writers, do you see your person in your mind's eye? Make sure it is someone who matters to you. Thumbs up if you can see your person in your mind's eye." All across the rug, thumbs popped up and heads nodded.

After checking that most thumbs were up, I wrote "My Dad" at the top of my paper and said, "Let me think of ideas about my dad. So, there was this one time that he came to a basketball game and he was wearing this crazy hat and he embarrassed me in front of all of my friends. No, wait." I stopped talking and sat straight up. "That's not *an idea*—that's *a story*. I need to list *ideas*. What do I think about my dad? What are my opinions and thoughts about my dad? Hmm,

FIG. 2–1   Isabel collecting ideas about her brother

I regard this kind of instruction as demonstration teaching, but in a really effective demonstration, students are participating in the same work that I am demonstrating. That is, really effective demonstration teaching has a layer of guided practice within it. I get students to join me, and then once they have begun to do some work, I show them how I do that same bit of work, voicing over to point out what I have done. If students just sit back and watch as I do a sequence of work, they're not going to learn nearly as much as they will if they are right there in the playing field with me, trying to do the same thing I am doing.

. . . One thought is that Dad doesn't let what other people think bother him. I'll write that down." I jotted, "doesn't let what other people think bother him.

"Now, let me think of another idea about my dad. I want to think of at least three. So, another thought I have about my dad is that he has taught me so much. I'll write that down, too." I jotted, "taught me so much" on the chart.

"Okay, I need one more idea quickly." Within a minute, the chart looked like this:

My Dad

- doesn't let what other people think bother him
- taught me so much
- helped me care about writing

Debrief quickly by recalling the strategy and pointing out that you thought of ideas not stories.

"Writers, did you see the way I thought of a person that matters to me and then jotted ideas I have about that person? I did this by pushing myself to say, 'A thought I have about (the person) is . . . .' Then I listed not small stories but big ideas. In a jiffy, I'm going to start writing about one of those ideas, but first, make sure you've done these first steps in the strategy."

Set writers up to list ideas about the person they've selected across their fingers.

"I bet you've already been thinking of your own person. Right now, use your fingers and list some ideas you have about that person. Push yourself by saying, 'A thought I have about (so-and-so) is . . .' and then jot that thought quick as a wink in your notebook, and then push for another and another."

I waited a long minute.

Demonstrate again. Choose one idea and start an entry in the air. Deliberately make a mistake, perhaps shifting to storytelling rather than writing general abstract ideas, and then fix the mistake.

"The next step is to choose an idea and start writing an entry. Watch me, because you'll do this soon. I'll choose an idea quickly because I want to get right to writing. Maybe—'My dad doesn't let what other people think bother him.'" I jotted the words quickly in my writer's notebook, voicing them aloud as I wrote. "Let me think." Then I started scrawling—and saying what I wrote:

My dad doesn't let what other people think bother him. He doesn't worry about making sure he does what people expect. This means that sometimes he does things that are odd, like using frozen peas as an ice pack, or wearing a red plaid hunting cap to school events.

You will notice that the form of this minilesson, like that of the first, does not exactly follow the template that undergirds most minilessons. I could have demonstrated a several-step process in the teaching section, then engaged students in those same several steps, but this is demanding work, and that would have meant the demonstration was not close to and supportive of students' own work. Therefore, instead, the teaching section of the minilesson involves a cycle that would normally have spanned teaching and active engagement. The sequence goes: I do, they do, debrief, I do, they do, debrief.

Sometimes, of course, there is no real way for students to participate in your demonstration. Youngsters can't help me think of ideas about my dad, for example.

Debrief again. Point out to writers that you wrote an entry about an idea.

"Writers, did you see the way I chose an idea and started writing about it? I pushed myself to say what I was thinking, to write more about my idea."

ACTIVE ENGAGEMENT

Set writers up to choose an idea and talk long about it with a partner.

"Now you're going to try this. Think of your ideas about the person who matters to you. In a minute you'll talk to your partner. Partner 1, write your entry in the air. And Partner 2, listen carefully so that your attention helps Partner 1 say more and more about his or her idea (thumbs up). Make sure Partner 1 says more about the idea."

I listened as Christina and Abby leaned toward each other.

"I have to pick my cat Brazil," Christina said eagerly as I hid a smile. "Our relationship is like a mother-daughter. She always looks out for me. She forgives me no matter what I do, like when she was very little and me and my twin sister Anara threw her on the bed." Abby began to wave her hands in front of Christina's face, and Christina stopped.

Abby said, "So you told me one idea about your cat. Do you have other ideas?"

I interjected. "Nice, Abby. You are a very helpful partner, although do you notice Christina's ideas aren't just about her cat—they are about a more focused topic: her relationship with her cat. Christina, getting ideas about your *relationship* with your cat is really sophisticated work."

Christina beamed.

I said, "Try starting your entry again. Push yourself to think of ideas, thoughts about your relationship." I moved onto another partnership.

LINK

Get students started writing while sitting in the meeting area, sending individuals off once they're writing.

"Writers, let's not waste a second of precious writing time. Let's dive right in, right here at the meeting area." Pointing to a chart where I'd recorded the first strategy, I said, "Remember, one strategy for writing about big ideas and issues is to think of a person who matters to you, list ideas, and then choose one to write long about. When you finish writing about one idea, grab another idea and write about it as well. Let's get started!"

One of the problems we see often in minilessons—including our minilessons—is that we, grown-ups, find it is such fun to talk or write at length about our ideas and our lives that we get going on very long-winded pieces of writing or spoken reflections. Kids meanwhile look on, passive, not grasping any of the points we hope we are making. We worked hard to keep this writing as brief as possible while still being detailed and provocative, and we write in our notebooks—where we can scrawl at 90 mph, voicing aloud as we do so, in a way that minimizes the time spent on this.

Soon we will channel children to move back and forth between writing about ideas and giving specific, precise details, which sometimes includes telling stories. At this stage in the unit we want to make the point to students that they can push themselves to stay in the realm of idea writing before moving into giving examples to explain the idea. This is often challenging work for students and this is not the only lesson where we will attempt to support writers in this work.

Teachers, we have not come back to the goal work we began at the end of the previous session. One of the assessment challenges with a unit such as this is that during the course of the unit, the students will engage in two types of writing. The first is "journey of thought" writing, the kind of freewriting that will not necessarily contain all of the qualities of opinion writing. The second type of writing will be the more formally structured essays, which are well suited to an opinion learning progression. You'll see us return to the opinion learning progression later in this unit as students get started on developing their essay. We'll ramp up the assessment work as the unit progresses and the later opinion writing unit The Literary Essay *will take up where this unit leaves off.*

Anticipate Ways to Keep Students Working, Despite the Brevity of Their Entries

THE WORK OF TODAY is to keep writers writing, filling up pages without stopping. This is no easy feat. Expect that the classroom will feel very different than it did early in the narrative unit. Although most of your students will by now be capable of sustaining themselves when they write narrative entries, you may find that many of them quickly run out of steam when writing entries that are idea-based. Today, your students will no sooner start writing entries than, in the blink of an eye, they'll be done.

It will be like popcorn, as one student and then another pops up to say, "I'm done." "I'm done." Others won't say they are done. They'll just finish their work and sit over the page, resistant and stuck.

The good news is that if you can anticipate this behavior, you can be ready to help. Today, see yourself as a circus performer, working hard to keep the multiple plates

---

MID-WORKSHOP TEACHING **Generating Ideas by Thinking of a Place or an Object**

"Writers, can I have your eyes and your attention? These essay entries that you have been collecting are briefer than the entries you collected when writing personal narratives, so you'll need to write more entries in a day. Let me teach you two other strategies that writers use to gather essay entries.

"One is, you can think of a *place* or an *object* that matters to you, list ideas around that place or that object, and then choose one of those ideas to write a lengthy entry about. Do you remember earlier this year when we made maps of the places in our lives and then recorded stories that hide in those places to get ideas for narrative writing? My map showed the swamp at the bottom of the sledding hill behind my childhood house. The trick is to jot little ideas that you think of, connected to those places. On my map, I could write ideas about that swamp. Let me try the tricks we learned earlier. 'One thought I have about this is that . . . I was pretending to be Huck Finn.'

"I want to push myself to think not just about one time, one story, but 'all the time' and 'in general.' Let me go back to that sentence: *That makes me think* . . . umm . . . *that all the time* . . . when kids play, a lot of play is all about pretending. I better say more about my idea. Umm . . . In kindergarten classrooms, they have dress-up areas where kids put on make-believe parties and go to make-believe stores, but

they don't put dress-up areas in classrooms for older kids. People act as if pretend play is just for little kids, but when kids play with Barbies, it is really pretend play, and when they stick squirt guns under their waistbands, they are doing pretend play.

"In the same way, I could choose an object that matters to me, like this necklace, and write ideas it sparks.

"Right now, try taking a place or an object—any place, any object—and then the challenging part (remember, this is very grown-up writing) is to list ideas about that place or that object. Do this now, quietly, listing across your fingers. Say to yourself, 'A thought I have about this is. . . .'" The room was quiet while children got themselves thinking.

The place Sarah picked to write about was the New Jersey boardwalk:

> The time I went to the New Jersey boardwalk it was cold, but being there with all my family made it a night to remember. The thought I have about this is being with your whole family in a new place makes the family come together.

"Jot what you are thinking. Just turn to the next page and start a new entry."

After a few minutes, I said, "If you feel yourself running out of steam with one thought, draw a line, and go up and grab a new thought and write about that. It is okay that your entries are short. The goal is fresh, new, interesting thinking." I added, "Some kids call these entries 'patches of thought.'" After most writers got themselves started writing, I voiced over, saying, "You have twenty minutes left in writing workshop today. Let's each fill up at least two more pages, front and back, in that time. Go! Fast and furious."

The objects Owen picked (see Figure 2–2) were his Christmas tree, Yankee Stadium, and the future. His first patch was his Christmas tree.

I love the annual event of decorating the tree. And the smell of the tree. I like hanging up decorations because it is good to get into the feeling. Smelling the Christmas tree just gets you even more eager for Christmas to come. I love getting in the feeling by playing Christmas songs. It just feels great.

When Sophie first tried out this work, she started her entry by recording what she noticed. If she had just stopped there, her entry wouldn't be much. But the great thing is that she pushed her writing to take a turn, and asked herself, "What does that make me think? What does this remind me of *in general*?" (See Figure 2–3.)

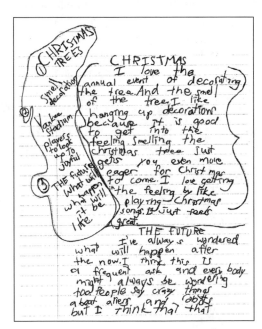

FIG. 2–2   Owen's page is a compost of ideas.

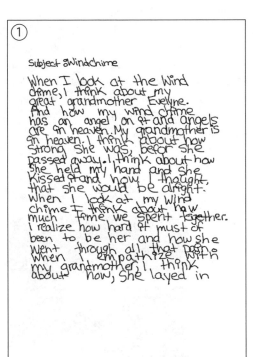

FIG. 2–3   Sophie's entry shows the way trains of thought yield new ideas.

spinning, the writers writing. Expect that for a few days, you will not have time to linger with any one writer, rereading and lifting the level of that writing. Instead, you will need to move from table to table, helping all the writers at a table keep going. Table compliments, where you compliment one writer and then share what the writer has done with the entire table, can help you reach multiple writers at once.

For example, at one table I said, "William, I *love* how you are working on one entry until you run out of steam, then skipping a line and starting a new entry right away on a different idea. You are showing *so* much stamina!" I called for the other writers at the table to listen. "I hope you have all noticed William's method of writing and writing until he runs out of steam on one idea, then skipping a line and starting another entry right away!"

You can also compliment an entire table on what you see them doing well or just beginning to do. To the table full of writers, you might say, "I *love* the way you guys are rereading the first thing you wrote and then thinking, 'What new ideas come to mind?' and then writing those ideas. Keep doing that!" Of course, you will have overstated what the children are doing, but Jerry Harste, coauthor of *Creating Classrooms for Authors and Inquirers* (1996) was wise when he said, "I see curriculum as creating in the classrooms the kind of world we believe in and then inviting children to role play their way into being the readers, writers, and learners we want them to be" (Calkins 2000, 18).

To another table full of writers, you might make a suggestion. "Let me teach you a totally cool trick that middle school kids do a lot. They reread their writing and underline just one key word or phrase or sentence, then they copy that part onto the top of a new page, and just 'write off from' that one word or line or sentence. Try it. It's really cool." Any time you suggest something to a writer or a table full of writers and then some kids try what you have suggested, this can be shared. "Class, all eyes up here." Once you have the class's attention, you can say, "Let me share with you this totally terrific thing that So-and-So came up with to do." Then you share the idea that, in fact, you gave to the writer in the first place. I can assure you, no child will protest, saying, "Actually *you* were the one to come up with that idea." And children are really keen to take up strategies that come from their classmates.

In all these ways, then, you will work to keep the children working.

So, teachers, approach today and this unit expecting that the work will be challenging for your students, and welcome the challenge! Be prepared to welcome approximation and to encourage children to keep going. Who was the writer who said, "Let the water flow until it runs clear?" Don't fuss over whether or not everything the child produces qualifies as an idea versus a story, a question, or a fact. Don't worry about clichés and platitudes. For today, encourage children to regard themselves as the sort of people who can generate important, new, surprising, fresh ideas, and help them keep going. Say, "Encore," even when their work is not perfect. Let the water flow, and it will begin to be more clear.

Generating Ideas through Reflection

Set children up to try one final way to generate ideas: that is, to think within a mental structure in which they shift between observing for a while, then reflecting for a while.

"You have already learned several ways to come up with ideas. You can think of a person, an object, or a place, and record ideas about that topic, then take one of those ideas and develop it across a page. When I said you can think of a place—you can just name a place, like you name a person, or you can mind-travel to that place. If you put yourself mentally in a new place, you can observe what is there, and then push yourself to have thoughts about what you 'see.'"

"I don't picture just any scene. I picture something that really matters to me, something about which I might want to write an essay. Since I'm really excited about the topic of my dad, I might picture a scene with the two of us—maybe him sitting next to me while I did my homework."

Set children up to observe a distant place that they must conjure up in their minds' eyes and then to articulate a thought about that observation.

"Let's try It. Close your eyes and picture something in your mind's eye that you care about. Your cat, when he was sick. Your friends at recess, when they are ignoring you. Put yourself in your kitchen, your living room, on the front stoop, or the branch of your climbing tree. Watch something—your little brother, while he's playing with your stuff, the pile of books beside your bed. Thumbs up when you've got something in mind that you are observing.

"Okay, Partner 1, start by just describing exactly what you see in your mind's eye. Say, 'I see . . . ' and keep going, listing what you see exactly. 'I see . . . I see . . . ,' being really detailed."

Nora said to her partner Jessie: "I am walking. I see a soft little body, with little wing flaps. It is the size of my hand. It is a baby bird, a newborn baby. It has fallen from its nest. I tried to help it."

After a minute, I again interjected, saying loudly and in a way that channeled the speakers' remarks, "And (repeat after me) the idea I have about this is. . . ." The children carried on, talking now about the ideas they generated from their observations. Nora said to Jessie: The thought I have about this is, no matter how hard you try, sometimes there is nothing you can do. You can't always fix things.

Debrief in a way that sets children up to draw on the cumulated list of strategies.

"So let's end class by just recapping all the strategies you have for writing entries that grow ideas. Do this not as partner talk, but as table talk." After children talked, I said, "You are listing the strategies we have on this chart. Always remember that if one slips your mind, you can find it up here."

Strategies for Generating Essay Entries

- We take a subject (a person, place, or object) that matters to us and list ideas related to that subject. Then we take one of those ideas and write about it.
- We observe and then write, "The thought I have about this is . . ."

COLLECTING IDEAS AS ESSAYISTS

Growing Small Particles/Sparks into Big Ideas

Writers, one thing that writers do is reread old writing and mark a bunch of places in their entries that spark new thoughts. Look for places that make you wonder or remind you of something or realize something new.

Tonight, I want you to do that, and then try to take some of those little sparks and turn them into longer pieces. Pretend they are like little hot embers. If you keep fanning and blowing and working on hot embers, they will eventually catch flame and produce a roaring fire.

Today, when they were working in a partnership, Alejandro showed Chris how he asked questions in his entry to get some new ideas. That helped Chris get some sparks for new ideas like "It's not okay to only think about yourself," and now Chris can write a whole new entry just about this little spark and see where it leads her.

So, tonight let's take our little sparks of thought and push ourselves to keep working and writing about them. Let's keep pushing ourselves to write, "What's really important about this is . . ." and "this matters because. . . ." Let's keep working at our little sparks of thought until our ideas become fiery and passionate!

I notice that some kids are not dressed nice on picture day. Why do kids not dress nice on picture day? Do they even care how they look for their pictures? If they don't I certainly do? I think that their parents should make their kids wear nice clothes for picture day don't you? The kids responsibility is to make shure they look nice because they are going to have that picture forever and it is not fair for the kids who look nice. The kids who look nice really care that their picture looks good. I am one of those kids who wants to look nice.

FIG. 2–4 Alejandro asks questions as a strategy for developing ideas in this writing-to-learn entry.

Writing to Learn

ONCE YOU HAVE FILLED your students' mental backpacks with a collection of strategies for generating a type of writing, it is always a wise idea to step away from teaching minilessons that present strategies for generating writing so as to teach something altogether different, thereby nudging young writers to draw from their repertoire of possible strategies rather than waiting for you to channel them in the direction you select. For this reason, I generally suggest that your second or third minilesson in *any* unit be one in which you shift from providing strategies for generating entries to one in which you lift the level of those entries. If you remember, in the fiction writing unit, after equipping students with a few strategies for generating entries, you taught lessons on qualities such as focus and show don't tell—qualities of good writing that are essential to narrative writing. And last year, in third grade, your students spent just a very few days learning strategies to get started writing persuasive speeches and then they were taught to consider audience as a way to raise the level of that work.

So the challenge in planning this lesson is to decide on qualities that are equally fundamental to the writing you are now asking students to do. This is a unit on essay writing, so your mind is probably going to the question, "What are the qualities of good expository writing?" And you are right that answers to that question will undergird this unit. But actually, during this early portion of the unit, your goal is not *essay writing* so much as writing to grow ideas. That is, the writing your students are doing now, in the early portion of this unit, is not even a specific genre of writing. And the entries your students are writing certainly aren't meant to be structured like the very controlled, boxes-and-bullets essays they'll eventually write. So what should writers aim for?

Let's start by agreeing that writers should be aiming for their writing to be thoughtful and provocative. During this session, you'll see some examples of that sort of writing, and you'll be able to generate your own descriptors for it. But you also need to ask yourself, "What does a writer do to produce writing that qualifies as thoughtful and provocative?" These are important questions.

IN THIS SESSION, you'll orient children to the genre of writing to learn, helping them see how writers freewrite to grow new ideas.

GETTING READY

✔ Untangled Knots freewriting sample to use as a mentor for students to study to notice the moves the writer has made (see Teaching and Active Engagement)

✔ A copy of the freewriting sample for each student tucked into their writing folders prior to the lesson

✔ Blank chart paper and markers

✔ Writing materials and writing tools for students

✔ Student freewriting text, such as Civilization for students to study to notice additional moves the writer has made (see Mid-Workshop Teaching)

✔ Chart paper with "Qualities of Good Freewriting" at the top to fill in with students (see Active Engagement and Share)

COMMON CORE STATE STANDARDS: W.4.1, W.4.5, W.4.8, W.4.10, RL.4.1, RL.4.4, SL.4.1, L.4.1, L.4.2, L.4.3, L.4.5

In his book, *Writing Tools* (2008), Roy Peter Clark, vice president and senior scholar at the Poynter Institute, one of the most prestigious schools for journalists in the world, encourages writers to shift between writing with detail and writing in abstract generalization. He writes, "Good writers move up and down a ladder of language. At the bottom are bloody knives and rosary beads, wedding rings and baseball cards. At the top are words that reach for a higher meaning, words like *freedom* and *literacy*" (107). This ladder of abstraction was popularized by S. I. Hayakawa—and the terms themselves illustrate its meaning. The first noun—the *ladder*—is a tool that you can hold in your hands and climb on. Clark writes, "You can do things with it. Put it against a tree and rescue your cat Voodoo." The second noun is *abstraction*. "You can't eat or smell it or measure it . . . It is an idea that cries out for exemplification" (108). Clark illustrates the power of jettisoning the abstract with the specific when he quotes Updike, who has written, "We live in an era of gratuitous inventions and negative improvements. Consider the beer can." Updike then complains that the pop-top on a beer can ruins the aesthetic experience. Our point, in citing this, is that when aiming to write writing-to-learn entries well, it helps to blend concrete, specific detail with abstraction, with big ideas.

To help children write with big ideas, you will want to nudge them out of being grounded in just one specific example. Once several examples are laid alongside each other, it is a small step for writers to compare one thing with another, and doing so moves the writer between concrete detail and generalization. So if a child is an expert on something—say, baseball—and compares that thing to another topic, this often leads to more abstract thinking. "Writing is like playing baseball. There are different ways to be good at it."

Then, too, one can move writers up the ladder of abstraction by nudging them to think about motivations, about underlying causes. Because this is a unit on personal essays, it will especially pay off for writers to think about motivations behind their own opinions or feelings. If the writer's first entry, then, lays out the thesis statement, "I like birthdays," it will often pay off for the teacher to ask (and to teach the writer to ask) the simple question, Why? The writer can actually follow a train of thought by continuing to press on that Why? question. "I like birthdays because you get presents. (Why?) I don't have as much stuff as other kids do. (Why?) I think my parents don't want me to be spoiled. (Why?) My parents think it is important for people to work for stuff."

To help writers feel comfortable in the world of ideas, it is helpful to let them know about things people do with their first thoughts. People do things with Lego® blocks—and in the same way, people do things with first thoughts. If a child writes, "I like birthdays," it helps for the child to know ways to do more thinking with that thought. One can rank: "My best birthday came when I was 8." Or "I like birthdays but I like Christmas even better because. . . ." A person can categorize: "There are four different kinds of birthdays." A person can compare: "Different families celebrate birthdays differently." Teaching children to use their initial thoughts as springboards toward thoughtful and provocative writing, to think and grow ideas on paper and to use writing as a tool for thought, is no small feat and the importance of doing so cannot be emphasized enough.

Today's session aims to help lift the level of students' entries by involving them in an inquiry into what makes for effective freewriting. It is important to note that the session does not take the form of a traditional minilesson where students learn a strategy to add to their repertoire and then go off to continue to work independently. Instead, students will be engaged in investigating around a question, and so they will remain on the rug for a bit longer than usual. The work of today places a high cognitive demand on your writers. They will be pushed to work at high levels of Webb's Depth of Knowledge as they consider and conjecture just what writers do to create powerful freewriting. Be prepared to guide their efforts—helping them toward their ideas more precisely, closely read and reread exemplar freewriting, and take risks to transfer and apply what they notice to their own writing. The work of today is challenging, intellectually demanding, and critically important.

Writing to Learn Inquiry

CONNECTION

Support your students' identities as writers. Then name the question that will guide the inquiry: What makes for good freewriting?

"Writers, you've all been freewriting about big ideas and issues. I've been trying to do some of this freewriting myself and it's challenging. It's challenging because I can't just go to Barnes and Nobles and find some freewriting on the shelf, right? Most authors do their freewriting in their notebooks, so examples of this kind of writing are not out there in the world. I have been thinking about what I should aim for when I am freewriting—and what you should aim for, as well. That is, when we are writing to learn, writing to think on the page, to grow new ideas, what makes for good freewriting?

"Today, instead of a regular minilesson, we will do an inquiry. This means we will investigate to answer a question that *all* of us have—myself included. I won't be able to teach you the answer to the question because it is *my* question as well."

 **Name the question that will guide the inquiry.**

"The question we will be researching today is, 'What is good freewriting?' And what, exactly, does a writer do to do a great job at this kind of writing?"

TEACHING AND ACTIVE ENGAGEMENT

Remind students that to inquire into the characteristics of any kind of writing, it is important to study an example of that kind of writing, asking, "What did the writer do to make this?"

"So, I do not know what makes for good freewriting, but I do know how to go about answering that question. I know that there are things I can do when I want to understand what makes for a good poem or a good fantasy story or a good picture book. I bet you know this as well. When we want to know what makes for a good poem, we find some great poems. We read them over and over, we find the best parts and study them, and we think, 'What did the poet do to make this so beautiful?' Give me a nod or a thumbs up if that's what you were thinking too." The children signaled, and I added, "So, I think maybe we need to find some good freewriting and do that same kind of thinking."

Pace your minilessons. This is an inquiry mini-lesson, so you want to reserve time for students to talk and think together. It's appropriate, then, for the connection to be especially lean.

Just as with guided practice, there are specific reasons and purposes to teaching using the method of inquiry. In this case, I want to involve the students in looking deeply at free-writing to consider its qualities, rather than simply tell students about these qualities. My aim is to help students take ownership of what they notice and transfer and apply it to their own writing.

Set writers up to study and then discuss what the writer did. Give them *a lot* of time to talk.

"Writers, I started this unit off saying that it will be challenging, and what I am asking you to do today—talking about what works in this sort of writing—is d*efinitely* challenging!

"Here is the hard thing about it. Usually, if you look at a piece of writing and talk about ways in which it works, you can say back the words we already have on our chart. You can look at a Small Moment story and say, 'It is focused,' 'The writer shows not tells,' and things like that. But this time, we haven't got that chart yet. We *don't know* what makes this kind of writing good! The whole idea is that we are supposed to really look at the writing and to think up stuff that *no one has ever said to us*. This kind of talking takes courage because you don't know if you are 'right.'

"I've got a couple of pages of freewriting here (see Figure 3–1; the remainder of this piece can be found on the CD) and I've also put a copy in each of your writing folders. Will you take that piece out and look with me for a few minutes at this freewriting and try squeezing your mind, coming up with something you could say about what the writer maybe, perhaps, has done that the rest of us could try as well. Let's study it and think, 'What is strong about this writing?' And 'What did the writer do that we could try?' You can talk, but you should probably also jot your thinking."

Coach writers to go out on the thin ice of conjecturing, to restate what they are trying to say in more precise language, to ground ideas in specifics. After they jot and discuss, reconvene the class to elicit, refine, and chart selected ideas.

For a minute, I did the same work as students were doing, and then I began coaching into their writing and thinking. As I crouched among the writers, I called out voiceover comments based on what I was seeing:

"Guys, when someone says something vague and you don't get what they mean, say, 'Can you say it more exactly? I'm not following you.'"

"Try for exactly true words to describe what you see. Make them up. These might be words no one has ever used before, but it is what you are seeing and thinking."

"Pause sometimes to recall all that you've said, making sure you have the exactly right words."

"Point to the part of the text you are discussing. Reread it. Then I should hear a bunch of you trying to name what the writer is doing in that part."

"Well, I'm not really sure," David was saying as I pulled up to listen to his partnership, "but it is sort of like the writer just keeps going. 'Cause there's a lot of ideas in here all just put together."

"What parts make you think that?" I asked him, coaching him to refer to the text.

① Friends are like a untangled rope. I think this because friends are always friendly and barely making arguments. It is like friends are always strait until there is a arguement that forms a knot. But friends always say sorry and the knot gets untied.

It is like there is lots of kids lining up to form a huge rope. I imagine friends as friends who help each other and treat each other kindly.

In my life I had friends helping me a lot. Having a friend that you could trust is one of the best things to me. Like whenever I have a hardtime with something I just have to ask Takeshi to

② explain it for me. (Except when I am doing a test.) Friends are always a big untied knot

FIG. 3–1 You can set your writers up to study freewriting from previous students such as this piece from Jonah.

Teachers, the rest of this piece is included on the CD-ROM accompanying this series so that you can make use of it in small groups, conferences, and so on.

This little turn-and-talk may not look huge but we cannot overemphasize enough the importance of the students having this chance to talk with their partners and conjecture about what the writer is trying. Students are not just pointing out or repeating what the teacher has said but rather they are trying to find their own words.

"Like here?" David said, sounding unsure. "Like where it says that friends say 'sorry' and the knot gets untied and then it says there is like a huge line of kids making a rope. That's two different ideas."

"So, maybe . . . ," I said, helping him put into words what he had noticed, "Maybe we might say that the writer keeps writing, just letting different ideas come out. What else do you notice? Keep looking."

Meanwhile, I also charted some of the things I heard children saying (and others I wished they had said) on a chart that I kept angled so the children couldn't yet see my list. After a bit, I said, "Think about all you have said about the qualities of good writing-to-learn and choose one quality to add to the class chart." I gave the children a few seconds to think. "Thumbs up if you have something to add." When the majority of children had their thumbs up, I said, "I've heard and recorded some amazing things—and a bunch of these are things many of you were saying. Let me show you some of the things I've charted, and as I say something, put a thumb up if you and your partner noticed that very same thing." Then I revealed the chart I'd made as they talked:

Qualities of Good Freewriting

- The writer keeps writing freely, letting any thoughts come out.
- The writer seems to try to make ideas that get better and better as she writes longer.
- The writer sometimes compares things to make you get what she means.
- The writer doesn't cross stuff out.
- The writer sometimes says the big idea over and over (in different ways) as if trying to get it right.
- The writer stays for a long time on one big idea.
- The writer goes from big ideas to small examples back to big ideas.

The cardinal rule for any lesson is to watch time. Any time spent in the meeting area is time away from writing and every second has to count. Here I'm highlighting what I've heard to keep the lesson tight and to allow for plenty of coming writing time, but also to ensure that I can help students precisely word their observations. What they are noticing is not always easy to put into precise terms. If you choose to have students share out, be ready to keep the lesson moving, guide their responses, and help rephrase their responses to get at the heart of what they are really trying to say.

LINK

Launch students directly into freewriting, charging them with transferring and applying all that they have just noticed.

"Writers, let's work on getting stronger at this type of writing. I bet right now you are already thinking of a new idea that could start a new entry or you are thinking of an old entry that you might revise. Will you put a thumb up when you have in mind exactly the kind of work you want to do to today?" I waited until I saw thumbs. "So, I might decide that I want to start my writing from writing I've already done. I have this great line in one of my entries—'Teachers are not the only ones who help us learn lessons'—and I'm going to box out that line, put it on a new page, and just start a whole new entry. That might be something else you could try.

"Okay, let's dive into writing, right here, right now. Open up your notebooks and get started." I bent my head over my writer's notebook and started scribbling furiously. After a bit, I said, quietly so as to avoid interrupting the writing, "Remember to keep your pen moving, writing and writing and writing, not stopping." The room was silent.

After another long moment in which one could hear the scratch of pens, I began tapping students and sending them back to their seats to continue working. Nora was already well on the way toward writing a page about talking in school (see Figure 3–2).

Nora's ideas about herself have led to a plea for wider change. She is coming to new thinking through the act of writing.

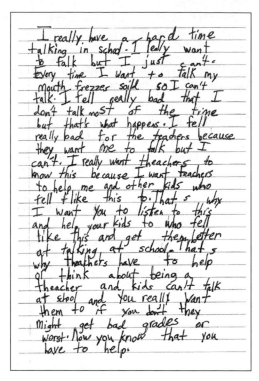

FIG. 3–2 Nora wrote the sentence "I have a hard time talking in school" and then wrote a new entry off of that sentence.

Providing Guided Practice

I F YOU NOTICE that several students are having difficulty making the transition from writing stories to writing about ideas, you may want to do a shared writing activity to support these children. Grab chart paper and a marker, gesture for the children to join you in a huddle (quickly), and then suggest the group work on one shared entry, just so they can get the feeling for how different it is to freewrite about ideas, rather than to write a story. To hurry past the topic-choice portion of writing and focus on the harder aspect of it, suggest a topic on which everyone in the group has some authority. Perhaps you'll ask the group to write ideas about recess, and suggest that one way to start writing ideas on any topic is to either observe that subject matter for real—or to observe in one's memories. To get started writing ideas about recess, then, the small group of youngsters might for a moment recall what happens at recess, picturing it, and then say what they observe. Sydni started. "All the kids are running around like crazy at recess."

Then I said, "So, if we want to write an entry starting with Sydni's observation, we need to say our thoughts about 'All the kids are running around like crazy at recess.' Right now, think about that." While they thought, I recorded the observation. Then I repeated Sydni's observation and asked, "What thought do you have about that?" Aidan clearly had something to add. "Recess is when we get to be free."

I guided, "When you are writing your ideas, try to say your thought and then say more about that thought—maybe tell a reason or give an example or make a comparison." Then I roped everyone into this work. "Let's all remember Aidan's thought and try to say more." As Aidan repeated the thought, "Recess is when we get to be free," I recorded it, and the thought hung in the air. Roy piped up. "There aren't any assignments."

I wrote this and pointed out that it helps to reread and say, "What more do I think about this?" and for a minute, the children did this while I waited. Then I quietly muttered, "We've got to say more," and eyed those who hadn't spoken. "What is your idea about recess and how there aren't any assignments?" I added, explaining, "We try to

MID-WORKSHOP TEACHING **Learning from Writers**

"Writers, show your partner your writing and talk about whether you think freewriting is working for you—which means talk about whether you are coming to new ideas that surprise you."

After children talked a bit, I said, "Let's listen to Miles' freewriting (see Figure 3–3), and notice the things he did that are already on our chart, *and*, also, let's notice things he did that we haven't gotten on our chart yet but that could be added. Jot notes so we can talk later."

I've been thinking about civilization. Civilization is a big word. When I hear it I conjure up images of the beginning of nations and empires.

"Hmm, . . . that's an interesting move. Writers, are you taking notes on what this writer is doing? I'm going to reread that part." I did, and then I said, "Hmm, . . . Writers, what are you noticing? What are the moves Miles is making? I'll read on."

What does it really mean? I think it describes the essence of our race, it is our culture, our technology, and our cities all combined. It is the computer program Civilization II that made me really think. Evan and I always call it. Civ II. I wondered why. I now think . . .

"Writers, keep checking the chart as you listen. See what the writer is doing. When you come up with something, see if it is on our chart and if not, think whether we should add it. I'll reread."

I wondered why. I now think it is because Civilization is such a massive word to describe this game, Civilization II is a big and complex . . . but it might not be big enough.

"Writers, I'll stop there though this entry keeps going. Talk to the people at your table about what moves the writer made that are on our chart and what we need to add to the chart." (See Share for revised chart.)

(continues)

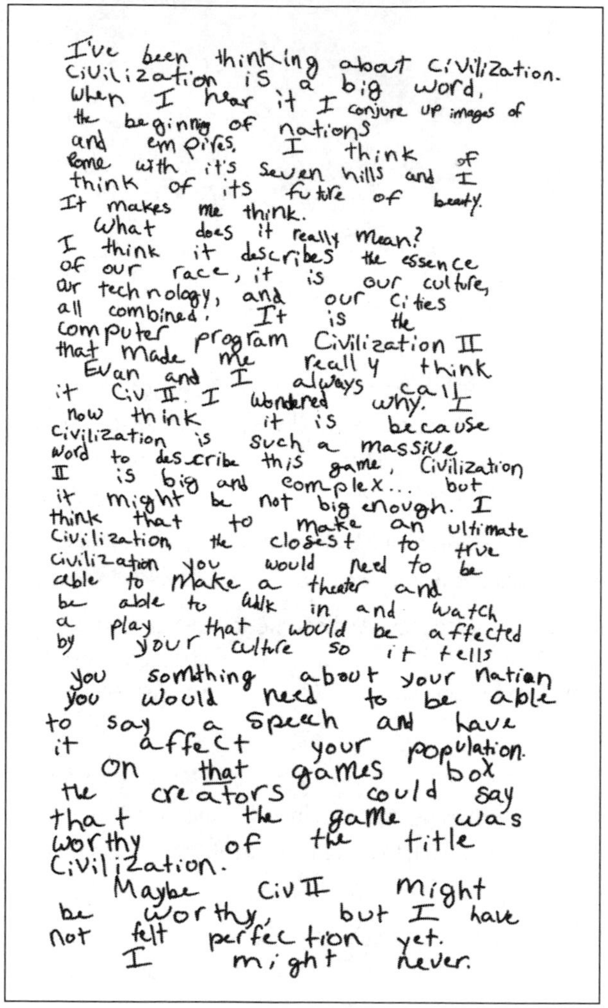

I've been thinking about civilization. Civilization is a big word. When I hear it I conjure up images of the beginning of nations and empires. I think of Rome with it's seven hills and I think of it's future of beauty. It makes me think.

What does it really mean? I think it describes the essence of our race, it is our culture, our technology, and our cities all combined. It is the computer program Civilization II that made me really think. Evan and I always call it Civ II. I wondered why. I now think it is because Civilization is such a massive word to describe this game, Civilization II is big and complex... but it might be not big enough. I think that to make an ultimate Civilization the closest to true Civilization you would need to be able to make a theater and be able to walk in and watch a play that would be affected by your culture so it tells you something about your nation you would need to be able to say a speech and have it affect your population. On that games box the creators could say that the game was worthy of the title Civilization.

Maybe Civ II might be worthy, but I have not felt perfection yet. I might never.

FIG. 3–3   Miles talking about civilization

think of more to say about the main thought." I reread it again. Chris dictated, "Kids should have more recess!" and I recorded this at the growing edge of the paragraph.

In this manner we continued to write an entry together about recess. The entry consisted of a list of related ideas, each written in a sentence. This wasn't perfect writing, but my goal wasn't perfection. After a few minutes of work, I reviewed what we had done together, asking the children to talk about how it felt to write about ideas instead of writing stories. Then I told them to use that "idea-writing feeling" as they switch and try writing another idea in their own notebooks—this time on their own topics. "I'll see how you're doing soon," I said, and moved on.

Of course, you'll intersperse small-group work with one-to-one conferences. Certainly one of your main goals will be to teach elaboration. Find writers who think and write in "sentences of thought," giving just a line or two to each mental operation. For example, a writer may have used the strategy of observing to spark thinking, but the writer's observation involves just a sentence or two. "I see the green plant. It has one long stem which only has two tiny leaves." Notice if this is a pattern. Does this writer tend to do just quick bouts of thinking with a pen? If you see this pattern in one child's writing, then you have a choice. You can teach that one child that it helps to reread one's own writing, noticing patterns in what we do as writers, and then you can point out this pattern in the writer's writing and suggest the writer return to some of those underdeveloped "sentences of thought" to try extending them. Alternatively (or in addition), you can make this into a mid-workshop teaching point or a share or a small-group teaching point.

Freewriting to Generate New Ideas

Harvest the class's observations about qualities they notice in the exemplar freewriting, adding to the chart.

Qualities of Good Freewriting

- The writer keeps writing freely, letting any thoughts come out.
- The writer seems to try to make ideas that get better and better as she writes longer.
- The writer sometimes compares things to make you get what she means.
- The writer doesn't cross stuff out.
- The writer sometimes says the big idea over and over (in different ways) as if trying to get it right.
- The writer stays for a long time on one big idea.
- The writer goes from big ideas to small examples back to big ideas.
- The writer comes up with new ideas.
- The writer raises questions

Ask students to assess their own most recent entry based on the qualities listed on the class chart, giving themselves a thumbs up or down, and helping them clarify goals for going forward.

"Writers, what if we put your writing in the center of this class and asked people to think about what *you* do as you write? I'll read off the items on our chart, and you give a thumbs up if you see yourself doing what we have listed or a thumbs down if you aren't doing that. And hopefully, this will give you some ideas for how you can make the writing to learn that you do in the next fifteen minutes more powerful than any you have ever done before—because that is your goal. Not just more writing, but better writing."

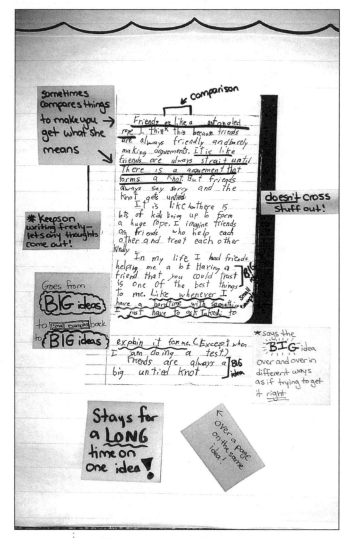

FIG. 3–4 Some teachers hung freewriting annotated with the qualities the class had noticed.

Channel writers to celebrate if their writing yielded new ideas.

"Writers, earlier we said that our goal when freewriting is to grow new ideas. Pause and reread what you have written, and box places where you've gotten a new idea. Star that idea like crazy—or give it a fireworks if you want—to show how totally cool it is when ideas burst out of the page (see Figures 3–5, 3–6, and 3–7). I've put some colorful marker pens on your desks. If you have time, reread earlier entries and do the same.

"Okay, now share your work with a partner and discuss how you came to your new thinking. Try to tell your partner what *you* did that helped you come to new ideas." Christina read her writing:

Family is who you always want to talk to no matter what. Family is who you are never afraid to fight with. Family doesn't have to be a direct relative. Family can be your very best friend. Family can be your dog that you take a walk with every day. Family can be your first doll that sits on your bed every day waiting for you to come home from school. Family can be your first-grade teacher. Family can be your next-door neighbor. Family just has to be someone or something you love and care for. Family is like a puzzle because when family is broken apart it always comes back together just like a puzzle. In other words, family can never be taken apart forever.

"'Family is like a puzzle' is my new big idea!" she announced. "I kept thinking about what else I could say about family."

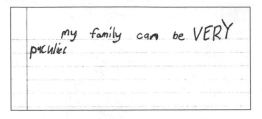

FIG. 3–5   Jonathan pulled out an idea to write long about.

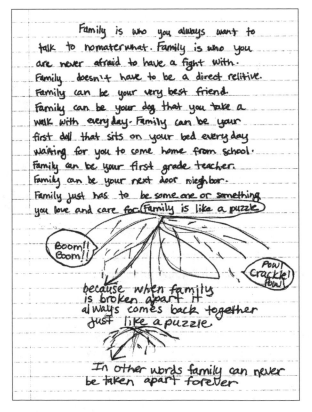

FIG. 3–6   Christina celebrates her writing by drawing fireworks around a new idea.

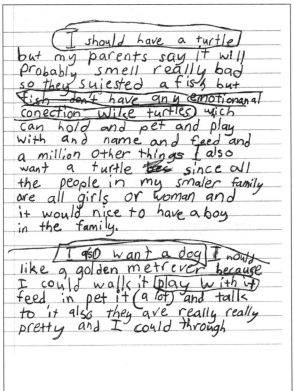

FIG. 3–7   Jonathan reads over an entry and circles some ideas he is having.

Using Elaboration Prompts to Grow Ideas

T HE WONDERFUL THING about teaching writers is that every teacher has a built-in staff developer on hand every day. You teach, and then before the sun sets that day, you get feedback on the precise ways in which your teaching has been effective and the ways it has not been so effective. This feedback is an extraordinary gift because research has shown that learners of anything—and certainly that includes learners of teaching writing—improve immeasurably when they are given feedback. What a bonanza it is, then, that teachers of writing have built-in staff developers!

For you to reap these benefits, you do need to put a bit of time into receiving the feedback that is right there for you. And in this world, when all of us are so strapped for time, so busy busy busy, it is entirely possible that you'll allow yourself to be so engulfed in all that you have to do and to reach and to get to and to accomplish that you won't pause long enough to take in the feedback that is right there for you. Don't do that. Doug Reeves has shown that 20% of what we do yields 80% of the payoff. You need to learn which parts of your teaching are yielding that payoff, and you need to alter your teaching based on that feedback.

The feedback that is there for you—the built-in staff developer—is in your students' work. You teach, your writers' write, and *their* work is an immediate assessment of *your* work. You need to collect their work and to sit with it, thinking, not, "How are my students doing?" but instead, "How am *I* doing?" Read their freewriting from three days ago, two days ago, and yesterday and think, "Are they getting better?" Compare their writing to your image of good freewriting/writing to learn, asking, "Are they getting better in obvious, concrete, dramatic ways?" And, if not, be ready to reconsider your own teaching.

Be ready to notice especially the sources of trouble, because the storyline of your teaching is going to emerge from you (the main character in this story) encountering difficulties (as main characters always encounter in a story) and then inventing responses to those difficulties. Those invented responses will be where the rising action occurs in the storyline of your teaching.

IN THIS SESSION, you'll teach children that writers linger with their ideas, extending their initial thinking by having conversations with themselves as they write and using elaboration prompts to grow their ideas.

GETTING READY

✔ "Qualities of Good Freewriting" list from Session 3

✔ "Ways to Push Our Thinking" list of prompts, written on chart paper. Feel free to use ours or add your own that your students are already comfortable using. (see Teaching)

✔ Your own entry of an idea and ways you pushed your thinking by using prompts. Prepare to demonstrate the process in front of students.

✔ Idea the whole class can build on using prompts

✔ A chart with some noted qualities of freewriting that you can use to create small groups (see Conferring)

✔ Examples of big abstract ideas and small precise details (see Mid-Workshop Teaching)

✔ A cut-out photo or drawing of a ladder (see Mid-Workshop Teaching)

✔ You'll want to be on the lookout today for a great example of freewriting that leads to new thinking that you can highlight (see Share)

COMMON CORE STATE STANDARDS: W.4.1, W.4.5, W.4.10, RL.4.1, RL.4.3, RL.4.10, SL.4.1, SL.4.4, L.4.1, L.4.2, L.4.3

This extra-powerful, extra-fun session emerged from just this sort of grappling with difficulty. Time after time, teachers found that when teaching essays—and when teaching free-writing as well—students found it hard to write about ideas at length, and part of that difficulty was that they found it hard to think about ideas in depth. Many students approached this unit, writing (and thinking) in what the great writing researcher, Mina Shaughnessey, referred to as "sentences of thought."

"It is no small thing to teach students to elaborate. Today, then, is just one of many days devoted to this challenge."

As mentioned earlier, I have come to realize that when working in expository genres, elaboration is especially difficult because the writer needs to learn to go from thinking in one-liners to thinking in paragraphs (or better yet, in essays!). It is no small thing to teach students to elaborate. Today, then, is just one of many days devoted to this challenge.

It's easiest to teach children to elaborate on their ideas in writing if they've already done this in conversations. Many teachers first teach youngsters to grow ideas by engaging them in accountable discussions after read-alouds. If you want to do this, read aloud a text, and when you pause, ask children to turn and share their ideas with a partner. Listen in as they talk, locating a child who has an idea that could generate an effective conversation. After a few minutes, ask, "Could someone get us started in a conversation about what we just read?" and call the child whose comment you heard earlier.

Let the class see you mulling over that one child's idea, restating it as you do so. Then say to the group, "Let's *all* talk and think more about Raffi's idea." You might say, "Talk with your partner about ways you agree with what Raffi said and ways you disagree with his idea." Soon afterward, convene the class and help them work together to add on to and talk back to that one idea. At first, you'll need to provide the conversational prompts. "Raffi said. . . . Who'd like to *add on* to that idea? Do the rest of you agree or disagree? Tell Raffi. Tell him why you agree. Give him examples."

Whether or not you begin by leading these accountable talk book conversations, you will want to teach children to grow ideas as part of writing to learn. In this session, you'll teach them to use the same phrases that they're apt to use in conversation—phrases such as "the important thing about this" or "As I say this, I'm realizing . . ."—to elaborate as they write. Last year your students likely learned strategies to elaborate, which consisted of helping them shift from declaring opinions and reasons to providing concrete examples to show their thinking. Thus, you'll probably find them comfortable with phrases such as "an example of this is . . . ," "for instance . . . ," or "like this one time. . . ." Now you will want to ratchet up the level of that work by pushing them to also elaborate through other means. You'll want to also equip them to linger at the level of ideas before shifting into the more familiar world of retelling instances. "In other words . . ." and "This is making me realize . . ." and "The important thing about this is . . ." can all help children elaborate first by saying more about their ideas. What important work!

Using Elaboration Prompts to Grow Ideas

CONNECTION

Celebrate that children are writing provocative ideas and point out that they could be saying even more.

"Writers, I brought your notebooks home last night. I made myself a cup of tea, wrapped myself in a blanket, and put the pile of notebooks beside me. You know what happened? I read a few sentences in one of your notebooks, and then those sentences got me thinking and I'd look further on the page to learn what *you* thought about the topic you'd brought up, and then—Whoa! I'd find you had jumped onto a whole new topic!

"I kept wanting to phone you guys and say, 'You got me thinking that. . . . Isn't it also true that . . . ? This makes me realize. . . .'

"I think we've turned a corner in this unit of study. You have gotten really great at coming up with entries that spark all kinds of thoughts."

❖ **Name the teaching point.**

"Today, I want to teach you that *you need to hold on to those thoughts for longer stretches of time*. It helps to hold conversations with yourself about your own first thoughts. Some writers keep a list of 'ways to push our thinking' close by while they write and use those elaboration prompts to prompt them to talk back to their own first ideas."

TEACHING

Recall that yesterday, students noted that when doing strong freewriting, writers linger with and elaborate on an idea. Explain that writers conduct conversations with themselves as they write—conversations that allow them to develop their own first thoughts.

"The other day, when you studied Jonah's freewriting, you guys noted that it was effective in part because he stayed on one idea for a long time, saying that big idea in more than one way until he got it right. When a writer stays on one idea for a long time and finds a lot to think and say about that one idea, people say the writer is 'elaborating.'

I'm hoping children will understand the need for elaboration if I situate this within the context of an interested reader who's dying to get into a grand conversation over their ideas.

Remember that our goals always extend beyond the reading and writing workshop. It is important to teach writing in part because writing is a powerful tool for thought. This session goes a long way toward helping children use writing as a tool for growing ideas on the page. We're explicitly teaching children to say more and think more, to extend their first thoughts, and to know what it is to see new ideas emerge from the tips of their pens. This is important!

"Here is the secret. If you are thinking something—like, thinking, 'It's hard to be a good friend'—the best way to get yourself to think a lot more about that is to have a really great talk with someone about that idea, right? And that other person might say things like 'Yeah, I agree,' and then she might say the idea (It's hard to be a good friend) in *her* words. Then you might nod and say, 'Yeah, that's it!' And who knows, you might say the idea *again* before giving an example.

"So here is what I need you to know. Essayists let the words on the page be sort of like the other person in a conversation. So they have a thought, and they put that thought on the paper. Then they listen to the paper saying their own thought to themselves, and say, 'Yeah! I agree' (with themselves) or say 'One example of that is . . .' or 'That's partly true and partly not true.' It is as if essayists are in conversation with themselves. That conversation with themselves is what allows them to elaborate—to say more about one idea, to connect the idea to other things, to say the idea in more than one way, to go from big ideas to specific examples.

"Sometimes it helps to keep a list of ways to push our thinking close by while we write and to use those elaboration prompts to extend our thinking, prompting us to talk back not just in conversations with others but also when writing more about our own first ideas."

It is crucial to teach children to talk back to each other's ideas. The single most common limitation in children's writing is that ideas are underdeveloped. By teaching children to talk back to each other's ideas, you also teach them to talk back to (and extend) their own ideas.

Earlier we taught children to use prompts to turn the corner from simply observing to having a thought about what they observed. In this minilesson, you use a wider array of prompts to promote thoughtfulness, channeling children toward different kinds and even levels of thinking. A prompt such as, "For example . . ." or "To add on . . ." can lead children to provide examples and think associatively. "This makes me realize . . ." or "This is giving me the idea that . . ." can lead them to progress from one thought to another, often in a free-association fashion. "On the other hand . . . ," "But . . . ," and "I partly disagree because . . ." can lead a child to question, while "This is similar to . . ." and "This is different from . . ." can lead to comparison.

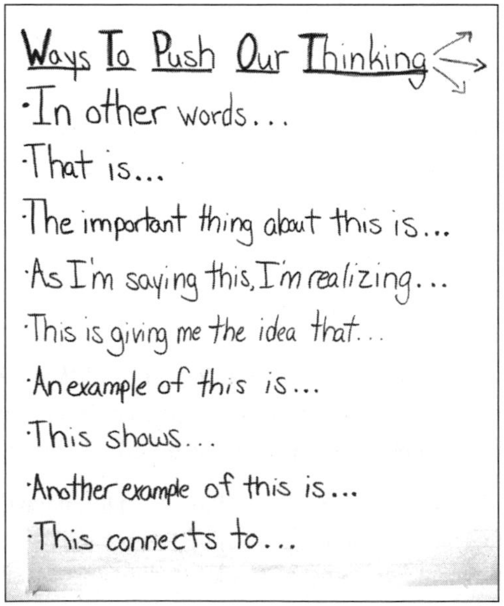

Ways to Push Our Thinking

- In other words . . .
- That is . . .
- The important thing about this is . . .
- As I say this, I'm realizing . . .
- This is giving me the idea that . . .
- An example of this is . . .
- This shows . . .
- Another example of this is . . .
- This connects to . . .
- I see . . .
- The thought I have about this is . . .
- To add on . . .
- I used to think that . . . but now I think that . . .
- What surprises me about this is . . .
- Many people think . . . but I think . . .

Ways To Push Our Thinking

- In other words . . .
- That is . . .
- The important thing about this is . . .
- As I'm saying this, I'm realizing . . .
- This is giving me the idea that . . .
- An example of this is . . .
- This shows . . .
- Another example of this is . . .
- This connects to . . .

FIG. 4–1

Involve writers in helping you to use elaboration prompts to help you talk back to your own first ideas.

"I'm hoping you can help me try this in my writing, and then you can try. Here's a teeny start to an entry:

> When I was a kid, my father taught me a lot.

"Maya, would you choose from the 'Ways to Push Our Thinking' list," I said, signaling to the list. "Coach me by saying a prompt you want me to use, and I'll use that prompt to think more about my claim. I'm going to write-in-the-air, but in real life, I'd be writing on the paper." I repeated my entry, "When I was a kid, my father taught me a lot."

Maya interjected, "*In other words . . .*" I repeated my claim and the prompt, paused in thought and then completed that sentence. "*In other words*, my father was one of my first teachers. I had others at school, but my father was a teacher-at-home."

Then Maya said, "*For example . . . ,*" Repeating her prompt, I nodded at her and used it to spur an additional thought to my writing-in-the-air. "*For example*, he taught me that a person's job should also be that person's hobby. Every Christmas he made waffles and took them to the hospital where he worked. He never complained about having to go into his job on Christmas."

Before long, Maya inserted, "*This gives me the idea that . . .*" I again repeated her prompt and said: "*This gives me the idea that* everyone should have work that they love. I now realize people who love their work are lucky."

ACTIVE ENGAGEMENT

Set children up to practice using elaboration prompts to extend an idea you give them.

"Now it's your turn to practice this. I'm going to give you a shared, whole-class idea, just to practice. Partner 2, you'll take the part of the writer. Partner 1 will prompt you, acting almost like the other person in the conversation, saying elaboration prompts that can help you think longer about your idea. I'll give you the idea, and then Partner 2 you repeat it. Partner 1, use the chart to help you use elaboration prompts to help your partner grow his or her thinking. Remember to give Partner 2 some space to write-in-the-air whatever his or her thoughts might be.

"Okay, here's the idea: Kids have more problems with friends as they get older. Partner 2, repeat it and go."

As I do this, I try to demonstrate that a writer can use one of these prompts without knowing what she'll say next. As we articulate the words of a prompt, our mind leaps ahead, thinking "Why is it important?" In this fashion I aim to demonstrate that writing can be a tool to grow brand-new thoughts. Children already know that we write to record well-fashioned ideas that we've decided to present to the world; now I'm helping them learn that we also write to muse, speculate, risk having new insights.

When children begin to bring these phrases into their writing, you'll notice a child may write a phrase such as "This makes me realize . . ." without being aware of the meaning of that phrase. If you see a writer write that phrase, point to the words and say, "Oh! This tells me you are having a brand-new idea right now. I can't wait to see it!" If the writer writes, "This is important because . . . ," you will want to exclaim, "I can't wait to see what you figure the real significance of this is! I can't wait to see your decision." In this fashion, you teach children what those hard-to-pin down words mean.

LINK

Restate the teaching point. Rally writers to use elaboration prompts as scaffolds to help them extend their own ideas as they write.

"Writers, listening to you, I'm hearing your first ideas become more insightful. Remember, if this writing can get you thinking deep into a conversation with yourself about your ideas, using elaboration prompts to talk back to (and think with) your own ideas, this can push you to grow insightful, surprising ideas. Later you can box them out, put them on top of a new page, and think off from them.

"How many of you will start today by putting the writing-in-the-air you just did onto the page?" Some hands went up. "Great. Get started. You'll probably be able to do a second one today, too. And how many of you are writing a new entry today?" Others raised their hands. "Great. Remember, you can use our chart, 'Ways to Push Our Thinking.' And try to use these elaboration prompts to help you stay longer with an idea. If anyone feels a little unsure about what you are doing, stay here on the rug and we'll work together. Off you go!"

As most of the class moved off, I gathered the few writers who remained and did another quick round of using prompts, this time charging them with writing their ideas on paper rather than writing-in-the-air. I left them to continue working as I moved off to confer and pull small groups, checking back on their progress from time to time.

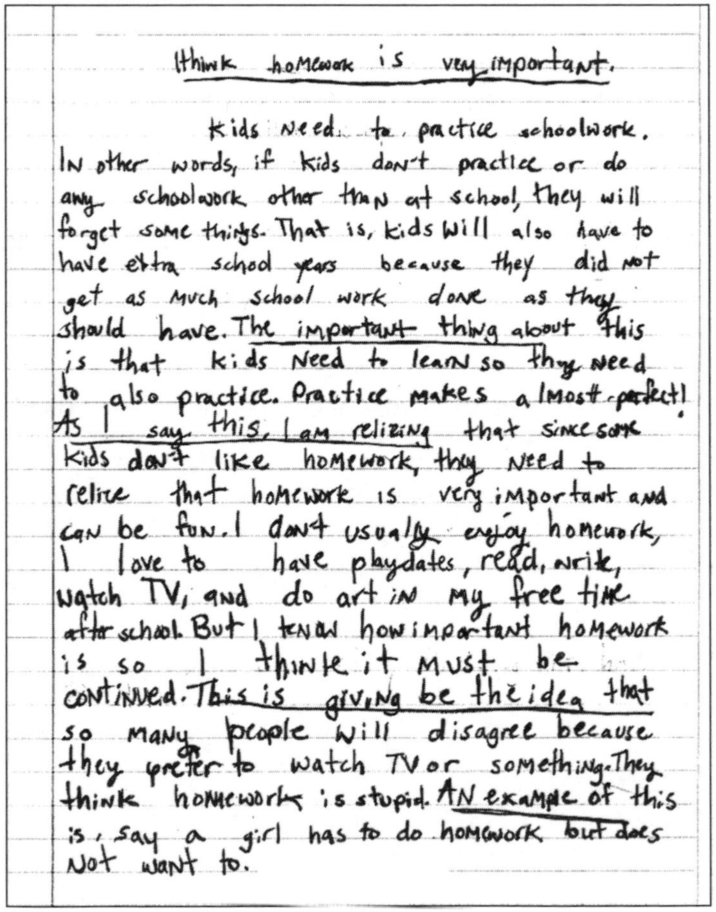

LaKeya used conversational prompts to extend her first thought (see Figure 4–2), and Maya elaborates using prompts (see Figure 4–3).

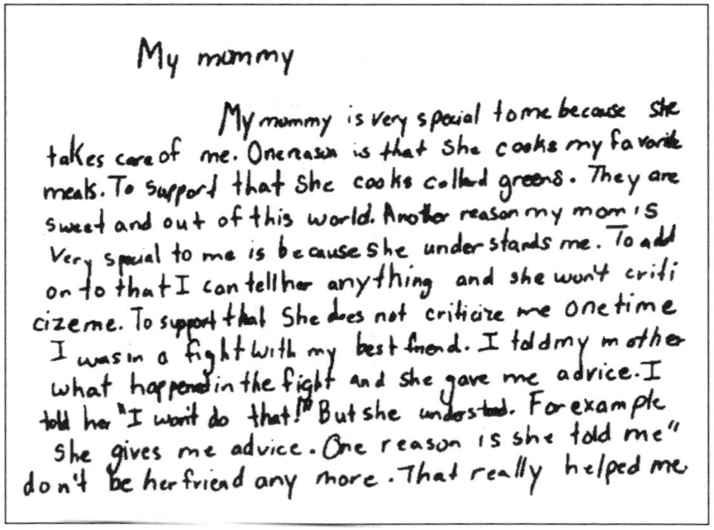

FIG. 4–2 LaKeya has used conversational prompts to extend her first thought.

FIG. 4–3 Maya elaborates using prompts.

GRADE 4: BOXES AND BULLETS

Noting Qualities of Good Essay Writing in Children's Work

WHEN YOU CONFER WITH CHILDREN, try to let their entries teach you (and your students) ways to talk and think about essay writing. Notice entries that children have written that for some reason work especially well, and then join children in trying to put into words why those particular entries work. Be very specific and ask children to be specific, too. For example, ask, "What do you mean when you say, 'It's detailed?' Point to the details you used. What works about them?" The Common Core State Standards make it very clear that it is important for youngsters to grow up not only writing well, but also able to talk about effective writing, turning texts inside out to discuss what writers have done to create effects. Any time you recruit students to talk about effective writing, you support this important skill. *(continues)*

MID-WORKSHOP TEACHING   **Moving Up and Down the Ladder of Abstraction**

"Writers, can I have your eyes and attention? I'm noticing you move back and forth between writing about big ideas and showing them through small specific details. Totally cool! You're writing about huge ideas like 'I care about my friends' and then showing those ideas through details like the time your friend was sad and you sat next to her on the steps, even though you really wanted to join the kickball game. Emma, for example, is writing about the big idea that good friends can be any age and then shows that idea by writing about her friend who is two years older. (See Figure 4–3.)

Emma moves up and down the ladder of abstraction (see Figure 4–4):

> My brother is older than me.
>
> Older siblings don't always act their age.
>
> I am two years younger than my friend, but she acts as though I am her age.
>
> Good friends can be any age.
>
> Parents don't always understand kid issues.
>
> My parents don't always understand what I am dealing with.

"Writers, a guy named Roy Peter Clark, who is a really important writing teacher for grown-up writers, calls what you are doing 'going up and down the ladder of abstraction.' At the top of the ladder," I said, waving my hand above my head, "are the times you write about big ideas like friendship and being true to oneself and peer pressure. At the bottom of the ladder," I continued, and I brought my hand down, "is

FIG. 4–4   Emma moves up and down the ladder of abstraction.

(continues)

when you show these ideas through detailed examples and Small Moment stories. I confess, I sometimes keep this photo of a ladder beside me when I write to remind myself to go up and down the ladder of abstraction when I am writing.

"Let's practice thinking about where an idea is on our ladder. Show me with your hand whether I am writing at the top or the bottom of the ladder. Let's see. I could start by writing about how my father taught me so much. Show me with your hand where that is on the ladder." The children all raised their hands above their heads, and I nodded, "Yes, that is a very general idea about all the times, not just about one time.

"Let's try another one. So, I could tell about how one time my father taught me it was okay to cry. You are right. That's lower down. It's a specific example.

"I could write, 'Some grown-ups, like many kids, care a lot about fitting in, but others don't think that matters.'" The children stretched their arms over their heads, and I nodded that yes, this was a big, abstract idea.

"I could say that my Dad wore frozen peas on his head at our Christmas party." (Specific.)

"Writers, remember, the best writing moves up and down the ladder of abstraction. If you find yourself staying at the top of the ladder and writing on and on about big ideas, push yourself to say, 'For example, this one time . . .' because that will help you move down the ladder.

"On the other hand, if you find yourself only writing about the details, push yourself to say, 'This makes me think . . .' because that will help you move back up the ladder."

I ended by saying, "Before you continue writing, reread your writing and mark in the margin whether it is high or low on the ladder of abstraction. Decide if you are writing at the top of the ladder or the bottom. Then push yourself to move back and forth. Okay, back to writing."

It will also be important for you to notice problems that you see in children's entries and to help children put those problems into words. This, too, will help children develop a vocabulary for talking about their goals as they write.

As you talk about writing with students, one of the things you will notice is that writers can always write at greater or lesser levels of abstraction. For example, earlier I jotted ideas I had about my dad. One idea was that he was one of my most important teachers. That is a fairly general idea, high on a ladder of abstraction. Think of it as Roman numeral I in an outline. I could move down a notch in the level of generalization and write, "My dad taught me to fail with grace." Think of that as the A in the outline. Or I could move toward an even more specific/less abstract idea (the number 1 in the outline) and say, "When my dad was fired, he taught my brothers and sisters and me the truth of the saying, 'When one door closes, another opens.'" Expository writing works best when there is only a little bit of writing at the highest level of abstraction and much more writing at the lowest level. But writing at the lower levels of abstraction needs to fit under the province of the writing at the higher levels of abstraction. As mentioned earlier, it is important for children to learn to shift between higher and lower levels of abstraction and for our teaching to support that flexibility.

Then, too, as you talk about writing with students, you will probably talk and think about whether the writing feels honest. I suspect you will generally find that when writing feels fresh, it is characterized by honesty. The writer may not use fancy words, but he or she seems to reach for the exactly right words.

Writing about ideas also works when the writing is cohesive. The entries students produce now will not tend to be that, but you may find sections that do feel cohesive. Chances are good that those sections will contain repetition and parallelism, as these are ways writers create a unified message. You may notice that in some essay entries, a key phrase or word recurs, almost like a refrain. As the text unfolds, bits of the text harken back to earlier passages. This creates resonance, and it is often what takes my breath away in an essay. When children do this it is usually a lucky accident. Find these accidents and let the young author (and his or her classmates) know the effect on you!

You might also consider how you can set up small groups around qualities of good freewriting. You might set up a chart with different qualities you want to see in the writing and jot quickly the names of students who seem to need more help in these areas. Then you'll have your small groups set.

Shifts from big ideas to details	Stays with one idea	Reaches for precise words
Grows new thinking	Writing has parts that feel cohesive	

For any of these groups, you can always create a piece of your own demonstration writing or show a short excerpt from a previous student that showcases the quality you want writers to notice and involve them in a mini-inquiry as to how the writer of the exemplar piece has reached for precise words, or stayed with one idea, etc. Chart what they notice and get them to try it out in their own writing immediately.

Celebrating Extended Thinking

Ask partners to talk over the development of the thinking in their notebooks—with or without prompts.

"Writers, can I have your eyes and attention? Get with your partner and share an entry in which you really pushed yourself to stay with those ideas so they led you to new thoughts. And talk about whether you used the elaboration prompts from our chart to stay with your idea or whether you did something else. We're inventing ways of writing here, and I'm dying to learn about what you are doing that works for you."

"I definitely used the prompts," David told Maya. "Me, too," Maya said. "But I also tried to ask myself questions and that helped me keep going, too."

Convene the class and highlight an example that you want the rest to emulate.

"Listen to these examples from your classmates! See how their thinking grows and grows? You'll notice that Ellie definitely uses elaboration prompts, and she uses more and more sophisticated ones as her entry progresses along. First she uses 'for example,' but soon she's nudging her thinking with 'I realize . . .' and 'what surprises me is . . . .'"

> I hate it when I am doing something important and then I get interrupted.
> For example, when I'm reading a book and my mom calls, "Ellie, it's time to go to sleep" but I really want to finish the book because that's what I am into. I realize that this happens a lot to me, like when I'm watching TV or having fun with my friends. What surprises me is I always have a lot of time and no one interrupts me when I am doing things I don't like, like homework or practicing my oboe or other things.

"Let's each set a goal for ourselves for our next entry. Right now, think of something you want to try doing in your next entry. Maybe you want to try writing a full page on one idea. Maybe you want to make sure you move up and down the ladder of abstraction. Maybe you want to try pushing your thinking by using all of the prompts, even the more sophisticated ones. Make a goal for yourself, right now. Write that down at the top of a new notebook page and box it out. When you return to your notebook, you'll see your goal and be reminded of what you want to accomplish the next time you write. Okay, share your goal with a neighbor right now and say how you will hold yourself accountable for meeting your goal!"

We got a dog when mom came from Africa becquse she said we could when she left. We all thought she would not keep her word, but I should have known better because she did, the weekend she came back. Mom was also the first person who the dog, Monty, really loved. Both Monty and I really have a lot of emotion for mommy. Mom takes care of me, cooks for me, and makes me feel happy.

I love her so much. I also love my dad so much because he is the nicest guy I know, he works five days a week - just so he can support my family and me. Sometimes he even goes to work on the days you usually have off. And he does our house, our food, our clothes. And I am gald to have a father like that. But sometimes I don't think I

appreciate him enough, even thought I should. There are alot of people/ things that I think we should appreciate more. There should be a holiday called 'National Appreciation Day' when we take time to appreciate the things that we usually forget to. There are many people in the past that invented things for us, our troops who give their lives for us, teachers.

FIG. 4–5   Max's entry represents a journey of thought.

USING ELABORATION PROMPTS TO GROW IDEAS

Elaborating on First Thoughts

Tonight, practice using some of the elaboration prompts at home. Have a little conversation with yourself while you are walking down the street or brushing your teeth or looking out the window. For example, you can walk down the street and pick a prompt out of the air. Say to yourself "I'm learning that. . . ." Fill in the sentence in a way that surprises you. Then add on. Say another prompt: "For example. . . ." Or try more complicated elaboration prompts (they're the later ones on your list), like "I used to think that . . . but now I think that. . . ." "What surprises me about this is . . ." or "Many people think . . . but I think. . . ."

When you do this work, try to make sure that you don't only say these phrases but that you use them. Use the phrases to make your initial idea become richer, more complex, and more original. Suppose I say, "I like dogs" and add, "This is important because. . . ." But then I simply say, "It just is," and add, "Furthermore, I like cats, too." I wouldn't be using these terms as tools for thought. What a difference there would be if instead my thought train went like this:

> I like dogs. This is important to me because my mother's dogs sometimes seem to matter as much to her as we, her children, do. I find myself growing up to be like her. Furthermore, now that my oldest son is going off to college, I've been thinking of getting myself a new puppy.

Most of your homework tonight won't be written. It will instead be thought, said, or lived. But also, in your writer's notebook, re-create and extend one train of thought, one that leads you into especially provocative areas.

Mining Our Writing

IN THIS SESSION, you'll teach children that writers mine their entries and their lives for insights, developing these into more fully formed ideas and thesis statements.

GETTING READY

✔ Previous notebook entries from the narrative unit so you can demonstrate rereading these to find new ideas laying within the lines (see Teaching)

✔ A seed idea and relevant examples that you could imagine using in an essay so that you can demonstrate developing a thesis statement for your own essay

✔ "Questions Writers Ask of Earlier Entries" chart (see Teaching)

✔ Students' writer's notebooks

✔ "Strategies for Generating Essay Entries" chart from Session 2

✔ "To Develop a Thesis Statement, I . . ." chart (see Share)

✔ Chart paper and markers for the Share

COMMON CORE STATE STANDARDS: W.4.1.a,b, W.4.3, W.4.5, W.4.8, RFS.4.4, SL.4.1, L.4.1, L.4.2.d, L.4.3

KATHERINE PATERSON, author of *Bridge to Terabithia*, says, "Writing is something like a seed that grows in the dark . . . or a grain of sand that keeps rubbing at your vitals until you find you are building a coating around it. The growth of a book takes time . . . I talk, I look, I listen, I hate, I fear, I love, I weep, and somehow all of my life gets wrapped around the grain" (1981).

This quote exactly matches my understanding of how writers build depth and intensity in a piece of writing. For example, I might jot down an anecdote. When I reread it, something stirs inside me. I find myself layering the anecdote with an insight. I drive to work, thinking of my writing, and pass something by the side of the road that somehow fits with the original anecdote and its accompanying insight. By now my mental seed idea has taken on extra layers, like one of those surprise balls given as favors at a child's birthday party, the kind with reams of crepe paper hiding all sorts of embedded treasures. I write, I reread, I remember, I listen, and all of this gets wrapped around the initial idea.

One way to teach children to layer their ideas and memories is to teach them to reread entries—and to catch the thoughts they have as they do this rereading. For example, I might reread my entry about my father with his improvised ice pack, and suddenly I'm thinking of how teachers, too, are always jerry-rigging things to make do with whatever we have. Hardship leads to resourcefulness. All of a sudden I am thinking of creativity as a willingness to live off the land, to improvise. Suddenly what began as an idea about my dad has become an idea about people in general and life and creativity—what it is and where it comes from. Where will I go next with this trail of thought?

In this session, you'll teach children to reread and rethink to layer their experiences with insights. You'll teach them to reread entries and ask themselves questions: "Why did I write this? What surprises me here?" This session, then, is about finding meaning and messages in the stories and lessons of our lives. I hope it can bring you and your children to the heart of writing.

Mining Our Writing

CONNECTION

Compliment students on elaborating on ideas, reminding them of the importance of doing so. Stress that the goal is not saying more, but rather growing better ideas. Spotlight a writer who did this.

"Writers, yesterday I watched you push yourselves to stay with one idea in your writing by growing new thoughts about that idea. I am so glad you are remembering that the goal is not just *longer* writing about a topic or an idea, but also better thinking. The goal is to lift the level of your own ideas. When you write something like 'It is important to have a best friend' and then reread what you have written and push yourself to think more, your ideas become more complex. Listen to what Tyrone wrote recently, when he made a goal to push himself to say more." I read with great seriousness, stressing the growing profoundness of his words.

> It is important to have one best friend. This is important because having one best friend is like having a home in the world. Some people think that it is best to have lots of friends and to think of them all as equal, but I find it comforting to know that Amy will always be there for me no matter what.

"Did you see Tyrone start with 'It is important to have a best friend' and end up thinking, 'Having one best friend is like having a home in the world.' Whoa! Give me a thumbs up if you sometimes found yourself starting with a ho-hum idea," I gestured toward the ground to show this meant a low-level idea "and then you ended up lifting the ideas sky high." I gestured toward the sky as students put their thumbs up. "Great job!

"I think you are ready to learn one of the most important lessons of all." I lowered my voice and leaned forward. "Ready? Here it is."

❖ **Name the teaching point.**

"Today, I want to teach you that instead of coming up with *new* ideas all the time, writers often reread and mine their old writing, looking for jewels. It is especially powerful to look not only at *one* old entry and then another, but to look across a bunch of entries and see the topics that resurface often. It is powerful to discover that there are ideas or themes underneath the surface of our notebooks and our lives."

You plan for your students to write in paragraphs of thought, not sentences of thought. Over time, watch whether their initial ideas always fit into the confines of one sentence. As writers become more sophisticated, they'll use the whole paragraphs not so much to elaborate upon a one-sentence idea, but to lay out the idea in the first place. If you wanted to do so, you could explicitly teach this.

TEACHING

Involve the students as you demonstrate returning to your own earlier entries to look for underlying ideas.

"I'm hoping you will help me try some of this work with my writing. Let's reread one of my earlier notebook entries—a story—and look for some ideas that might be lying between the lines. I'll jot some of those ideas in the margins and choose one marginal idea to write as a longer entry. Then, in a bit, you'll be able to try this with your writing.

"Okay, so let's start by looking back at one of my previous entries. You know that I'm sort of getting onto the topic of my dad, so I'm going to go to an entry about him, just any one." I leafed through the pages of my notebook, scanning the narrative entries until I settled on one. "To get started coming up with ideas, let's reread just the ending of this entry and keep some questions in mind. Here's a whole list of possible questions, but let's just think of the first one or two as I reread my entry."

Questions Writers Ask of Earlier Entries

- What is the important thing about this entry?
- What does this teach about me? About life?
- Why do I remember this one time? How does it connect to who I am or to important issues?
- What other entries have I written that connect to this one?
- What does this make me realize?
- What do I want readers to know about this?
- What surprises me about this?

"Keep those questions in mind and help me think about what ideas this entry might have laying between the lines," I said, and flipped open the chart tablet to read my entry:

> When the [basketball] game was almost over, I glanced toward the doorway and saw my father striding across the gym floor toward me, his red plaid hunting cap perched on his head, his rubber galoshes flapping. Why couldn't he wait in the car like all the other dads, I thought. Then, in a voice that boomed through the room, my dad called "Lukers!" and began to climb the bleachers toward me and the other kids. I wanted the floor to open up and swallow me.

"Okay, let's think about that first question: 'What is the important thing about this entry?' Hmmm. . . . Well, I wrote about it because I was so embarrassed. I still remember that when Dad came to sit with me, I wanted the floor to open up and swallow me.

One important reason to keep a writer's notebook is that this allows us to revisit earlier writing. There are many reasons to invite children to reread their notebooks. During word study, you may want them to practice their new high-frequency words by rereading early entries, correcting any instances where they've misspelled them. If you have taught children to think about structures in their writing, you can ask them to reread old entries and categorize them according to the structure in which they are written. Today, you are showing children how they can take inspiration from these early pieces. Once you have a narrative and some big ideas about that narrative, you have the ingredients for a strong essay.

This is far too long to write in class. I had already written it.

Whenever I model, I try to make my processes transferable. Notice that these questions could be asked of any personal essay entry. I want to teach kids to ask (as well as to answer) questions such as these.

"So, what are *the ideas* this entry gives me?" I reread it. "This entry is about the idea that when I was a kid, I really wanted to fit in. And dad didn't act like other fathers." Then I said, "I'm going to annotate this entry. That means I'm going to write some quick notes in the margins to help me remember my ideas." I jotted into the margins of my writing, "Dad doesn't act like other fathers." and "I wanted to fit in."

"Thumbs up if you were thinking about ideas along those lines as well." Thumbs popped up. "Hmmm . . . so, I could look and scan to see if I have other entries about my dad or about wanting to fit in. I know a famous author once said that most of us only have two or three themes that run through a lot of our writing, so it may well be that those same topics reoccur."

Debrief, naming what you've done in a way that is transferable to other days and other topics.

"Did you see how we reread an already written entry and then asked just one or two questions about it? In that way, we're mining the entry for underlying ideas. You know, I might find some of those same ideas under the surface of a lot of my work."

I waited a minute until more thumbs had gone up. "Okay, now annotate your entry. Just like I did, jot your ideas in the margin. Just a few words, not a full sentence." Again, I gave them a minute to scratch quick jots.

Kimberly turned to her partner and said eagerly, "I asked myself why it was important and it's important because it showed I did something for myself and how happy I was about that." Kimberly read her entry to her partner, pointing out the way she annotated an idea in the margins (see Figure 5–1).

> I remember the first time I caught a lizard. I've held one before of course, but catching one was different. I was working around the garden in my grandma's house in Florida. Then I saw it. Climbing on the fence. I cupped my hands and . . . caught it! I picked I up by my two fingers. I could feel it heart beating and it squirming. I put it up to my face and looked at it in the eye. "Hey little fella, you shouldn't be playing around at this time, my uncle is going to mow the lawn." I walked to the front yard and set him down on a palm tree. He stood on the branch looking at me. I catched him again. He let me. I said, "Go on, go to your family." I set him down again. He stood there. I gave one last look and ran to the door. "Goodbye!" I was so happy, and I told my dad how happy I am to do something for myself.

Continue to involve your writers in watching as you generate new writing from your previous entry.

"So now writers, I'm just going to let some ideas come out of my pencil." I began scribbling on my clipboard and voicing aloud as I wrote. "Why is this story about the basketball game important to me? I think I wrote about being embarrassed by my father because when I was young it bothered me that my dad didn't act like other fathers.

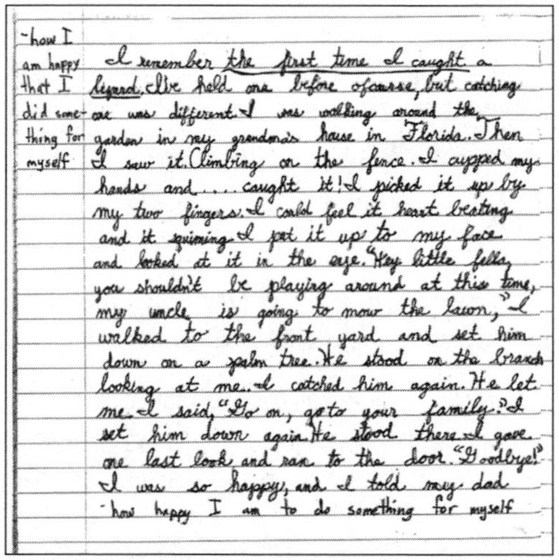
-how I am happy that I did something for myself

I remember the first time I caught a lizard. I've held one before of course, but catching one was different. I was walking around the garden in my grandma's house in Florida. Then I saw it. Climbing on the fence. I cupped my hands and . . . caught it! I picked it up by my two fingers. I could feel it heart beating and it squirming. I put it up to my face and looked at it in the eye. "Hey little fella, you shouldn't be playing around at this time, my uncle is going to mow the lawn," I walked to the front yard and set him down on a palm tree. He stood on the branch looking at me. I catched him again. He let me. I said, "Go on, go to your family." I set him down again. He stood there. I gave one last look and ran to the door. "Goodbye!" I was so happy, and I told my dad how happy I am to do something for myself

FIG. 5–1 Kimberly read an entry she wrote and annotated an idea she had about it in the margins.

"I could leave it at that, but I'll try to push myself to say more. Let's see . . . I'll reread and then just tell myself, 'Keep going.'

"For example, he didn't wait in the car like other fathers, but, instead tromped right into our basketball games. He didn't know parents were expected to stay in the background. He'd go up to my friends, introduce himself, and soon he'd be in deep conversations with them. My cheeks would burn because he didn't stay inside the traditional father role. That was long ago, however, and I've since come to see the beauty in my father's arrival at those games. . . ."

Debrief, naming what you've done in a way that is transferable to other days and other topics.

"Did you see how I kept pushing myself to explore the meaning of the first entry? Writers do this often."

ACTIVE ENGAGEMENT

Set up partners to practice what you demonstrate.

"Right now, Partner 1, please open your notebook and turn to a narrative entry from earlier. Reread the entry and push yourself to have some thoughts about it. You might want to annotate your entry by jotting a few of the ideas you see lying between the lines or you might just start writing another entry from that entry." I gave them a few minutes to work.

"Partner 1, will you read the entry you selected to Partner 2 and write-in-the-air your entry? Partner 2, you may want to ask one of the questions from our chart," I said, gesturing to the "Questions Writers Ask of Earlier Entries" chart.

"After you have said a thought and talked about it until you feel talked out, Partner 2 can interject prompts from our list," I gestured to the "Pushing Our Thinking" list, "one that might work to keep you thinking more. For example, Partner 2 might insert, 'This is important because . . . ,' 'To add on . . . ,' or 'This connects with. . . .' The goal is for Partner 1 to write-in-the-air what you could conceivably write in an entry."

LINK

Rally writers to use the strategies they have learned to explore seed ideas, sending them off to write after quickly conferring with their partners.

"Writers, soon you will choose your seed idea topics for your essays. You do not just want to just choose any ol', off-the-top-of-your-head idea. You want to choose an idea that truly matters to you, that you wonder about and question and wrestle with. Spend today using any of the strategies that we have learned to explore ideas that matter to you a lot.

"This means I am not telling you how to go about generating entries—and ideas. I'm leaving the choice up to you. You should have a lot of possible ways you could proceed in mind. Right now, look over our charts, think over your writing, and with your partner, *quickly* come up with two possible things you could do today to come up with thoughtful entries."

My writing has a quality that suggests I'm hemming and hawing a bit. I do this because I'm trying to support the concept of writing as a tool for thinking and not just a vehicle for conveying thoughts.

Notice that these minilessons contain echoes of each other. In prior lessons, children have already written-in-the-air, inserted prompts to nudge each other's thinking, and used language to elicit new ideas, so this should all be accessible for them.

You'll see that this link has a different spin to it than most. I ask children to list a few different options, instead of doing so myself. If you feel your kids need to be more active in more sections of your minilessons, you could do this sort of thing often.

Each child turned knee to knee with his or her partner and the room buzzed with talk.

Strategies for Generating Essay Entries

- We take a subject (a person, place, or object) that matters to us and list ideas related to that subject. Then we take one of those ideas and write about it.
- We observe and then write, "The thought I have about this is . . . "
- We let writing spark new thoughts, and we take those sparks and write new entries about them.
- We reread our earlier writing and ask questions about those earlier entries.

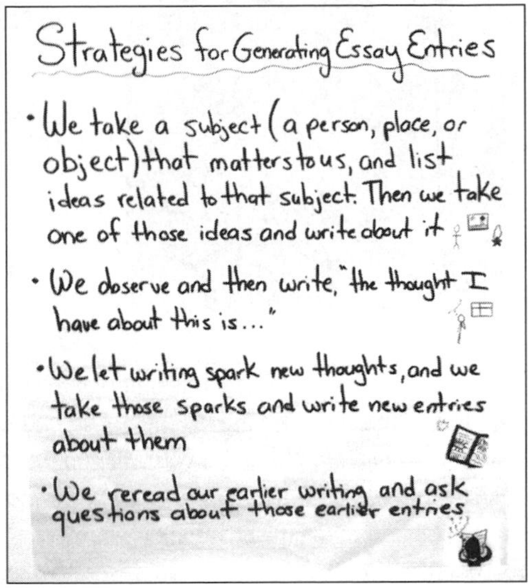

FIG. 5–2

Francesca shared her notebook entry with her partner (see Figure 5–3).

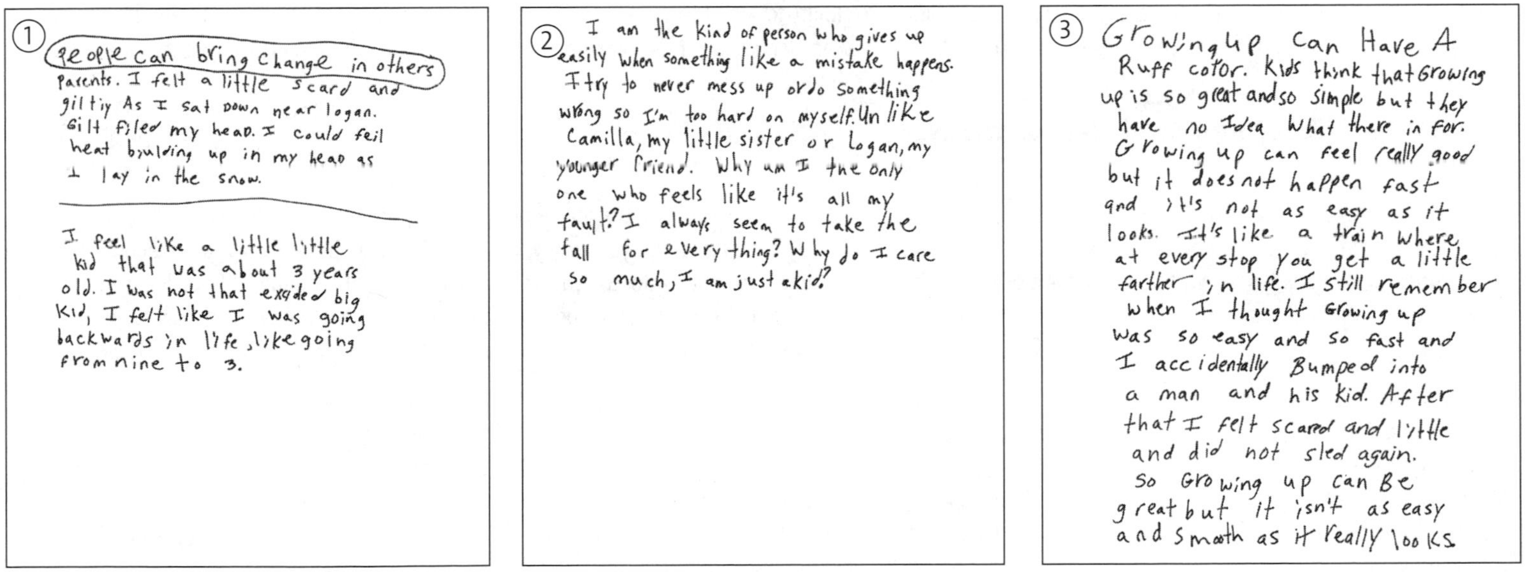

① People can bring Change in others
parents. I felt a little scard and
giltiy As I sat Down near logan.
Gilt filed my head. I could feil
heat bowling up in my head as
I lay in the snow.

I feel like a little little
kid that was about 3 years
old. I was not that excided big
kid, I felt like I was going
backwards in life, like going
from nine to 3.

② I am the kind of person who gives up
easily when something like a mistake happens.
I try to never mess up or do something
wrong so I'm too hard on myself. Un like
Camilla, my little sister or logan, my
younger friend. Why am I the only
one who feels like it's all my
fault? I always seem to take the
fall for every thing? Why do I care
so much, I am just a kid?

③ Growing up Can Have A
Ruff color. Kids think that Growing
up is so great and so simple but they
have no Idea What there in for.
Growing up can feel really good
but it does not happen fast
and it's not as easy as it
looks. It's like a train where
at every stop you get a little
farther in life. I still remember
when I thought Growing up
was so easy and so fast and
I accidentally Bumped into
a man and his kid. After
that I felt scared and little
and did not sled again.
So Growing up can Be
great but it isn't as easy
and smooth as it really looks

FIG. 5–3   Francesca's notebook entry

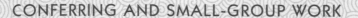

Encouraging Children to Make Choices

THE GOOD THING IS that this unit of study allows you to teach your students many things that will be new for them. The bad thing is that this unit is more directive than the others, and therefore you will end up spending less time trying to strengthen children's ability to make choices and work independently. That is, because this unit brings children to a new and challenging kind of writing, you'll often need to ask them to spend the workshop doing whatever you taught that day, instead of adding the day's strategy to a repertoire to be called on at will.

You have a little window of time now, before the complexity heightens, in which you can encourage children to make choices, so I suggest you make a special point of doing this. Begin your conferences by researching what it is they've chosen to do. Ask, "What are you working on as a writer?" and expect from their response not only a topic but also a strategy—one they've chosen for particular reasons to meet particular goals.

Be aware that children will quickly learn the words to use to impress you; nudge and probe to be sure they mean what they say. Ask, "Where exactly did you do that?"

Once you know what a writer is trying to do and the strategies he or she has used, you'll want to learn more. Ask that writer how the strategy is working and if he needs any help with it. Wait for the child to articulate an answer, so that the child feels responsibility for what to write and for how his choices are working. Try to help the child judge whether a strategy is working well by encouraging him to notice whether he is learning

MID-WORKSHOP TEACHING   Choosing a Seed Idea for an Essay

"Writers, come gather in the meeting area. You've probably started to feel like there are one or two topics you keep returning to as you write. For example, I notice that I keep writing about my father. Right now, let the writing you have done over the past few days run through your mind, and think, 'What are the topics that reoccur for me?' If it helps, flip through your notebook."

After a minute, I said, "Put a thumb up if you have one or two topics that you find yourself writing about over and over again." I waited a few moments, watching pages turning and thumbs going up. As I watched, I voiced over possibilities for topics/seed ideas. "Maybe you notice you write a lot about how you hate to make mistakes. Maybe you write a lot about how your friendships are complicated. Maybe you write a lot about how growing up is hard. Maybe you write about how you are competitive. Or about fights with your sister. . . ."

I waited until the majority of thumbs had gone up and then said, "Jot your topic, quickly.

"You've just found one possible writing territory. In a few minutes, you will zoom in on a specific topic that you may want to write about, but for now, think about the bigger things that matter to you." Then, a minute later, I continued. "I'm talking about a writing terrain, or territory, because it helps the writer to have some sense of the bigger terrain he or she might explore before trying to zoom in on a specific topic.

"Once you have a sense of possible territories for your writing, reread your notebook, looking for specific seed ideas that are part of those important territories. Like I might know I want to write about my father and I might, in the end, decide to write about ways that my father taught me to be my own person or ways that he is unusual. When you look for a seed idea for your essay, you are looking, quite literally, for a seed *idea*. When you wrote narratives, you really selected seed *stories*, but this time, you are writing *essays*, so it helps to find an idea that you want to explore or to argue for. We'll be turning that seed idea into a thesis statement in the end of today's workshop, and into an essay next week."

during writing. Ask, "What did you learn by writing this entry?" and "What new idea did you form as you wrote?" Your questions show that writers can expect to learn new things as they write and can choose ways to make sure that happens.

Remember that after learning what a child is already doing, you'll want to find something to compliment. Then tell the writer that if she is game, you could give a tip, a pointer. Say, "Let me teach you one thing that'll make what you are doing even more effective." After this, your conference will resemble a mini-minilesson.

If you feel unsure of what to teach during the teaching component of the conference, keep in mind that the class charts can be a resource for you as well as for young writers. If the child is unsure of what to write, and a chart is posted titled "Strategies for Generating Essay Entries," then you'll want to remind the writer that when she is stuck she can reach for a strategy from her mental toolbox or from the classroom charts.

Another resource you and the child can draw on is the writing that you shared as an example of strong freewriting. For example, if a child doesn't know how to develop an entry, writing more than a line or two about a thought, you could say, "Well, let's look at what some of our mentor authors have done that you could try. That's what I often do when I'm stuck." Then a glance at the mentor text might suggest that one way a writer can say more is to shift from the level of abstraction to that of specificity, using a phrase such as, "For example, one day . . . " to help.

Remember as you confer with children that they are still writing entries and are not writing formal essays. The authors haven't intended to write these entries in an essay shape, with a topic sentence and then support, and there is no reason their entries need to follow this pattern. The goal has been thoughtfulness and insight.

Developing a Seed Idea into a Thesis Statement

Demonstrate the step-by-step process of choosing a seed idea and developing it into a potential thesis.

"Writers, there is one last bit of really important work for you to do today. I'm hoping you will help me as I try this work with my writing, and then you will have a chance to help each other do it as well. I'm hoping you will help me choose a seed idea and develop a thesis. I wrote down the steps I usually take." I uncovered a chart.

To Develop a Thesis, I . . .

1. Find a territory, and sometimes a part of this territory, or an issue or idea within it: my topic.

2. Review and collect relevant examples, ideas, information, and stories that could perhaps go into an essay on that topic.

3. Ask myself, "What do I really, really want to say about this topic?"

4. Reach for the exact words and say the idea as a sentence. Think, "Is this the general idea I actually want to explore?" And if not, try another.

5. Center on an idea, then try saying it again, a bit differently. Do this a bunch of times until it feels just right and exactly true.

"As you see me go through each step, help me keep on track by giving that step a little check." I demonstrated raising my hand into the air and giving a little "check-off" gesture. "Then you'll get a chance to try developing a thesis for *your* essay. Step one is to find a topic. I already think I want to write an appreciative essay about my dad." I jotted the word "dad" down in the center of a large piece of blank chart paper (see Fig. 5–5). "Writers, you should be giving me a check." I watched as the class raised their hands and "checked off" that step.

"Step two. What do I want to put into an essay about my dad? Hmm, . . ." I flipped through my notebook, scanning pages. "Maybe I could put in the story about sailing with Dad on the last day of vacation when he confessed he couldn't

To Develop a Thesis, I . . .

1. Find a territory, and sometimes a part of this territory, or an issue or idea within it: your topic.

2. Review and collect relevant examples, ideas, information, and stories that could perhaps go into an essay on that topic.

3. Ask myself, "What do I really, really want to say about this topic?"

4. Reach for the exact words and say the idea as a sentence. Think, "Is this the general idea I actually do want to explore?" And if not, try another.

5. Once I have centered on an idea, try saying it again, a bit differently. Do this a bunch of times until it feels exactly right and true.

FIG. 5–4

wait to get back to work." I jotted the words "took me sailing" and "excited to end vacation" on my paper in the start of what would become a web. "Maybe I could also put in the story of how he makes waffles every Christmas for the interns who are still working at the hospital." I jotted "making waffles" and "happy to leave festivities for work." "There is a lot more I could write but I've collected some examples so let me move on to the next step." The children checked.

"Step three. Let me look over what I have so far and ask, 'What do I really, really want to say about my dad?'" I was quiet for a minute, studying the web I had made. Then I tapped the fourth step on the chart to signify that I was moving on and watched the writers check off my work for step 3.

"Step four. So far, it seems like my dad shows me important things. So maybe I could write, 'My Dad Shows Me Important Things.' But is that what I really, *really* want to say? No. I really want to say that he is like, part of me. I learned so much from him.

"Final step. Writers, do you notice how I keep pushing myself to think of what I really want to say? Let me try to reach for the exact words and to say it in a simple, clear sentence." I paused, then said, "I learned so much from my dad. He is a really important teacher to me. He is one of my most important teachers. Maybe even my most important. 'My father is my most important teacher.' Hey!" I sat straight up. "I think that is a strong start for a thesis." I wrote the words "My father is my most important teacher."

Get writers started doing this work and coach into what individuals are doing.

"Okay, writers, you already have some topics in mind that you've been exploring in your writing. Right now, choose one so you can try developing a thesis. Put a thumb up when you have that topic in mind and this time instead of a physical check, make a little mental check for step one." I waited until I saw the majority of writers with their thumbs up. "Okay, now go through the rest of the steps. You'll make a sort of flowchart or map or web that captures the main things that could go into an essay, like I did. Then reach for the exact words and say your thesis as a sentence. Try it a number of times before writing it on the bottom of your paper. You'll come in tomorrow with a thesis that you feel says exactly what you want it to. Get started on this work now, while I come around and watch how you use the checklist."

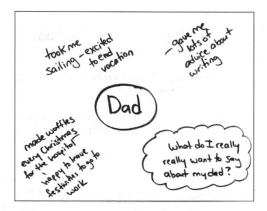

FIG. 5–5

FIG. 5–6   Emma develops her thesis by webbing out examples for an essay about her brother.

FIG. 5–7   Next, Emma lists possible seed ideas for her essay.

FIG. 5–8   Sam webs out ideas for his essay.

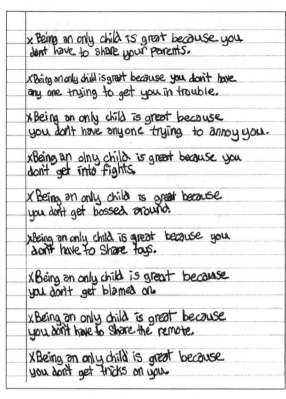

FIG. 5–9   Sam lists possible seed ideas for his essay.

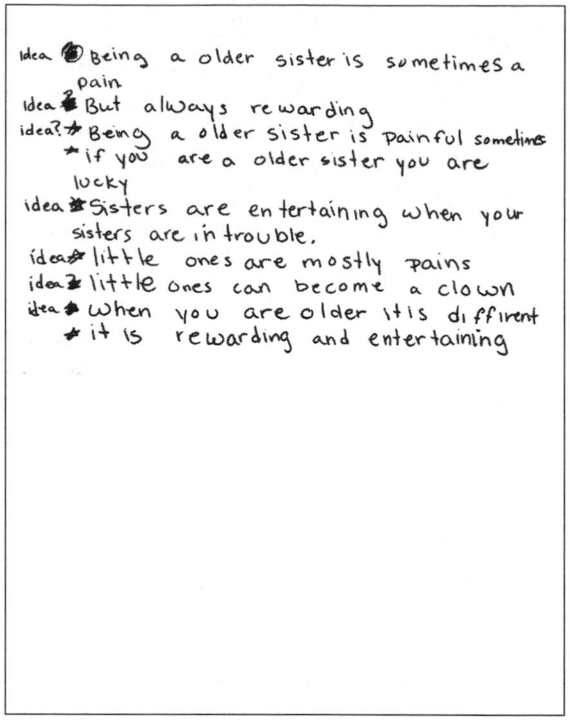

x Being an only child is great because you don't have to share your parents.

X Being an only child is great because you don't have any one trying to get you in trouble.

X Being an only child is great because you don't have anyone trying to annoy you.

X Being an olny child is great because you don't get into fights.

X Being an only child is great because you don't get bossed around.

X Being an only child is great because you don't have to share toys.

X Being an only child is great because you don't get blamed on.

X Being an only child is great because you don't have to share the remote.

X Being an only child is great because you don't get tricks on you.

Idea ① Being a older sister is sometimes a pain
Idea ② But always rewarding
Idea ③ Being a older sister is painful sometimes
    ✱ if you are a older sister you are lucky
Idea ④ Sisters are entertaining when your sisters are in trouble.
Idea ⑤ little ones are mostly pains
Idea ⑥ little ones can become a clown
Idea ⑦ When you are older it is different
    ✱ it is rewarding and entertaining

FIG. 5–10   Josy lists various seed ideas for her essay.

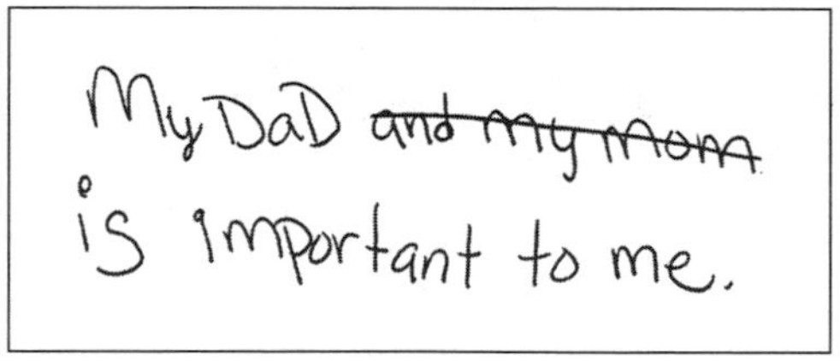

My DaD and My Mom is important to me.

FIG. 5–11   Randolino's thesis

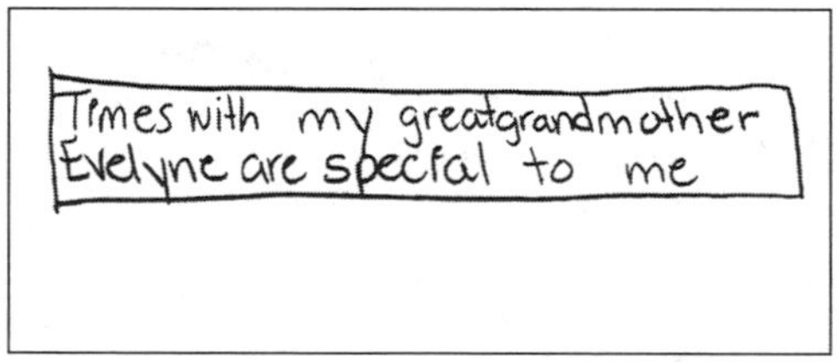

Times with my greatgrandmother Evelyne are specfal to me

FIG. 5–12   Sophie's thesis

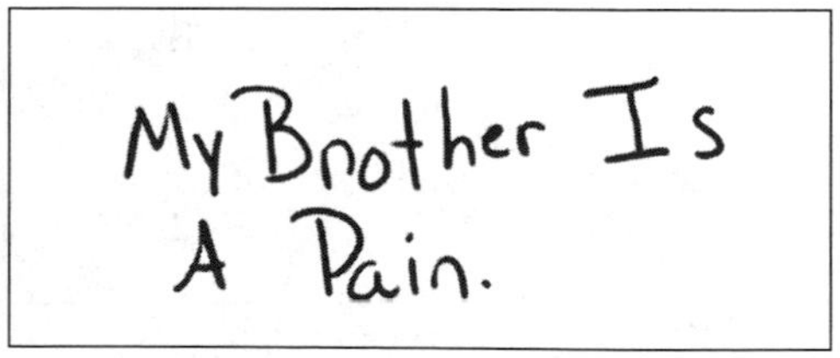

My Brother Is A Pain.

FIG. 5–13   Tray's thesis

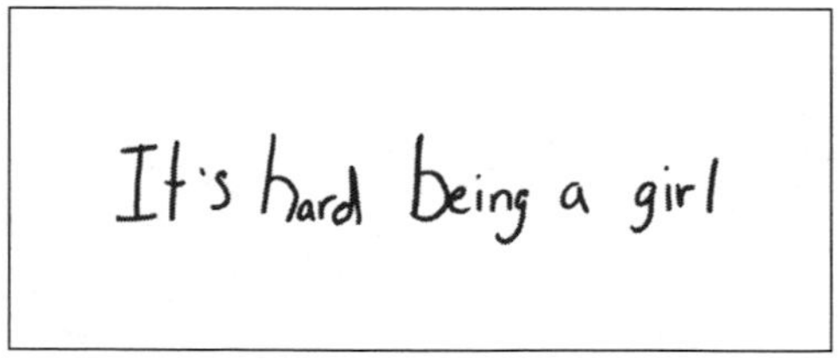

It's hard being a girl

FIG. 5–14   LaKeya's thesis

MINING OUR WRITING

Exploring Different Theses

Writers, tonight for homework, use the checklist and work to develop a thesis for other topics you might want to write an essay about. Or, if you like the thesis that you worked on today in class, make sure it says precisely what you want it to say. You may need to try saying your thesis a couple of different ways.

Alejandro's already started to do this work. He reread his notebook and found an entry he'd written about his friendship with Mike and how it's hard to be friends sometimes. He figured this might be a topic he'd like to write an essay about, so he reread his entry, looking for a single sentence that summed up the entry and his feelings for Mike. Listen.

> I have been thinking about my friendship with Mike. I thought that it is sometimes hard to be friends with Mike because he is interested in things that I am not interested in. For example, he is interested in movie making and I am not, he likes to make up comic book characters, he likes to play video games and I don't, he likes to watch the Simpsons and I don't. I sometimes have fights with him. For example, we play card games that he made up and he sometimes changes the rules in the middle of the game. On the other hand Mike is a good friend because the games that he makes up are fun.

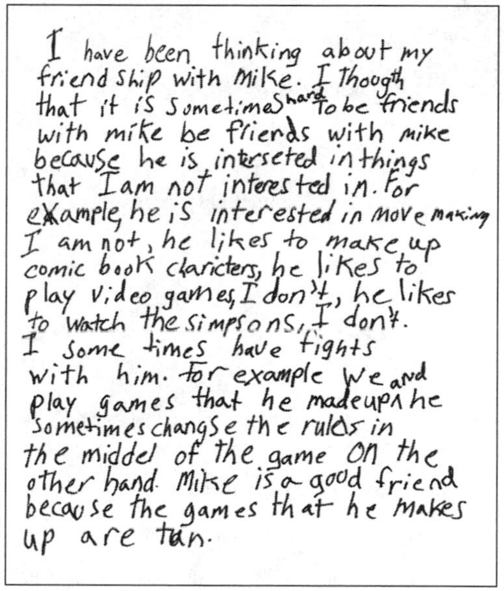
I have been thinking about my friend ship with Mike. I thougth that it is Sometimes hard to be friends with mike be friends with mike because he is interseted in things that I am not interested in. For example, he is interested in move making I am not, he likes to make up comic book claricters, he likes to play video games, I don't, he likes to watch the simpsons, I don't. I some times have fights with him. for example we and play games that he madeup, he sometimes changse the rulds in the middel of the game On the other hand. Mike is a good friend because the games that he makes up are fun.

FIG. 5–15 Alejandro's notebook entry

Alejandro realized that he didn't have one line that captured what he thought, because he had both good and bad feelings about Mike. So he thought, "Maybe the one thing I am saying is that my friendship with Mike is complicated." He wrote that down.

> My friendship with Mike is complicated.

Then he tried to revise that idea by saying his feelings more precisely. He tried to compare the friendship to something everyone knows. Here's what he wrote next.

> My friendship with Mike is like a seesaw. Sometimes it is up and sometimes it is down.

Then he tried to write this in a stronger fashion, adding in his emotions.

> It is hard to be friends with someone who is so different from me.

Tonight, you may need to do this kind of work to find or craft your thesis too. Be sure you come in tomorrow with your thesis written as a sentence so we can start planning our essays.

Boxes and Bullets

Framing Essays

IN THIS SESSION, you'll teach children that writers support their thesis by developing different types of reasons.

GETTING READY

✔ Your thesis and different ways you might support it (reasons, ways, and times) to use as a demonstration (see Teaching)

✔ Chart paper to write on in front of your students

✔ Students' theses from yesterday's Share session

✔ Writing materials and tools for students including note cards for them to write their theses on

✔ Your web from Session 5, where you collected stories and possible ideas about your territory/topic

✔ Students' webs from Session 5

✔ Students' writer's notebooks

✔ Your example of how you could revise your thesis or a student's thesis (see Share)

COMMON CORE STATE STANDARDS: W.4.1.a,b; W.4.5, RI.4.2, RL.4.3, SL.4.1, L.4.1, L.4.2, L.4.3

BEFORE YOU EMBARK ON TODAY'S SESSION, you will definitely want to have a thesis in mind so you can write your own essay along with your students. Unless you try your hand at this work, you won't grasp why and how it is challenging. To an outsider, the process described in this book may look simple, but it's vastly more complicated and more interesting than it appears from a distance.

Today's work is foundational for the writing students will do for the bulk of this unit and different in key ways from the opinion writing work in which students engaged in previous years. Last year your students came up with categories to support their claims, which were not necessarily parallel or totally distinct. And writers did not have those categories in mind from the start.

Your goal today will be to help your children imagine several alternative plans or outlines for an essay. You will teach children that essayists sometimes support their thesis statements by providing reasons for a claim, sometimes by offering times when the claim is true, and sometimes by explaining different ways in which a claim is true. Students will begin with their theses and then mull over the smaller points they want to make. Will they support the claim by providing reasons? Times? Ways?

If you look closely at what your children do in response to today's teaching, you'll find that this work is more challenging than you ever imagined—and hence it will present you with lots of teaching and learning opportunities. Your students won't produce a lot of work, but the work they do produce will be worth hours of study on your part—and lots of responsive instruction. Because today's session involves foundational work, it is especially important for you to devote time to helping each individual develop a credible essay plan. For this reason, as well as others, the work children do during today's session will spill over into tomorrow, giving you more time to work with individual writers.

This session will not follow the usual pattern of a writing workshop. At the start of the minilesson, let children know that the schedule and format for today will be unusual. You needn't explain the details to them, but it is important that you realize that children will write while sitting in the meeting area, and your conferring and small-group work will happen as they sit around you in that space. This responsive teaching will be important. If children leave today with some workable plans for essays, the work over the upcoming days will all click into place, but if you only reach a third of the class, chances are good that the infrastructure of many essays will need to be addressed soon. Today, then, you'll definitely want to move quickly from child to child, helping them explore and learn from the writing that emerges on their pages. You

Because today's session involves foundational work, it is especially important for you to devote time to helping each individual develop a credible essay plan.

will be helping each child draft and revise what will amount to a frame—an outline—for an essay. Children will learn not only to write a thesis, but also to rewrite it, and they'll do this countless times over. The revision work will teach lessons in logic and cohesion, which means children won't be doing the usual sort of revision—reaching for sensory details or questioning whether a text is focused. Instead, the revision will revolve around thinking about the relationship between theses, reasons, and evidence. All of your students' revision will culminate in a grand total of about thirty words. I promise that although the products may not seem as luscious as other writing you've seen across this series, the lessons in logic and language that you and your children can learn through this work are crucial and long lasting.

Tonight's homework will be especially important as you will ask your writers to do another on-demand, giving themselves forty-five or fifty minutes to produce a quick essay. Tomorrow you will involve your writers in self-assessment and revision of those on-demands, so tonight's work is critical for tomorrow.

Boxes and Bullets
Framing Essays

CONNECTION

Restate the cake metaphor, rallying children for the work of planning out the essay frames for their claims.

"Writers, I hope that right now each of you has a thesis that you feel fired up about, one that you can hold in your two hands like this." I showed the children how I had jotted my thesis in a box on the top of a clean sheet of notebook paper. "Take one minute and write that thesis on the card in front of you just like I did." I gave them a few minutes to scribble. "Hold them up!" I said, as I made a big deal of looking across the rug. Then I motioned for the students to lower their cards.

"Writers, today marks a big day in our unit. Today, you will start to plan out your essays. This means that you will be thinking about both the content of your essays, that is, your big ideas, *and* the form, the structure of your essays. This is challenging. It will be kind of like you are making a big cake and you have to make a cake that looks beautiful in form *and* tastes amazing, too! You have to keep structure and content in mind at the same time."

You'll see that this connection harkens back to the reference we made earlier about cakes that look lovely but taste awful. You are again rallying your students to balance a focus on form with a focus on content.

❧ **Name the teaching point.**

"Today, I am going to teach you that one way to make sure that your essays are strong in both form *and* content is to have a clear plan before you start writing. You can plan by writing your thesis and your reasons to support that thesis, by planning your boxes and bullets."

TEACHING

Demonstrate how you generate reasons for your own thesis, and deliberately model that you weigh and reject some possibilities.

"Essayists back up their claims with reasons. They write, "'I think this . . . because. . . .'" And here is a key tip: Essayists use different types of reasons to back up their claims. One, their reasons might show *when* their thesis is true. Two, their reasons might show *why* their thesis is true. Three, their reasons might show *how* their thesis is true. Watch me and research how I try out reasons that show when, why, or how my opinion, my claim, is true.

I have taught this session using fairly physical props, such as a construction paper "plaque" on which each child writes his or her thesis. When I do that, I'm trying to convey subtle messages through the use of materials. The plaque helps children feel as if they've made a commitment to a single thesis. The entire rehearsal and entry-gathering phase culminates in the commitment to this one- or two-sentence claim.

"So I have my claim: 'My father is my most important teacher.'" As I said these words, I held up the page on which I had written this in large letters. "Let me look at what I want to put in my essay and see what type of reasons I'm going to provide." I uncovered my web from the day before and studied it silently for a moment.

"Okay, I want to write about my father making waffles for the people he works with on Christmas and telling me when sailing on the last day of vacation that he couldn't wait to get back to his job. So maybe my reasons are really showing *when* my thesis is true, *when* my father was my most important teacher. So I could say, 'My father is my most important teacher. My father is my most important teacher *when* he makes waffles on Christmas. My father is my most important teacher *when* he takes me sailing. My father is my most important teacher *when* he gives me advice on writing.' Is that what I want to say?" I was quiet for a moment and then shook my head.

"No, times don't work for me. I don't just want to write about *when* my father is my most important teacher. I think I want to write about *why* he is my most important teacher."

Continue demonstrating the next steps in the process of creating reasons for your opinion statement. Again, deliberately model making mistakes and fixing them.

"Okay, so I want to write about *why* my father is my most important teacher. That means my reasons need to show *why* my thesis is true. I'm going to repeat my claim and then say 'because. . . .'" I dragged out my articulation of the word to imply that more came after it. "First, let me think over all I have already written about what my father has taught me." I glanced at my web and then closed my eyes briefly, letting the students see me struggle.

"Okay, my father is my most important teacher becauuuuuse . . . he taught me to love work. My father is my most important teacher becauuuuuse . . . he taught me to love writing. My father is my most important teacher becauuuuuse . . . he took me sailing." I stopped. "Wait, 'took me sailing' doesn't prove that my father taught me anything. I need to find a third reason that 'My father is my most important teacher.' Let me try again. I'll repeat my claim and then say 'because.' My father is my most important teacher becauuuuuse . . . he taught me that one person can make a difference." I jotted the three reasons on my chart under the box with my thesis.

> My father is my most important teacher.

- My father is my most important teacher because he taught me to love work.
- My father is my most important teacher because he taught me to love writing.
- My father is my most important teacher because he taught me that one person can make a difference.

Debrief by articulating what you did that you hope children will also do.

"Writers, do you see the way I repeated my claim—my thesis—and then said 'because' to help me think of reasons to support my claim?"

It runs against all our training for children to be so repetitive! If you decide to encourage children to word the stem differently each time, know that we tried this too. But we have come to believe that if children don't repeat their stem (at least during this unit of study), they end up with categories (bullets) that aren't cohesive. This disjunction becomes increasingly problematic when the main idea is elaborated upon in an entire paragraph that also doesn't align. I strongly recommend that you stop worrying that the topic sentences will be dull if children repeat the stem.

In this unit, the work you do in response to kids' efforts will be especially important because the intellectual work of the unit has everything to do with muddling through the hard parts. So insert yourself into partner conversations and listen for what you can support and teach. You may find that you need to convene the whole class' attention several times, intervening to lift the level of children's work during the prolonged active engagement. For example, often a close look will reveal that two of the reasons a child has produced are the same, just worded differently—you could mention that now or save it for a later time. Perhaps the child's points don't sound aligned—you could adjust them subtly by repeating them, with small tweaks that make the child's language fall into parallel structure.

ACTIVE ENGAGEMENT

Set children up to practice coming up with reasons for their own claims.

"You each have your own thesis statement. In a minute you are going to try supporting your thesis with reasons. Right now, think over all you have written about your claim. Glance back through your notebook if it helps." I gave them a minute to do this work. "Now, you will practice trying out finding types of reasons that support your claim and that match what you want to say. For now, just practice coming up with one reason that shows why your thesis is true, unless others rush out. First, mentally say your thesis, then say 'becauuuuse . . . ,' and a reason will pop into your mind right then, as you talk. Do that now." I gave them a minute to do that work.

"In a minute you will share your thesis and reasons with your partner. Today both of you will get a chance to share. Partner 1, you'll go first. You'll state your claim and first reason. Partner 2, listen and give a thumbs up if that reason supports the claim and thumbs down if it doesn't. Then you can switch roles. Okay, turn and share." The room erupted into talk.

Emma's thesis and supporting reasons are shown in Figure 6–1.

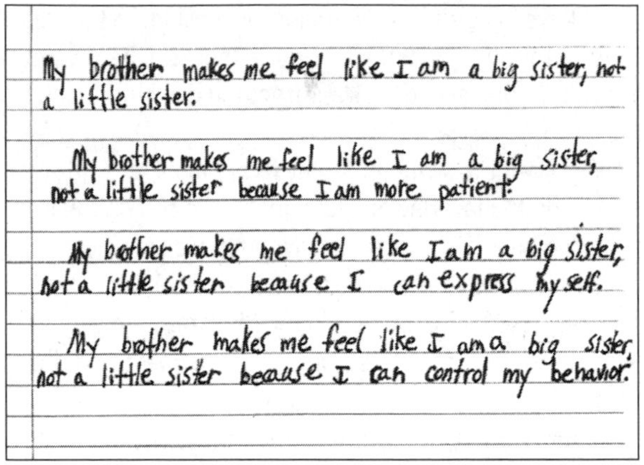
My brother makes me feel like I am a big sister, not a little sister.

My brother makes me feel like I am a big sister, not a little sister because I am more patient.

My bother makes me feel like I am a big sister, not a little sister because I can express myself.

My brother makes me feel like I am a big sister, not a little sister because I can control my behavior.

FIG. 6–1 Emma's thesis and supporting reasons

LINK

Set writers up to continue to work to develop their own theses and reasons.

"Writers, today is going to be a bit different than usual. Instead of sending you off to work on your own, I'm going to suggest you spend the rest of today's writing workshop right here because you have work to do that must be done today. By the end of today, you each need to have an opinion statement and three reasons to show why that thesis is true. Right now, sitting here, work to find reasons to support your claim. You want those reasons to match what you want to say. Write a box (your thesis) and bullets (your reasons) in your notebook. Help each other. I'll be coaching, and I'll collect your plans at the end of today's workshop."

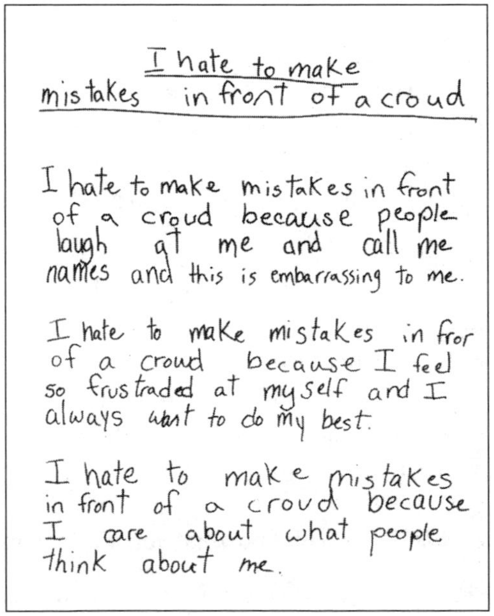
I hate to make mistakes in front of a croud

I hate to make mistakes in front of a croud because people laugh at me and call me names and this is embarrassing to me.

I hate to make mistakes in fror of a croud because I feel so frustraded at myself and I always want to do my best.

I hate to make mistakes in front of a croud because I care about what people think about me.

FIG. 6–2 Rie, trying to grow her first thesis

Anticipating Predictable Problems

TODAY'S LESSON will create some challenges for your writers. These challenges are best addressed through quick one-to-one conferences and small-group strategy lessons. By anticipating the predictable problems, you can be ready for the conferences and small-group work you'll need to lead today.

Some writers will still need help developing and articulating strong, clear thesis statements. Some will write questions rather than statements. Teach them that instead of writing, "Why do I love my dad so much?" they need to make a stand, to claim a position: "I love my father because he makes me improve myself." Some children will resist making clear, concise statements and instead hedge their opinions: "One of the reasons why I love my dad is that some of the time he doesn't let me be anything less than my best, but other times he isn't like that." Help writers who hedge to create a lean, clear thesis statement that doesn't waffle.

Steer children away from a claim that has two branches, as in "My mother and my father are important to me." That essayist would have to prove that both his mother and his father are important. It is simpler to start with one single claim. Then, too, sometimes a thesis is really making two points, as in this example: "Because children care a lot about their parents, sometimes they are embarrassed by them." There is nothing wrong with this opinion statement, but defending it poses an extra layer of writing challenge, because now the child needs to show not only that kids can be embarrassed by their parents, but also that this feeling is motivated by care. Later, writers can always address counterarguments or further claims, but for now, help children write straightforward, clean, crisp thesis statements.

Some kids will write a fact in lieu of a thesis or merely name a topic. The child who writes, "My father picks me up after school" has written a fact, not a thesis. I prompt children to go past the fact to an idea by asking, "What are your ideas or your feelings about this?" Soon the child will have a thesis: "I love it when my father picks me up after school." The child who writes, "My strong opinion is about war" may need practice in simply learning how to state a clear thesis. When I pulled up to confer with

MID-WORKSHOP TEACHING
Finding Alternative Ways to Support a Thesis

"Writers, can I have your eyes and attention? I want to tell you that there are other kinds of categories apart from times or reasons. Perhaps a different type of category will better match what you want to say. So watch me think about kinds of ways to back up my thesis." Gripping my construction paper plaque on which I'd written my thesis, I said, "Okay. I'll go back to my claim, 'My father is my most important teacher.' I'm going to think of all I've written and all I've thought about that topic and then ask myself, 'Do I want to tell different kinds *of ways* my dad has been a teacher?' I would need to repeat my thesis and then say '*by* . . .' to help me think of kinds of ways he has been a teacher.

"So let me try it. 'My father is my most important teacher *by* . . . listening to me. My father is my most important teacher by . . . pushing me. My father is my most important teacher by . . . setting an example,'" I said, writing these in boxes and bullets format on chart paper.

"Writers, do you see the way I've considered different *ways* my father is my most important teacher? Now, this plan may not be exactly right for the essay I want to write. I'm pretty sure I want to write about *reasons* my father is my most important teacher, but this plan might match what you want to say.

"Try out different ways to support your thesis until you find a plan that matches exactly what you want to say. You'll be revising your boxes and bullets over and over and over."

Tanya, I decided to provide guided practice during our conference to make sure my teaching would stick. "Let's practice," I urged her. "I'll name a topic and you say a claim. Cafeteria food. . . ."

"They have chicken nuggets on Thurs—"

"Tell me what you think about it!" I interrupted. "Give me a claim! How do you feel about cafeteria food? Cafeteria food. . . ." "Is gross?" "Smoking. . . ." "Is bad for you."

Then, too, you can anticipate predictable problems your writers will encounter as they go about creating reasons for a claim. Typically, when writers run into pitfalls in this work, they have created categories that don't support their claim, overlapping reasons, reasons that are not parallel, and so on. You can anticipate conferences and small-group work that push writers to reconsider their reasons and help them to recognize why the current plan will not support the thesis. I like to show students an example of strong boxes and bullets, such as Sophie's to help them to see how she made two drafts of her boxes and bullets, with the second more specific than the first.

Here's Sophie's first draft of her boxes and bullets (see Figure 6–3).

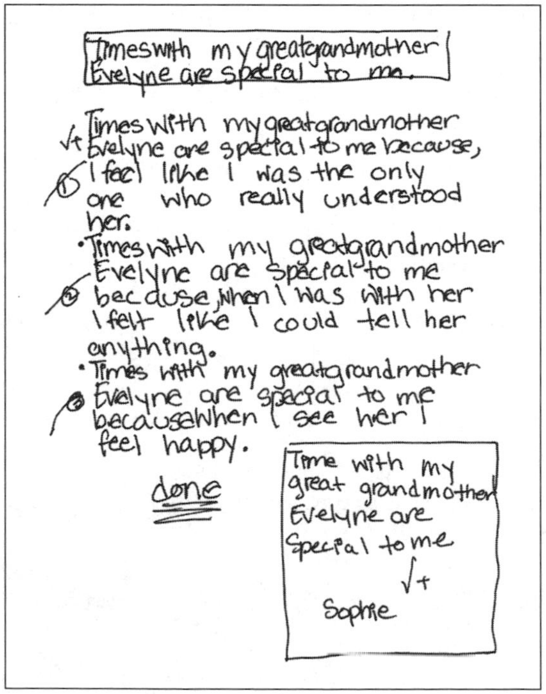

FIG. 6–3   Sophie's first draft

Sophie's second draft is more specific than her first:

FIG. 6–4   Sophie's second draft

As I crouched among the writers in the meeting area following the lesson, I helped one child after another set up possible frameworks for an essay, and I encouraged nearby children to listen in as I worked with their classmates. I especially helped kids "try on" a variety of optional ways their essays could go. My conversations sounded like this:

"So what is your thesis, Diana?"

"My mom is important to me."

Although ordinarily I wouldn't accept something as vague as "My mom is important to me because she is nice," in this instance I keep in mind that I have asked kids to write *big ideas*. I have asked for generalizations. Although it is true that even big ideas often become more compelling when they are more specific, it can then be harder to elaborate on them when they are more specific. I don't necessarily push for more specificity. My goal is to help all kids grasp the concept of an umbrella idea, a claim that is supported by several distinct and parallel subordinate categories (or reasons).

As I work with one child and then another, I am sure to come across the problem that one reason does not support the thesis. When I see this, I often try to showcase the problem by telling the child about another kid whose reasons did not all support the thesis. "Your list reminds me of this other kid who said, 'My dog is like a friend because he listens to me, he keeps me company, and he wins dog shows.'" Do you see that the third bullet may be true of my dog, but it doesn't explain why he is like a best friend?"

When I create examples that I hope will make a point to children, I choose very clear-cut ones. I once said, "I like oranges because they are juicy. I like oranges because they are tasty." Then, for the third bullet, I said, "I like oranges because one day I saw an orange plant in a rain forest." That last reason was obvious and dramatic enough that I made my point easily.

One thing I like to do is collect all of the boxes-and-bullets plans on Post-it® notes and tape them on two pages of loose-leaf paper. I stick these in my conferring binder so I can see at a glance whose plans will likely lead to an effective essay. I first categorize these by "workable" and "needs help" and then I categorize the "needs help" according to predictable problems and plan to do more small groups like today.

Here are some thesis statements and thesis statements with reasons that illustrate predictable problems you might be seeing. You can use these to support students in noticing these types of problems. You will find other groups of thesis statements with reasons that illustrate predictable problems as well as exemplars—and you can use these for small-group work, conferring, homework, and so on—on the CD-ROM.

Problem—Thesis is not personal:

> Mars would be a fun place to live.

Problem—Reasons do not support/match the thesis:

> My mom is my best friend
> - because she is a good cook
> - because she dresses well
> - because she works hard at her job

Problem—Reasons are not parallel:

> My mom is my best friend
> - because she buys me things
> - now that I am older
> - when I am at home

Problem—Thesis is two-pronged. Writer would need to prove both parts and gather reasons to support both:

> My dad is my friend and my mentor.

Problem—Fact not a thesis:

> My grandmother is old.

Problem—Reasons are overlapping:

> My mom is my best friend
> - Because she is fun
> - Because I have a good time with her
> - Because she listens to me

Revising Our Thesis Statements

Share an example of a writer who revised a thesis when it did not match what she wanted to write about in her essay.

"Writers, now that you are developing your reasons for your thesis statements, you'll get a much clearer sense of what you want to put in your essay and how your essay will go. Sometimes when you think and talk more about your essay, you realize that your original thesis no longer matches what you want to say. When that happens, revise your claim. Sydni's original thesis was 'It is difficult being an only child.' But as she thought about what she wanted to write, she realized that her thesis did not match what she really felt, that being an only child is complicated. On the one hand it is difficult. But on the other hand it feels special. Sydni lucked out. That is also a form that often works for essays; you say that your ideas on whatever the topic is are complicated. Then you say, 'On the one hand . . .' and then, 'On the other hand . . .' or you could say, 'I used to think . . . but now I think. . . .'"

Have students go back to their plans to see if this strategy might be helpful to them and let them know they will be handing these in to you.

"Right now, check your current plans for your essay. Will you have a lot of evidence to go with your reasons? Does your thesis match what you plan to say about it? If not, you have the option to revise your thesis like Sydni did.

"I am going to collect these plans at the end of the workshop to look at tonight. You have a few more minutes to review your work, then jot down your box-and-bullets and your name on a Post-it and put it in this basket."

If you believe that children have already revised their thesis statements well enough, you may want to use this share time to again emphasize the importance of building essays with parallel supporting paragraphs. You could list thesis statements and then supporting paragraph ideas, each with one that is off-kilter, so that children can learn to spy the ones that need revision. In addition to the samples in the conferring section, you can find additional predictable problems on the CD-ROM.

BOXES AND BULLETS

Fast and Furious Flash-Drafting

Writers, we are about to start a new bend in our unit. You will be developing your essay. To do this work well, you will want to keep your personal goals right in the front of your minds. Tonight I am asking you to do another on-demand. Set your clock for a half hour or forty minutes and write fast and furiously to support a strong opinion. Bring that piece with you tomorrow because you'll spend tomorrow assessing your work and reminding yourself of your personal goals as you head into the next part of the unit!

Return to Boot Camp

ear Teachers,

One of the most wonderful and challenging things about this unit is that it essentially channels students to write two very different types of writing. Writing to learn, to explore on paper and think in thought patches on a page, is a type of writing that calls upon students to use writing as a tool to grow ideas. It is not far from the formality of the five-paragraph essay. Essay writing, on the other hand, is a type of writing that asks students to keep form in mind and to think and work within a clear structure.

For your students who have spent the last few days freewriting in their notebooks, essay boot camp and the notion of the importance of the structure of the essay may seem a bit far away. Yet as the unit turns the bend, students will be starting to develop their personal essays and they will need to recall the vision of what they are ultimately working to create. This is a day, then, when we will suggest a return to essay boot camp.

In the previous version of the unit, as students collected stories, then quotes, then a variety of outside evidence, they were focused on the work of gathering each of these types of materials. In this version, we have tried to keep students focused on the work at hand as well as how that work fits into the bigger picture of what they are endeavoring to create. In other words, we have tried to help them keep the forest in sight as well as the trees.

So today we suggest that students again be immersed in the process of creating an essay, and that you raise the level of the work they did during the last boot camp. During that session, the focus was on helping students to write within the frame of an essay, and you will want to see students applying and transferring that work, yet now you might also ratchet up the level and give students a preview of the work they will soon undertake, by teaching them to incorporate a variety of evidence to support their thinking as they write within the essay structure.

Another reason to involve students in a return to essay boot camp today is to give yourself another day to check over the boxes-and-bullets plans that your students developed

COMMON CORE STATE STANDARDS: W.4.1, W.4.5, RFS.4.4, SL.4.1, SL.4.4, L.4.1, L.4.2, L.4.3

yesterday. By now, you are likely feeling that while some students have solid thesis statements and supportive reasons, others may not. Thus, today's workshop is another chance for you to help students to revise their plans and set them on the right road toward success in developing essays.

To plan for today's work, you can look back at Session 1 to help you take students through the process of creating a shared class essay. You will want to give students opportunities to work on quick on-demand essays as well as one single, beautiful essay across a span of time. Thus you will see that, throughout the second bend, students have opportunities to write on-demand flash-draft pieces for homework. We know that you might not follow every homework suggested in the book, but we urge you to pay particular attention to these flash-draft opportunities so that your students can practice writing whole essays with formal structure at the same time they are working to develop mini-stories and lists in class to support their longer essay. Tonight's homework is the first opportunity to write a flash-draft that students will self-assess at the start of tomorrow's work.

MINILESSON

You might start by letting students know that since they will soon be starting to develop their essays, this unit has turned a bend. You can remind them that writing an essay means keeping both form and content in mind, in much the same way as baking a cake. Then you can let them know that they have spent the last few days working on making the content of their writing strong and now you want to remind them that they need to start putting form and content together. So today we will return to essay boot camp and work together to create a shared essay that you will then each go off to flash-draft. Let students know that today you will raise the level of the boot camp work.

You can tell writers that today you want to remind them that essays are strong in both content and structure. One way that writers achieve this is to include a variety of evidence to support their opinions as they write within the frame of an essay.

After this, you might put up the same charts that you used in Session 1. You'll want the chart about how to frame an essay as well as your boxes-and-bullets plan for the essay "I love ice cream." Then you can let your students know that you will work as a class on developing the first reason, and that they'll want a variety of evidence to support that first reason—some facts, some mini-stories. You can put up a piece of evidence you found to support that first reason, perhaps a fact such as:

- At the ice cream store near my house, there are over 20 different kinds of toppings!

Let your students know that while that is one kind of evidence that could support the reason, but that to make a strong essay, we'll need others, like little stories. Remind students that they gathered personal examples to support their opinions in third grade so they already know how to do this. Then ask each person in the class to think of a personal story that could support the first reason you love ice cream. To scaffold students, providing a quick model and perhaps jog some ideas for them, put up a mini-anecdote of your own to support this reason, something such as:

> I remember when my friend, Kate, and I went to get ice cream, we stood for a long time at the counter. There were so many toppings we couldn't decide what we wanted most. Kate said, "We'll just have to come back again soon so we can try out the other toppings!"

Ask students to put a thumb up when they have a quick mini-story and ask them to write-in-the-air with a partner. Listen in and coach as they do this. You'll likely want to coach students to just tell the part of the story that is most important, asking them: "Does that support the reason that you love ice cream because there are so many toppings?" After you convene the class, show them the essay frame chart and remind them that when they write a section of their essay, it should start by repeating the thesis, then the reason, and then giving the evidence. Remind them that they can give details the way they did on the first day of the unit and also add these new kinds of evidence. Ask students to practice writing their first section in their minds, using either the evidence you have gathered just for today, or their own evidence. Then have them turn and write that section in the air to a partner. You'll want to coach in again. Likely you'll remind writers to use transitions and to incorporate all of the evidence they can. Listen in for an example of a section that you want to highlight to the class, or add to your own:

> One reason why I love ice cream is because there are so many toppings. You top your ice cream with different kinds of nuts or chocolate or fruit or even shredded coconut! I've also seen people putting crushed cereal on top. At the ice cream store near my house there are over 20 kinds of toppings. I remember when my friend and I went to get ice cream, we stood for a long time at the counter. There were so many toppings we couldn't decide what we wanted most. Kate said, "We'll just have to come back again soon so we can try out the other toppings!" The toppings are a big reason why I love ice cream!

Point out that the section is strong because it uses the frame of the essay and starts off with the thesis then the reason then gives a variety of evidence. If it does not close by repeating reason and thesis, remind writers that this is important and have the writer repeat the revised section.

Let writers know they will now write the entire essay in the air. They can take the highlighted writer's first body paragraph as their own or they can use the one they wrote-in-the-air. You can also provide them with a few pieces of evidence that you found to help support them in this work. So you might give them a few facts and a mini-anecdote of your own, reminding them that these facts and details have come from your experience, observation, or research. You can let them know that you've already thought a little bit about what reasons these pieces of evidence might best support. So you might hand them a sheet that looks something like the following:

| I love ice cream |

| I love ice cream because you can add different toppings. |

- At the ice cream store near my house there are over 20 kinds of toppings.
- I remember when my friend and I went to get ice cream, we stood for a long time at the counter. There were so many toppings we couldn't decide what we wanted most. Kate said, "We'll just have to come back again soon so we can try out the other toppings!"

| I love ice cream because there are so many flavors. |

- On Ben and Jerry's website, there are close to 50 flavors of ice cream listed.

| I love ice cream because it's refreshing on a hot day |

- I remember the time last summer when it was so hot, I felt like I was dying. It was too hot to read or go to the park or THINK! So I ran to the store and I bought some ice cream. When I tasted it—"Ah!" I said. All of a sudden, I felt coolness in my throat and I wasn't hot anymore.

Then get writers started on writing their entire essays in the air. Be sure that you hear them writing-in-the-air, not just talking about what they will write. If they are turning to their partners and saying, "I think I could put in how…," interrupt and coach, "Write it in the air! How would it sound? Another reason why I love ice cream is…."

As you hear writers writing their essays in the air, send them off to quickly flash-draft the entire essay they have just written in the air. Give them loose-leaf paper and tell them they have ten minutes so they need to write fast and furiously!

CONFERRING AND SMALL-GROUP WORK

Last night you likely took home the Post-it notes with your writers' boxes-and-bullets plans and now you are aware of those writers whose plans need intensive support. You'll need to decide if you want to pull away any of your writers from writing now or if you want to find other time during the day to talk to those writers who still need help with their boxes-and-bullets plans for their personal essays. Either way, today is a final chance to get them on the right track toward developing essays, and you want to take advantage of it. You may want to pull in close to the writers who most need your help today in planning and do some intensive coaching. As your students work on their flash-drafts you might crouch down next to an individual writer whose plan needs help, pulling them away from their flash-drafting for just a few minutes. You will want to push the writer to tell you what they really want to write their personal essay about. Listen carefully to try to grasp the main categories the writer seems to want to address. Then you can say these back to the child in a way that is clearer.

You might start with, "So what you're saying is…" and then lay out a clear boxes-and-bullets plan that matches the writer's intention. You might even scribe a quick boxes-and-bullets plan on a Post-it note as the writer talks so you can make the most efficient possible use of time. You will want to make a note of the writers who will need this kind of intensive support and writers to give them repeated practice in creating boxes-and-bullets plans over the course of this unit, so that by the end they can be independent in this work.

MID-WORKSHOP TEACHING

For today's mid-workshop, you will want to remind writers that last year they likely learned some ways to hook their readers into reading their pieces at the start. Ask writers to think of a way they learned to hook a reader and then turn and talk. Likely, you will hear writers mention strategies like, "Giving a startling fact, creating a strong image, beginning with a mini-story," and so on. Give writers a quick minute to share out some of these ideas, and then charge them with doing their best adding introductions and conclusions to their flash drafts. "Just give it your best shot," you can tell them. Remind them to use everything they know about how to hook readers. Let them know they need to have their entire essay done by the end of the workshop.

Enjoy!

Lucy, Kelly, and Cory

Composing and Sorting Mini-Stories

IN THIS SESSION, you'll teach children that writers draw on narrative writing and use mini-stories to support the ideas they want to advance.

GETTING READY

- Students' on-demand homework assignments from the night before which they will self-assess
- Opinion Writing Checklist, Grades 4 and 5 copied on chart paper
- A copy of the Opinion Writing Checklist, Grades 4 and 5 for each student
- Sample student thesis statement and reasons, written on chart paper (see Connection)
- A sample booklet like the one used in the third-grade opinion writing unit where each page is labeled with a different reason to support the opinion
- One large folder and two smaller folders for each student for gathering and organizing evidence for their essays
- Lined paper for students
- Your thesis and reasons written out on folders for demonstration (see Teaching)
- Your web/mosaic from Session 5
- A step-by-step mini-story that you can demonstrate telling as evidence for one of the reasons supporting your thesis (see Teaching)
- A student or teacher example of a mini-story that did not support the topic sentence
- Students' writer's notebooks and mosaics/webs from Session 5 to demonstrate where to find mini-stories to support your thesis and reasons
- "Guidelines for Writing Supporting Stories for Essays" chart or copies to hand out to students (see Share)

COMMON CORE STATE STANDARDS: W.4.1.a,b; W.4.3, W.4.5, W.4.9.a, RI.4.2, SL.4.1, SL.4.3, SL.4.4, L.4.1, L.4.2, L.4.3.a, L.4.6

I REMEMBER THE FIRST research report I ever wrote. My older brother and sister had each written reports, so I knew in advance that I'd need to buy index cards, a file box, and pens of different colors. I traveled by bus to the big library in the center of Buffalo, spending several Saturdays surrounded by books, proudly accumulating index cards full of information.

Now when I write nonfiction books, I no longer record information on index cards. But I do still collect bits and pieces of related information: quotes, stories, examples of student writing, data, and ideas. Later, when I prepare to write, I lay the bits alongside each other, noticing that two citations say almost the same thing, that this one text illustrates that citation, that some of my sources contradict each other. I realize some people do most of this work on the computer, but I still rely on the old fashioned system of collecting, sorting, making headings, and so forth.

To bring children into the realm of writing that is organized logically instead of chronologically, it is helpful that they have opportunities to manipulate their information in physical and concrete ways. When teaching children to add and divide numbers, we initially ask them to combine and share buttons or blocks. In similar ways children benefit from physically manipulating bits of information and ideas. In this way, they can grasp that two chunks of data are similar, that one story literally fits under a main idea, that a large pile can be divided into two smaller piles.

This session directly builds on and extends the work of the third-grade opinion writing unit from this series. In that unit, your students learned to organize their writing and create categories. Students wrote long about their claims then created categories by studying their writing and grouping evidence. They cut and taped the different pieces of evidence into booklets with each page labeled as a different category. Now, you will extend that work by helping students to use folders to create similar systems of organization that allow for them to collect material for their essays that will be filed according to the reason that it illustrates. Later you will teach children to transfer this physical system to a mental one and proceed through this work on a more abstract level.

It is important to note that writers will only be gathering evidence for their first two folders. You'll be taking them through the process of gathering, selecting, and organizing evidence for these folders in a relatively step-by-step fashion. Then, in a few days, you'll push writers to develop their third reason with much greater independence, letting them take themselves through the process again so you can see how their learning is transferring.

Some of you may decide to forego the step of working in folders and physically manipulating a collection of passages and other sorts of material. You may decide to channel students to write straight into an essay format, as we do eventually. That will be your decision. Our instinct is to remind you that this work is more complicated for youngsters than you may imagine, and to encourage you to provide this extra round of scaffolding. Either way, in this session you'll teach children to collect stories that illustrate their ideas, knowing that this is a task they should be able to do with confidence and skill. Last year, students likely learned to collect small examples to prove their points and now you will teach them to write examples with greater sophistication, choosing the words that will angle the story to support and bolster a particular reason.

Your teaching needs to rally children to rely upon what they already know about writing stories, and to help them with the new challenge of angling (and unpacking) their stories to support their main ideas.

Composing and Sorting Mini-Stories

CONNECTION

Involve writers in some quick self-assessment of the on-demand pieces they wrote for homework last night.

"Writers, each of you has your on-demand that you wrote at home last night and I also have a copy for each one of you of the Opinion Writing Checklist for Grades 4 and 5."

"Take a minute and look at your piece against this checklist. Which of these goals do you see it already starting to meet? Which do you think could be future work? Do some quick self-assessment."

I coached in among the writers, quietly pushing them to find evidence for what they were saying.

Compliment writers on finding and setting new goals. Encourage them to post these.

"Writers, this is wonderful. It seems that a lot of you are seeing yourselves growing, but you are also noticing some great next steps for yourselves, too.

"Today, during writing workshop, I'm hoping you'll take some time to post your goals publicly so you can hold yourself accountable to them."

Turn writers' attention to continuing to work on their larger piece.

"Right now we are going to move to continuing to raise the level of your work in developing one beautiful piece across time. Let's close our notebooks, put our on-demand away, and listen up, because I have something important to tell you."

Tell children that the boxes and bullets they wrote earlier will provide the frames for their essays.

"Writers, thumbs up if you have ever walked past a construction site and witnessed a new building being built." Many of the children put their thumbs up. "Amazing, right? Well, there is this new building being built on my block. I walked by it this morning and saw iron beams reaching into the sky and forming the shape of the building. Even though only the frame was up, I could see how the building would go. And I started thinking right at that moment that constructing buildings and developing essays have a lot in common. Just like the frames of a building give a sense of what the finished building

Teachers, you should be noticing how we are working to help students get stronger at writing both quick flash-draft essays and longer pieces, developed across a span of time. Both of these types will be important to students' academic careers. One of the goals of this unit is to ensure that students are ready and able to write both, so we're aiming to keep students focused on both kinds of writing. The self-assessment work at the start of this session is reminding students that every piece should be best work and giving them an opportunity to see growth.

There are lots of advantages to using a metaphor in a minilesson. When trying to teach abstract and complicated ideas, sometimes a metaphor can make your ideas more concrete and memorable. It is important, however, to avoid using multiple metaphors. You can't one day liken the frame of an essay to the frame of a building and then the next day suggest that an essay is shaped like a butterfly with separate but similar wings or like a three-leaf clover or a tree with branches. You'll see that I return often to this session's metaphor, that an essay is like a building, and that I generally return later to any metaphor I use in a minilesson. Before you choose a metaphor, then, be sure it can be sustained across more than just one minilesson.

will look like, the boxes-and-bullets plan for your essays give you a sense of how your finished essays will go. They are the frame.

"So now, you need to take the same next step that builders of buildings take: you need to gather and organize materials. When I passed the construction site, I saw a big pile of lumber and another big pile of bricks and another one of stones. Builders gather the materials they need and put them into piles so they can keep materials that belong together organized. They gather and organize material. And you need to do the same thing. Builders make piles; writers create files."

Explain that writers use files to store the materials that will fill in the frame of an essay. Provide an example.

"Before you start gathering material, you need to figure out how to organize it so you can keep related material together. Remember last year when you wrote persuasive speeches and used booklets to tape evidence into different categories?" I held up a booklet like the one used in the third-grade unit and the students nodded. "So remember that if you wanted to write about how you thought that kids should stand up to bullies, you might have made one page all about times when you have seen bullying, another page about how kids feel about being bullied, and another page about what you think everyone can do to stop the problem. There was room on each page for you to tape examples, remember? Well, this year you might try a new system which will allow you to collect even more evidence and keep it all organized. I've given each one of you a large colored folder and three manila file folders.

"Let me show you how you can use these to organize your material. Look at Andy's essay in which he claimed that parents' fighting affects kids very much (see CD-ROM for complete essay). His skeletal plans—his boxes-and-bullets—for his essay looked like this." I uncovered a chart.

Teachers, you can also create these folders by folding large and small pieces of construction paper.

Opinion Writing Checklist

	Grade 4	NOT YET	STARTING TO	YES!	Grade 5	NOT YET	STARTING TO	YES!
	Structure				**Structure**			
Overall	I made a claim about a topic or a text and tried to support my reasons.	☐	☐	☐	I made a claim or thesis on a topic or text, supported it with reasons, and provided a variety of evidence for each reason.	☐	☐	☐
Lead	I wrote a few sentences to hook my readers, perhaps by asking a question, explaining why the topic mattered, telling a surprising fact, or giving background information.	☐	☐	☐	I wrote an introduction that led to a claim or thesis and got my readers to care about my opinion. I got my readers to care by not only including a cool fact or jazzy question, but also figuring out was significant in or around the topic and giving readers information about what was significant about the topic.	☐	☐	☐
	I stated my claim.				I worked to find the precise words to state my claim; I let readers know the reasons I would develop later.	☐	☐	☐
Transitions	I used words and phrases to glue parts of my piece together. I used phrases such as *for example*, *another example, one time*, and *for instance* to show when I was shifting from saying reasons to giving evidence and *in addition to, also*, and *another* to show when I wanted to make a new point.	☐	☐	☐	I used transition words and phrases to connect evidence back to my reasons using phrases such as *this shows that*. . . .	☐	☐	☐
					I helped readers follow my thinking with phrases such as *another reason* and *the most important reason*. I used phrases such as *consequently* and *because of* to show what happened.	☐	☐	☐
					I used words such as *specifically* and *in particular* in order to be more precise.	☐	☐	☐

> **Parents' fighting affects kids very much.**
> - Parents' fighting makes kids yell for things.
> - Parents' fighting makes kids choose sides between their parents.
> - Parents' fighting makes kids start not trusting people.

"He wrote his thesis," I said, pointing to a folded over sheet of construction paper. Then I held up the manila folders and showed students how they fit inside the colored folder. "Look how Andy made a separate place to collect and store materials for each of his bullets—one folder for each of his reasons. He made folders for two of those bullet point statements and he decided to write his third body paragraph without using a folder. He said he would use his mind as a mental folder to gather material for that body paragraph.

"I suggest you follow Andy's process because his system helped him keep his material organized. And folders allow for writers to gather *lots* of evidence. So right now, write your thesis across your colored folder and set up manila folders for your reasons. Right now, label your folders quickly because it is time to start gathering material. Whenever you write a non-narrative piece, one that will require a lot of materials, a lot of information, it helps to set up a system for gathering and collecting the materials you'll end up assembling."

❧ **Name the teaching point.**

"But today what I want to teach you is this. Some of the most important materials writers collect when writing essays are—stories!"

TEACHING

Demonstrate that writers bring knowledge of narrative writing to this new task, only this time they collect and write mini-stories that are angled to illustrate the bulleted topic sentence. First, they generate stories to support their thesis.

"Here's the great news: you can use all that you already know about writing good stories to help you support each of your reasons. Watch how I go about collecting stories in my folders, stories that could fit under each bullet in a boxes-and-bullets plan." I shared my plan.

> **My father is my most important teacher.**
> - My father taught me to love work.
> - My father taught me to love writing.
> - My father taught me that one person can make a difference.

Sometimes it is tempting to use the minilesson as a time to tell your students what you'd like them all to do. It would have been easy to state as my teaching point, "Writers, today I want to show you how I'd like you to organize and collect writing. You're each going to make three files. . . ." But we guard against letting minilessons become occasions to simply assign work to children, and we carefully watch our wording so that we are teaching children strategies that writers use often rather than nudging them to jump through a particular set of hoops on a particular day. Watch how we circumvent a teaching point that merely assigns today's work so as to hold to the principle that minilessons are occasions for teaching a strategy or an idea children can use often.

Teachers, note again that students are only going to collect and gather evidence for the first two folders. In a few days we'll return to the third folder.

"Let me take one bullet, 'My father taught me to love work.' Now I need to ask, 'What true story can I think of related to this?'" (Sometimes I already have stories that support a reason in my writer's notebook, or something I just need to remember a story from my original plan for the essay.) "Hmm . . . " I pulled out my web from Session 5 and studied it for a minute. Thinking aloud to myself, I listed possible story ideas—choosing stories that illustrated the idea that my Dad taught me to love work. "Hmm," I said. Touching one finger, I said, "I could show that Dad taught me to love work by telling the story of how on the last day of summer, when Dad and I sailed together, he confided that he couldn't wait for vacation to be over so he could return to work. Or, I could tell the story of (and I gestured to a second finger) the way that, on Christmas mornings, my father always went to the hospital to make waffles for the doctors and patients. I asked why he didn't send someone else. Dad admitted that he liked going to work. "It's my hobby."

Channel children to do similar work, brainstorming and selecting a story to tell to support one of their reasons.

"Writers, do you notice the way I took one of my bullet points, one of my reasons, and thought of several true stories that related to this point? In your mind, choose one of your bullet points, think 'for example . . . ', and list a few true stories in your mind that relate to that point." I gave them a minute to do this work.

Proceed to the second step of this work, selecting one story, then drafting it.

"Next, let me start writing the stories on my list. First, I need to remember what I know about writing focused stories." Collecting across my fingers, I said, "One. I'll make a movie in my mind of how the story unfolded, starting at the beginning.

"Two. Then I'll story-tell it step-by-step, bit-by-bit (but only the part that matches my thesis). When I write the story, I'll also keep in mind that it needs to highlight one particular idea—in this instance, that Dad taught me to love work.

"Three. I'll remember that this needs to be a tiny story." I closed my eyes. "So even though when I make my movie in my mind of Dad making waffles on Christmas morning, I see myself helping him—handing him the vanilla and the milk. Wait! That doesn't support my thesis that he taught me how to love work. I need to only tell the parts that show my thesis. So maybe I'll just story-tell the parts that show how watching him so happy to help the people at his work."

I opened my eyes, picked up my clipboard and began writing (on lined paper, outside the notebook) and voicing as I wrote.

> I remember on Christmas mornings after the presents had been opened my dad always went into the kitchen and began doing the one bit of cooking that he did all year. He stirred Bisquick and eggs in a huge bowl and set off for the hospital leaving us to finish Christmas celebrations without him. For Dad Christmas mornings were not just a time to be with family. They were also a time to serve hot waffles to the medical residents and patients. When I asked him once why he didn't send someone else with the waffles, he told me he loved being at the hospital on Christmas mornings. 'It's my hobby!' he said. Seeing him so happy to go to work made me realize that work can be wonderful.

I could have made my point in a briefer fashion, but when I write about topics that really matter to me I find it hard to be brief. I think children can tell when you are authentically engaged in your own writing, and they respond in kind. So I decided to forgive myself for offering examples that are longer than is ideal. You'll notice that I jotted this writing on my clipboard, not on chart paper. The advantage of the clipboard is that I can scrawl and abbreviate (and, if necessary, prepare a cheat sheet ahead of time to remind me of what I want to say) and talk more quickly than I actually write.

It is very powerful to write detailed stories that carry gigantic ideas. The writer Richard Price once said, "The bigger the issue, the smaller you write." I worked on this story before I met with the kids, trying to keep it brief, to make sure it was a step-by-step story, and to highlight the sections that illustrated my main idea.

This is dictated, on notebook paper, so that I can scrawl, lickety split (or pretend to write as I actually cheat and read something I've already written). The goal is to demonstrate—quickly.

Debrief, highlighting the process and pointing out that you told the story step-by-step, bit-by-bit, rather than summarizing it.

Then, pausing in the midst of the story, I shifted away from the role of writer and into the role of teacher. "Writers, I hope you saw that I collected this mini-story outside my notebook on loose-leaf paper. I did that because now I'm going to put the mini-story in the folder titled 'My father taught me what it means to love work.'" I did this.

"I hope you also noticed that to get myself started telling a story, I rewrote my thesis and reason and then wrote 'For example. . . .' Writers don't always use those exact words, but for today, use the phrase *for example* and then, maybe, *one time*. Finally, writers, I hope you noticed that when writing a story, I asked myself, 'How did it start?' I made a movie in my mind of what happened and wrote the story in a bit-by-bit way, and I told it in a way that highlights my idea."

ACTIVE ENGAGEMENT

Set children up to try this while writing-in-the-air. Ask them to think of a mini-story they can tell to support their first bullet.

"Writers, let's practice doing this right now. You have already thought of a bunch of true stories that match one of your reasons. Choose one. Say your thesis and first bullet in your mind and then say, 'For example, one time, I . . .' and quickly tell one little story that shows that reason. Thumbs up when you have that little story in mind." They signaled. "Okay, Partner 2, write your story in the air to Partner 1. Partner 1, listen to see if the story matches the reason. Give Partner 2 feedback. Go to it."

Katie turned to Michaela and said, "Sometimes I hurt people's feelings to get back at them. For example, one time I told my sister that I heard some sixth-grade boys talking about her. I said, 'I have something to tell you, but you are not going to like it.' She begged me to tell her. I told her about how I was going down 7th Avenue and I heard these boys from her class say she was ugly. She started to cry almost. But it was a lie, but she thought it was the truth."

Michaela whispered, "It is a strong story." Then she said, "But I don't think it all the way fits. What was your thesis statement?"

Together the partners figured out how Katie could add in a tiny bit about how she made the story up to get back at her sister. Then the story fit.

LINK

Restate the teaching point and remind students of the metaphor you established earlier describing their upcoming work.

"Writers, once builders and writers have constructed a frame, it's time to gather the materials needed to fill in around the girders. Builders truck in boards and cinder blocks; writers build with words. Today (and whenever you have built a boxes-and-bullets structure for an essay), you can bring in materials—stories—to build your essay. When you write stories that will be tucked into essays, remember to use everything you already know about writing powerful stories. Plan to write a couple of stories in one folder today, then a couple in another folder. If you don't get to the third folder, that's okay."

I tried to be explicit about the connection between this example and the overarching idea.

You will, of course, want to write your own story. Bring your dad into your teaching! Look ahead to Session 9, when you'll want to use the draft you write today again.

You'll find that when the challenge is to tell a story in such a way that it illustrates a point, writers often delete the beginning of the story (which means the story is not a story after all). For example, if my topic sentence is, "It is dangerous to drive to work," I could "tell the story" of yesterday's near accident by cutting to the chase in a way that relates to the topic sentence, saying, "Yesterday, I was almost in an accident." But that is not a story. To tell this as a story, I need to tell the start of the story, angling it toward the point I wanted to make: "Yesterday, I drove to work as usual, drinking coffee, talking on the cell phone, and steering around potholes. Suddenly . . ." That's an angled story!

As you know, we actually are planning on children not filling all three of their folders, allowing us to show them how they can write the body paragraph for an essay without first collecting, sorting through, and combining materials. We know we don't need to emphasize that the third folder can be left, for now, as writing a couple of stories in each of the two folders is work for a day.

Grouping Students to Tackle the Hard Parts

TODAY, YOU'LL WANT TO SPEND TIME supporting the work of the minilesson, which is key to the development of a strong essay. You'll want to confer and lead groups to help children gather stories that illustrate their ideas. You'll find that when children reach for stories that illustrate an idea, the idea usually comes at the end—the climax—of the story. Children, therefore, often bypass the set-up and wind-up

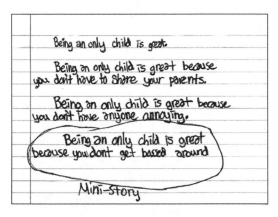

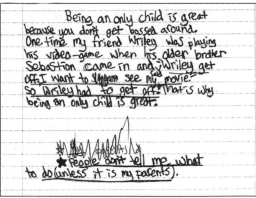

FIG. 8–1   Sam's notebook entries

SESSION 8: COMPOSING AND SORTING MINI-STORIES

MID-WORKSHOP TEACHING
Angling Stories to Support Thesis Statements

"Writers, can I have your attention? Eddy and I just discovered something important that I suspect pertains to many of you. Eddy's thesis is that he loves to spend time with his parents. In one of his folders, he's collecting material to support the reason. 'I love to spend time with my parents when we go on vacation together.' He collected a story about staying overnight in a hotel with his parents. I want you to listen to the story he collected and see if you can discern the problem that Eddy faces (and I suspect many of you face as well). Listen."

I love to spend time with my parents when we are on vacation together. For example, one time we went to a hotel in New Jersey. First we went to the zoo in the hotel. It had really cute baby animals. Then I went swimming. Then I watched three TV shows.

When I asked Eddy to tell the class what he'd discovered as he reread this, he said, "I realized I told a story of what I did, but I left my parents out—and my whole idea was that I like to spend time with them." So then he shared his next draft:

I love to spend time with my parents when we vacation together. For example, one time we went to a hotel in New Jersey. First we visited a zoo that was in the hotel. It had really cute baby animals. My Mom loved the baby sheep so much that she pretended she was going to sneak it up the elevator to our room. My Dad and I had to drag her away. We were just joking. Then we watched three TV shows; one that was my choice, one that was Mom's, one that was Dad's. We usually don't watch each others' shows.

(continues)

Nodding, I added, "Eddy made a really important discovery. If his story is going to illustrate that he loves vacationing with his parents, then he needs to angle his story about staying at the hotel so that the story shows that he likes to stay there because he gets to be with his parents! Listen to Eddy's next version of this story.

"Right now, before you do anything else, I want each of you to reread one of the stories you have collected and talk with your partner about how you could rewrite that story so that it really highlights whatever it is you need to show. Then rewrite that one entry, that one story. I'll be admiring the revisions you make."

> I love to spend time with my parents when we vacation together. For example, one time we went to a hotel in New Jersey. We visited a zoo that was in an hotel, I had really cute baby animals. My Mom. loved the baby sheep so much that she pretended she was going to sneak it up the elevator to our room. My Dad and I had to drag her away. We were just joking. Then we watched three TV shows; one that was my choice, one that was my Mom's, one that was Dad's. We usually don't watch each others' shows.

FIG. 8–2   Eddy's revised story

sections of their stories. When Jay Jay wanted to tell a story to illustrate that he loves being with his father because his father teaches him rollerskating moves, he wrote:

> One day my father taught me a skating trick and I like him cause he did that.

I helped Jay Jay see that he needed to back up and tell how the story started (though now the problem became the other extreme—too much windup!) Soon, Jay Jay's story went like this:

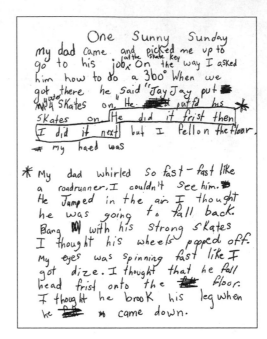

FIG. 8–3   Jay Jay's revised story about his father

Often children will tell a story without developing the part that illustrates the bullet point, the topic sentence. When I see this, I often say to the child, as I said to Jay Jay, "Would you box the part of the story that goes with your bullet point?" Then I state the child's bullet point, the statement labeled on the folder. In the example above, Jay Jay decided that only one line of the story, "He did it first, then I did it next," advanced his idea which was, "I love being with my father because he teaches me skating moves."

I typically then ask children to take the underlined/boxed section and write a long paragraph just about that. Jay Jay wrote this to insert into his original paragraph (see Figure 8–3):

> My dad whirled so fast–fast like a roadrunner. I couldn't see him. He jumped in the air. I thought he was going to fall back. Bang with his strong skates. I thought his wheels popped off. My eyes were spinning fast like I got dizzy. I thought that he fell headfirst into the floor. I thought he broke his leg when he came down.

The story tells more about Jay Jay's father as a skater than about the fact that Jay Jay loves his father because he taught him the 360° and other moves, but I let this go and moved on to teach one other tip. Once children have written a story, I often teach them to add a sentence at the end of the story that refers back to their bulleted reason. For example, Jay Jay's story at first had ended this way:

> I fell on the floor. My head was bloody.

I taught Jay Jay that essayists try to add a sentence at the end of a story that links back to the topic sentence. Jay Jay added:

> I came to in the locker room, still thinking how I love my Dad for teaching me skating moves.

The ending makes all the difference! Now he'd accumulated material in his folder which read like this:

> I love being with my father because he teaches me skating moves. One sunny Sunday, my dad came and picked me up to go to his job at the Skate Key. On the way I asked him how to do a 360°. When we got there, he said, "Jay Jay, put your skates on." He put his skates on. He did it first. My dad whirled so fast—fast like a roadrunner. I couldn't see him. Bang with his strong skates. I thought his wheels popped off. My eyes were spinning fast like I got dizzy. I thought that he fell headfirst into the floor. I thought he broke his leg when he came down. He did it first, but next I did it. I fell on the floor. My head was bloody. I came to in the locker room, still thinking how I love my Dad for teaching me skating moves.

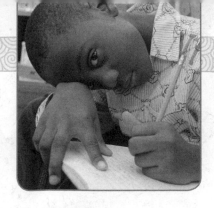

Self-Assessment for Writing Mini-Stories

Share your realizations about the process of essay writing to practice evaluating a piece of writing for what qualities are there and what qualities are missing.

"Writers, you've each collected a story that supports one of your topic sentences, or reasons. As I've worked with you today, I've realized that together we have figured out a bunch of guidelines to follow as you write mini-stories to support your ideas. I've written them out for you here, so you can refer to them whenever you want."

> Guidelines for Writing Supporting Stories for Essays
>
> - Writers usually include a transition into the story, such as _____ .
> - The story needs to have a beginning, middle, and end.
> - The story needs to be told to especially reveal the part of it that illustrates the thesis statement and the bullet point, the reason.
> - At the end of the story, it is usually wise to include a sentence that refers back to or repeats the main idea of the paragraph.

"Writers, let's listen to Tony's story, and as we listen, you and your partner check off (writing with your finger only and invisible ink) guidelines you notice he has followed, and then afterward, you and your partner can talk about the most important guidelines you think he still needs to follow. "

Drawing is really fun. I can express myself in drawing. One time I was mad at a kid for bothering me. Instead of settling it in a violent way, I controlled myself; for a minute I thought about all I knew about drawing. Then I took out a paper and a pencil. I drew him running around, screaming, with snake hair, a rat's head, and a slow turtle body. Drawing helps me express myself.

"Never underestimate the power of story as the conveyer of ideas. Many sections of the Bible are written in stories—parables, often—and these stories convey ideas. How lucky we are that Melville didn't write a book about whaling in general, but instead wrote about one man and one whale. And how lucky that Jane Austen didn't write about pride and prejudice, but instead wrote about one man and one woman struggling with and against their pride and their prejudice" (Zinsser 2004, 107).

FIG. 8–4 Tony's story to support his thesis "Drawing is fun."

"Now, students, reread your own writing and check off which of these guidelines you have already followed, and star the ones that you are going to work on next. For a minute, look through your own writing, and then in a bit I will ask you to share your thoughts with your partner."

COMPOSING AND SORTING MINI-STORIES

Angling Oral Stories

Writers, remember how much better our stories became after we rehearsed them, telling them before writing them down? Tonight practice angling another story to support one of your reasons. Tell it to someone before you write it down. Try telling the same story a second time, even if you need to recruit your dog as your listener! Once you are happy with how the story sounds, write it down.

Creating Parallelism in Lists

IN THIS SESSION, you'll teach children that writers gather a lot of different material to write their essays, including lists, and they decide which material should go in their essays.

GETTING READY

✔ Sample student text that uses a list to support a topic sentence that you can show to students as an exemplar (see Teaching)

✔ Your own example of using a list to support one of your topic sentences. Make sure your list demonstrates that you have repeated the stem of your reason. (see Teaching)

✔ Students' essay writing materials including their thesis and reason folders, their web or mosaic, and their writer's notebooks

✔ A teacher or student sample of a list that leaves out the main points the writer wants to tell that you can show writers how to revise (see Share)

✔ An example of a list where the writer has opted not to write in a parallel structure but instead used precise, powerful details (see Share)

✔ A sample text to demonstrate how to balance details and parallel structures (see Share)

I LOVE TO MAKE LISTS. I list my priorities for a day, a week, a vacation, a year. I list the names of flowers I've planted in my garden. I list names for the dog I'll someday get. I list books I've read and books I want to read. I list places I'd like to visit someday. I list the days when my sons will be away and the days when they'll be home again.

Lists reflect the human instinct to collect, sort, order, and select. When we cannot physically gather in our arms all the flowers we've planted and line them up on the counter, we list their names, and those names make the flowers present. Simply by naming them, we conjure them up: dahlia, daisy, lily—yes, I've got them all in my garden.

During today's session, you'll help children make lists that may help their essays. There are lots of possible ways to teach this concept. You could share your own propensity to list and to collect, and share also what you know of your children's similar tendencies. One child collects baseball cards, another barrettes. Both children spend time sorting these into categories. Writers do similar work.

Specifically, today you'll teach children to write what I refer to as "tight lists," or lists of items linked by a repeating phrase. The lesson, then, will be not only about lists but also about parallelism.

For writers, the challenge of this lesson will be to attend to both content and form. It would be easy to write tight lists of anything in the world, but remember, Rebecca's tight lists need to advance her claims about her fury with her grandfather, and Caleb's tight lists need to show that practice is essential to success in a sport. Trying to convey a meaning while writing within a tight list structure is like trying to tap your head and rub your belly at the same time—it is not easy. Try it and you'll see!

COMMON CORE STATE STANDARDS: W.4.1.b, W.4.3, W.4.5, W.4.7, W.4.8, RI.4.2, RL.4.3, SL.4.1, L.4.1, L.4.2, L.4.3.a,

Creating Parallelism in Lists

CONNECTION

Find a metaphor—probably from the world of construction—to helps students grasp that essayists collect a lot of different material, including lists, to write well-developed essays.

"Writers, I passed by that construction site on my block again this morning on my way to school. That building is really getting to be something. The builders have started putting in the windows, and it made me think about how many different types of materials it takes to build a building. You can't just use lumber. You also need glass and plasterboard and a lot of other stuff. Well, I started thinking about essay writing again while I was standing there. Just like builders build with plasterboard and lumber, writers build with words. I realized that you need to start gathering different types of materials, too."

❖ **Name the teaching point.**

"Today, I want to teach you that just as builders build with boards and lumber and windowpanes too, so, too, writers build with not only stories, but with other stuff as well. And lists are one of the most important materials that writers use when building essays."

I know this unit can be complicated. One day children learn to write personal stories; another day they learn to write lists. I try to consolidate all they've learned so that it feels simple and portable. I do that here when I say builders build with plasterboard and lumber, writers with words.

TEACHING

Share an example of a student who has used lists to support an idea.

"Let's study a piece of writing where lists as well as stories support one of the reasons in an essay. Let's look at this paragraph from William's piece. His thesis is 'My mom works hard for our family,' and his reasons are that, one, she wakes up early every day, and two, she never misses a day of work even when she is sick. As I read a section of the essay to you, look at how William chose to list ways his mother works hard, as well as to tell a longer story about one way she works hard. "Notice the differences between listing examples and storytelling." I read aloud, interjecting comments.

> She wakes up early every day to put my clothes in order. Depending on what activity I have.
> She wakes up early every day to check my book bag in case I forgot a book or a sheet.
> She wakes up early every day to see what is the temperature to see if I need a coat.

"Writers, notice that William is not storytelling. He's not storytelling what happened in a bit-by-bit way. He's instead giving us lots of quick examples that support the fact that his mom works hard for the family by waking up early every day. And he's starting each sentence of his lists the same way."

Involve children as you use the techniques the writer used to write a tight list pertinent to your topic.

"So I'm hoping you can help me borrow some of William's techniques as I collect lists to support my third bullet: 'My father has been my most important teacher because he taught me that one person can make a difference.' Will you make sure I do everything William did? Make sure that I repeat the stem of the reason and that each example matches my reason. If you see me make a mistake, give me a polite thumbs down so I can fix my work, okay? So let me see. . . ." I reread the topic sentence to what would be my third body paragraph.

> My father has been my most important teacher because he taught me that one person can make a difference.

"Let me think of a whole bunch of examples for how my father did that. I can only use a few words to say each one, in a list. And I need to keep repeating the start of the list. Here goes," I said, and dictated, writing-in-the-air, a possible list:

> My father taught me that one person could start a hospital clinic. My father taught me that one person could rally all the members of a family to write their memoirs. My father taught me that one person could turn a rainy drab day into an adventure. My father taught me that if there are a lot of doctors at a hospital, this can cheer up patients.

A few of the students immediately stuck their thumbs down and I stopped. "No, wait. That last one doesn't match, right? My examples are supposed to show how *one person* can make a difference. Let me try that last one again."

> My father taught me that one person could change the spirit at a hospital.

"Do you see how I repeated the key phrase at the start of each item in the list?" I put the entry in the appropriate file folder.

ACTIVE ENGAGEMENT

Set children up to turn their collections of possible mini-stories into lists.

"Right now, you'll get a chance to try. Look back at your notes from yesterday and remind yourself of all the true stories that relate to your first reason. In a minute, you'll repeat that reason in your head and then try listing two of your stories as examples. Remember to make sure you use precise words and that your examples match your reason. Okay, try listing in your head." I gave them a minute to do this work. "In a minute, Partner 2, share your lists with Partner 1. Partner 1,

① She wakes up early everyday to put my clothes in order. Depending on what activity I have.

She wakes up early everyday to check my book bag incase I forgot a book or a sheet.

She wakes up early everyday to see what is the temperature to see if I need a coat.

Perhaps the most important way why my mom works hard for the family by never missing a day of work even when she is sick.

One morning my mom told me that she was sick. She sneezed, she coughed she even wasted a pack of tissues. When she went to her job, that exact moment I felt that my mom could do anything. When she left I was worried. She left in an aweful condition when she got home she felt better.

"Hey, mom are you ok?" I said.

"I've never felt better!" she said.

② I was so relieved.

When she is sick she can still give me breakfast. She tries her best to give me something simply to eat.

When she is sick she can still put my clothes in order. She knows I put on whatever she gives me.

When she is sick she can still help me with my Homework. When I'm stuck she tries her best to help me.

FIG. 9-1 William's final draft

make sure the lists repeat the key words of the reason and that they match the reason. Give Partner 2 feedback. Okay, go ahead and try this." The room erupted into talk.

LINK

Remind writers of the importance of gathering a variety of materials for their essays.

"Writers, yesterday, most of you wrote stories that could support two of your three reasons. Today, make lists to support those same two reasons, even if that means one of your folders remains empty. I'll show you what you can do with that one later. Remember that just like builders use a variety of materials to construct buildings, writers use a variety of materials to construct essays. Today, fill up your folders with a variety of materials—with more stories, with lists, and with other things you think of as well. Later, you'll choose the very best material that will go into your actual essay. Okay, go to it!"

Toward the end of a minilesson, I often try to put the day's teaching point alongside earlier teaching points, and, if possible, show how they are related. In this instance, I refer back to the metaphor of writers as builders because this conveys the main concept of this minilesson. I also remind children that writers make choices, and that they can draw on previous teaching points as well as today's point.

Making List Items Parallel

ANY TIME YOU READ students' writing or have a conference with one child, you need to ask yourself, "Is this a lesson to teach one child, or should I pull in another writer or two?" You might think to yourself, "Sydni and Chris are both having trouble with. . . . Let me do a quick scan of the room and round up others who might benefit from this as well," and in that way, you might pull together a small group and teach all those children a strategy you suspect will help.

In one such strategy lesson, I said to the children who huddled around me on the meeting area carpet, "I gathered you together because I want to show you a trick I discovered when I was trying to make the items in my list parallel to each other. It's not easy to make them parallel, is it? I've noticed you guys are struggling with that, and you're not alone! So let me tell you what I learned from working on a list to go with my reason 'My father taught me to love work.'

"I had already written, 'My father doesn't just *like* his job, he *loves* his job.' When I read that line over, I knew it had a certain snap. I liked it. I didn't intend for the line to come out that way. I just wrote what I thought, and then I reread it and liked it. So I looked closely at the sentence to see if I could write more sentences in the same pattern. I noticed it has two parts, and they echo each other."

My father doesn't just *like* his job, he *loves* his job.

"So I built the next item on my list in the same way. I knew it had to go something like this: 'My father doesn't just *bing*, he *superbings*. My father doesn't just like (something), he super-likes (something).' You see how it had to go? So this is what I wrote:"

My father doesn't just care about his patients, he identifies with his patients.

"Do you see how I followed the pattern of the first sentence I wrote? I started with the same phrase, 'My father doesn't just . . . ,' and then I put in 'care about his patients.' I knew the next part had to be something he does more than just care about them. Instead of saying, 'He super-cares about his patients,' I chose to say, 'He identifies with his patients.'

MID-WORKSHOP TEACHING   Revising Lists

"Some of you are having some trouble getting started on a list. You aren't sure what to use as the repeating stem of the list. One thing to do is to think of a story, and then ask, 'How can I write this same information—or the important parts of it—as a list and not as a story?' So listen to the story Eddy wrote to go with his thesis statement, 'I love spending time with my parents when we vacation together.' Remember his story? You've heard it before, but this time listen so you can tell your partner what Eddy could write if, instead of story-telling, he was listing."

I love to spend time with my parents when we vacation together. For example, one time we went to a hotel in New Jersey. We visited a zoo that was in the hotel. It had really cute baby animals. My Mom loved the baby sheep so much that she pretended she was going to sneak it up the elevator to our room. My Dad and I had to drag her away. We were just joking. Then we watched three TV shows; one that was my choice, one that was Mom's, one that was Dad's. We usually don't watch each others' shows.

The partners talked, and then I intervened. "I heard you finding lots of ways to do this, and of course there is no one right way. Theo first tried this:

> At the hotel, my family went to the zool, my family watched TV, and my family rode the elevator.

"But then he realized he'd left out the part about the family doing this together (which is, of course, the main idea!). He also left out all the interesting details. So he tried it again, and this is what he came up with:

> I loved spending time with my parents when we stayed at a hotel. Together, we watched three TV shows (one that each of us had chosen). Together, we visited the hotel's zoo (where my Mom tried to sneak a baby lamb onto the elevator). And together we . . .

"Do you see that Theo has come up with a way for Eddy to repeat the important parts—that he, his mom, and his dad did these things *together*—and he has also included the details that bring his story to life? Coming up with this list isn't easy; Theo tried the list first one way, then another, then another. If you are working on lists that you can include in your folders, I should see draft 1, draft 2, draft 3 as you try your lists one way, then another, and then another."

"LaKeya did this, too (see Figure 9–2). Read this aloud in pairs and listen for the pattern, the song, in her words, and then look closely and point out to each other what she did that you could do as well."

After the children talked a bit about that passage, I said, "Try making your own list or revising the one you've started. Remember that first you reread what you've written and find a line you like, then you study what you did in that line to see if you can make another like it. I'll be right here helping you while you get started."

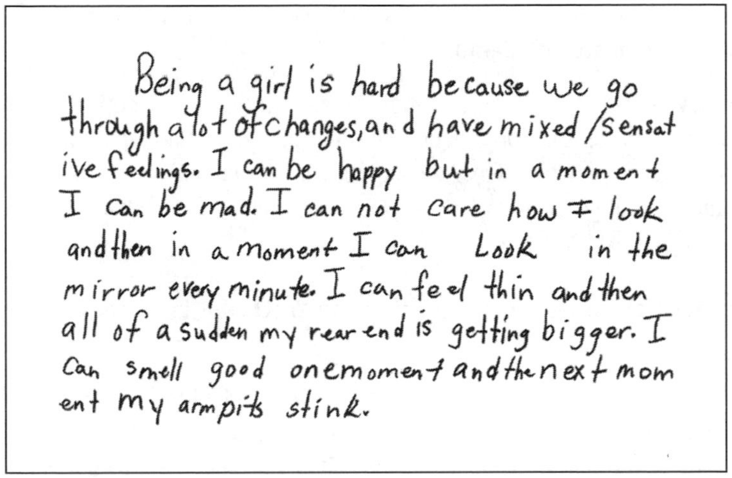

Being a girl is hard because we go through a lot of changes, and have mixed /sensative feelings. I can be happy but in a moment I can be mad. I can not care how I look and then in a moment I can Look in the mirror every minute. I can feel thin and then all of a sudden my rear end is getting bigger. I can smell good one moment and the next moment my armpits stink.

FIG. 9–2   LaKeya's lists

Balancing Details and Parallelism

Name the problem you have noticed. In this instance, children are so focused on parallelism that they forget the importance of honesty and detail.

"You are writing your lists in patterns, and that is great, but you know how sometimes when you try to write poems that rhyme, you get into trouble. Your poems end up having almost nothing *but* rhyme? Well, some of you are writing *lists* where one sentence matches with the next, but it's as if you are so worried about matching your words that you forget all you know about good writing! When you are writing a list (as when you are writing anything!), it is important to try to write well."

Showcase sections of an exemplar text that can teach the importance of using active verbs and precise details.

"There are a few qualities of good writing that you especially need to remember as you work on gathering lists. Using *specific* details really matters. When Eddy wanted to write a list about staying in the hotel with his parents, this meant that he'd need to squeeze his whole long story into items in a list. He was probably tempted to leave out the details about watching one television show that he chose, one show that his mother chose, and one that his father chose. He was probably tempted to leave out the detail about his mother wanting to adopt a baby lamb, but Eddy wisely knew those details were the strongest part of his writing, so he kept them.

"Sometimes when writing a list, the details can't fit into sentences that sound just right. In that case, sometimes writers decide to keep the details and let go of the parallelism. That's the decision Jamile made when he listed examples to show how his pets are good entertainers, and I think his decision was really wise. Listen."

> I think pets are good entertainers. My little sister has tea parties with my dog; he has carrots and she has bread. I read with my dog and he shares his thinking with me. Most of his thoughts have to do with snuffle, snuffle, snuffle.

"The items in Jamile's list don't perfectly match each other. He decided that content mattered more than sound, and he was probably wise to make that choice. I call this an elaborated—not a tight—list."

> I think pets are good entertainers My little sister have tea parties with my dog; he has carrots and she has bread. I read with my dog and shares his thinking with me. Most of his thought have to do with snuffle, snuffle, snuffle.

FIG. 9–3   Jamile's list does not have parallelism; he opted instead for details.

Debrief by naming what you did that is transferable to another day on another topic.

"So when you work on your lists, try to remember that strong action words and specific, precise nouns matter. And try to remember that even when you are squeezing a whole story into a sentence or two, you need to leave in the details like the dog eating carrots at the tea party and Mom wanting to sneak a baby lamb up the elevator to her hotel room!

"Right now, let's have you and your partner look over your lists, and think and talk about whether your effort to give your list a musical sound, with one line matching the next, may have dominated too much. Ask whether you have written the truth and used exact details. If you've sacrificed truth or detail, try rewriting your lists. Tonight you will be making sure your folders are full of evidence. Gather both lists and stories!"

CREATING PARALLELISM IN LISTS

Finding the Specifics that Bring Pieces to Life

Writers, you are learning that writers don't just write with words; they write with information. Don Murray, the Pulitzer Prize–winning writer, once said, "Beginning writers often misunderstand this. Young writers often become drunk on their way to becoming good writers. They dance to the sound of their own voices. They try to substitute style for subject matter, tricks for content, ruffles and flourishes for information. It doesn't work. The writer who has a warehouse of specific, detailed, relevant information has the advantage over any other writer."

And writers, you are collecting files full of information. So tonight, collect specific information related to your topic. Live like magnets. Last night Philip did this, collecting information about how his cat can be a lot of trouble, and he recorded this detail on his clipboard: "My cat trampled over me when she was catching a fly." What a detail—and he has it in his files because even when he was at home, he lived like a magnet, letting things related to his topic stick to him. Would you all do what Philip has done? Carry a clipboard with you, and let things that relate to your topic stick with you.

Specificity always helps. Make sure you come in tomorrow with your folders filled. You will need at least one or two stories and one or two lists per folder. Tomorrow we will start organizing all of our materials and get ready to draft!

When teaching children to write lists, after they do so in a way that repeats the stem over and over, you may want to show them that writers can collapse our lists. Instead of writing, "My grandfather is precious to me because he teaches me card tricks. My grandfather is precious to me because he lets me stay up late," you can tell a child to consolidate and write, "My grandfather is precious to me because he teaches me card tricks, lets me stay up late, and (whatever else the child wants to say)."

Organizing for Drafting

COMMON CORE STATE STANDARDS: W.4.1, W.4.3, W.4.4, W.4.5, RI.4.2, RL.4.3, SL.4.1, SL.4.3, SL.4.4, , L.4.1, L.4.2, L.4.3

IN THIS SESSION, you'll teach children that writers organize for drafting by checking that their evidence is supportive and varied.

GETTING READY

✔ Your folders with your thesis statement, reasons, and evidence, including mini-stories and lists

✔ "Steps to Take Before You Draft" list (see Teaching)

✔ Students' essay-writing materials including their folders and writer's notebooks, to be brought to the meeting area

✔ Colored pens or pencils to underline key parts in mini-stories (see Active Engagement)

✔ Extra folders for new topic sentences, if students need these

✔ "Questions to Ask of Writing Before You Draft" chart (see Conferring)

✔ "Essay Frame" chart from Session 1 (see Share)

✔ A mini-story that only partially supports one of your reasons that you can use to demonstrate checking and revising evidence (see Teaching)

✔ A mini-story that does not support your reason at all that you can show students to demonstrate how to cut evidence or revise boxes and bullets (see Conferring)

WHEN THIS COUNTRY WAS YOUNG, barn raisings were a common occurrence. When I close my eyes I can imagine the people gathering. They bring all types of supplies: hammers and saws, lumber and nails, watermelon and pies. I can see the whole neighborhood gathered, hauling ropes, lifting first one of the barn walls into place, then another. Those barn raisings were spectacular events. People had worked for weeks preparing the walls, aligning the structures of each, gathering all the materials in place; as a result, within a single day the smaller pieces could come together quickly, into a whole. Presto—suddenly, where once a flat field lay, now a barn stands tall, its completed form outlined against the sky.

The time has come in this unit for an "essay raising." After days of collecting, researching, writing, and planning the structure of the piece, after the long sessions of making sure the reasons and evidence are in place, it's time to pull together the full form of the essay! Today, you will ask children to take the two folders they've filled and all the material they've collected within each folder and decide which material does the job best and should be included in the final essay. Offer children a small set of questions to ask of the writing in each folder, questions that can guide their thinking whenever they are in this phase of essay writing.

Then, in the mid-workshop teaching and again in the next session, you'll ask children to nail together the pieces of writing into paragraphs. You'll offer them suggestions for making sensible arrangements and for organizing each little bit of information so that all the pieces fit together neatly to support the essay's thesis statement.

Organizing for Drafting

CONNECTION

Find a metaphor—probably from the world of construction—that helps students grasp that they will be readying materials that will be used to construct an essay.

"Writers, all this talk about building has made me want to start a home project. So last night I bought a kit to build a birdhouse. All these materials came with it! Wood, nails, paint, screws, and a whole bunch of other different stuff. I laid all that stuff out on my table and organized it into piles, just like we've been organizing our materials, and I got to work, putting one piece together with another, and another. So I started thinking that essay writing is just like this. Just as I choose and combine the right materials to build a birdhouse, I need to choose and combine the right materials to write my essay."

Name the teaching point.

"Today, I want to teach you that before writers put any project together, they organize their materials and make sure they have the right amount of materials. They test out whether all the materials really 'fit' with the project plan."

TEACHING

Explain how you check and organize the materials in one folder.

"Let me tell you how I usually organize my materials to get ready for drafting. I know that each folder is going to become one section of my essay, so I usually check one folder at a time. I lay out my materials and then I look them over and I go through a couple of steps. I've listed them here." I uncovered a chart.

> ### Steps to Take before You Draft
>
> 1. Reread a piece of evidence
>
> 2. Look for parts that match your reason (underline)
>
> 3. Decide if you need to cut or revise

◆ COACHING

You'll note the same notion of essay development as construction is raised again, with a slightly different spin—building a birdhouse. I want central metaphors to span multiple lessons, creating a sense of cohesion and consistency, but I also want to vary things a bit to keep the lessons feeling fresh. Here, I'm referring to building, but this time it is me who is building!

Involve the students in thinking along with you as you demonstrate checking one mini-story in your folder.

"Watch me go through the steps on my list. As I do each one, give it a little mental check. Remember, what matters most is that I only keep the materials that exactly support what I want to say. Let me start with this folder, this reason: My father taught me to love work.

"So here's all the material I wanted to include in this section":

- story of my dad taking me sailing and telling me he couldn't wait to get back to his job after summer vacation
- story of my dad making waffles for doctors and patients at work on Christmas morning

"First, I'll reread the first story and look for sections that match my reason: my father taught me to love work. When I find sections that go with my reason I'll underline them. That will help me check that this evidence matches my reason. I can only underline parts that match 'my father taught me to love work.' You read along with me and give a thumbs up when you see a part you think I should underline." Then I read this, interjecting comments as I did so:

At the end of summer my father took me sailing. We went off together in our little boat with lots of sandwiches and lemonade that Mom packed.

"Hmmm . . . should I be underlining? No, I don't see anything about how my father taught me to love work. Let me keep reading."

We sailed all day long and then we turned around to go home.

"Should I underline? No. Nothing about my father teaching me to love work."

My father whistled as we sailed back to the harbor as the sun set. <u>"I'm glad vacation is over," he told me. "Why?" I was shocked. "I miss work," he said.</u>

"Oh wait! That part shows he loves work. Finally, something to underline!"

<u>Seeing him so happy to go to work made me realize work could be wonderful.</u>

"Aha! I am definitely underlining this part! This part shows that he taught me to love work." I underlined the last part of the story then sat back.

"So now let me look at what I've underlined. I've underlined a part about my dad showing me that he loves work. And a part that shows he taught me to love work. So this story does match my reason. But not every bit of it matches, and I

As I teach this I want to convey that the construction of the essay does follow a set plan. The frame needs to be just right before the materials can be added in. Double-checking now that the topic sentences match the supporting evidence prevents instability in the final essay. Fixing the structure now is much, much easier than trying to revise a nearly complete draft.

When giving contrary examples it helps to be over-the-top obvious. You don't gain a lot by being subtle.

Notice that during my demonstration I was thinking aloud and going through a process in front of my students. Especially when I am teaching something that has multiple steps, I want to make sure that I convey the different parts by slowing down my teaching.

only have one bit that really matches my reason. I think I need to revise this. I'll add more to the parts that do support my reason and cut the parts that don't support my reason."

Quickly debrief, pointing out the replicable steps that you have taken that you want the students to follow, then set writers up to reread and underline one of their own stories.

"Writers, you should be making some mental checks. First I reread. Then I looked for parts that matched my reason, and now I'm going to revise and cut."

"Right now, just to practice this, take out your first folder and pull a story out. In a minute, reread this story and underline the parts that match your reason. Be critical. That means, be hard on yourself. If you aren't absolutely sure if a part matches your reason, don't underline it. Only underline parts that match. Remember to keep your reason in mind. Just like I did, ask, 'Does this show . . .' and then fill in your reason. Okay, quickly do that now."

Convene writers and continue to demonstrate going through the steps of checking and organizing your material.

"Let me keep going. Watch how I do the last step on the list. Make mental checks when you see me do it. Okay, so I need to cut and revise my story to make sure every bit matches my reason: my father taught me to love work. I have to add more to the parts that show that and cut the parts that don't. I'll make a movie in my mind and only story-tell the parts that show my father taught me to love work." I closed my eyes briefly, muttering to myself, "Only show the parts that show he taught me to love work."

As I spoke, I scrawled my words down on my clipboard.

> At the end of summer, my father took me sailing. I was sad that vacation was over, but Dad seemed happy. He whistled as we got back to the harbor as the sun was setting. "I'm glad vacation is over," he told me. "Why?," I was shocked. "I miss work," he said. Seeing him so happy to go to work made me realize that work could be wonderful.

Quickly debrief, pointing out the replicable steps you have taken so that the students can follow what you have done.

"Writers, did you notice the way I revised to add more to parts that matched my reason and cut parts that didn't? This is intellectually demanding, challenging work."

You'll see that this minilesson follows a different format. The work I'm asking students to do is complicated—check stories for angling, then revise—and each part is important. So I've decided to demonstrate the first part then let students try, then demonstrate the second part then let them try that. The format goes: I try, debrief, they try. I try, debrief, they try.

ACTIVE ENGAGEMENT

Set writers up to reread one of their stories, underlining the parts that support their reason, then coach them to revise those stories so they are more angled.

"Now you'll try this. You've already read one of your stories and underlined parts that match your reason. Right now, reread that story and decide again which parts match your reason. Be hard on yourself. Make sure you still agree with the choices you made before. Do that now." I gave them a minute to do this work.

After a minute, I said, "Remember that just like I did, you will want to revise your story to elaborate on the parts that support your reason, and you will want to cut the parts that don't. Try writing your revised version in your mind."

I gave them a minute of silence to begin doing this. "Okay, Partner 2, share your revised version with Partner 1. And Partner 1, be a critical friend and listen for parts that don't match the reason, giving Partner 2 that feedback. Okay, do that now."

I looked over Sam's shoulder and noticed that he did not have anything underlined in his first story, though he had penciled in a big question mark underneath it. I whispered, "Sam, do you understand what you are trying to figure out?" He nodded. "It's just that I have nothing to underline. I didn't show the bossing around in my story. I just got to eat my fries and not share them." I quietly complimented him on recognizing what was missing and trying the same strategy again on his second story. I prompted him to think about how he could revise the first story to make it work. I jotted a quick mental note to myself to check back in during partner talk to see how he planned to revise the story.

LINK

Restate the teaching point. In this case, remind children that they'll be checking and revising their materials before they draft, making sure their evidence actually supports their reasons.

"So writers, like I just demonstrated, you need to go through your folders. You will find that some of the material in a folder doesn't really belong in that folder, and so you'll need to tweak the story so it fits, or you may even decide that some material isn't going to work for this essay, and you'll tape it into your notebook to use as compost for a new writing project. Spend today being your own critical friend. Don't let any material slip by into your essay that isn't exactly right."

I want children to see that although essayists do develop a plan for what they'll say and they search for material that can support the ideas they plan to advance, they also know that the material they collect will often lead them to revise their original plan.

Revising Evidence to Support the Reason and Claim

THE WORK YOU HAVE TAUGHT STUDENTS to do today will be complex, and you'll probably feel as if you need to put on roller skates and move quickly among them, coaching in to support one child, another, and another. If you find yourself sometimes needing to almost do a bit of this work for some students, don't worry too much about the fact that you are "taking away students' ownership" because the good news is that children have two folders within which to do this work. If you provide more scaffolding than usual as they try to grapple to understand ways to revise stories so that they support a reason, the good news is that students will have plenty of opportunities to work with increasing independence within a second folder of work.

You may decide that some students need more time practicing this work before they are expected to implement it with any independence in their own writing. If so, you can always convene a small group to help you angle stories in a second one of your folders. For example, I gathered a few students during a lunchtime small group that I created to provide extra help, and said, "I also have another Christmas day story in my folder, and I've made copies for you! It's the one from earlier in the year, and it tells that my father got a cut on his head and used a bag of frozen peas as an ice pack." Then I suggested the children in that small group work in partners, rereading this story and thinking about whether the story supported the reason. This was the entry I showed students:

> On Christmas Day, my dad went to move a log in the fireplace and gouged his head on one of the nails from which the Christmas stockings hung. To stop the ferocious bleeding, he held a bag of frozen peas on the top of his bald head. Guests arrived for our Christmas party and he greeted them with the bag of frozen peas draped over his forehead. The guests weren't surprised to see Dad's odd ice pack because he's always done what he pleases without much concern for fitting into social norms. It isn't important to him to dress "right." He wears his red plaid hunting cap

MID-WORKSHOP TEACHING
Organizing Writing for Varied Information

"Writers, can I have your eyes and attention? I want to tell you another way that writers check material before drafting. They also check to make sure that they have material based on different information. So I can't write one story about my dad going to work on Christmas when I was nine and then write another story about my dad going to work on Christmas when I was ten unless they show different information.

"I want to share with you what Chris figured out when he was looking through his stories to support his thesis statement and reason, 'I love soccer because you can have lots of fun.' He read one story he had. It went like this:

> One time I had the ball and dribbled past all of the defense and I had a perfect shot. Our team was already winning so on purpose I turned around and scored on my own team! The other team though I switched teams so I was right in front of the goalie and he passed to me! Then I scored for the team I was originally on. It was hilarious. I was a riot.

"Then he looked at another story about how he loves soccer because you can have lots of fun and he realized that it was about another time he tricked the other players on the team. Chris realized that they were both showing him having fun by tricking. He knew he could only pick one of those stories to put in his piece. He picked the one I read to you first.

"Writers, see if you, like Chris, have stories that prove your thesis statement and reason by telling the same kind of story. If you do, pick the story that best shows what you are trying to say."

everywhere. When I was a teenager and he wore that hunting cap to my school events! I was often embarrassed by him.

As students worked, I asked them to think about these questions, specifically:

Questions to Ask of Writing Before You Draft

- Does each bit of material develop the thesis statement and reason?
- Is each bit based on different information?
- Does the material, in total, provide the right amount and right kind of support?

After children talked among themselves, I called on Rebecca, who said, "It is a good story but I don't think it really goes in this folder 'cause it doesn't show anything about his job. It only shows about his *ways*."

Of course, I had deliberately set out to do this by using a text that does not support my topic sentence. When one of the students pointed this out, I feigned surprise. "Oh dear," I said. "You mean I can't use this? Could it go in another one of my folders?" I reread the thesis statement and topic sentences:

My father is my most important teacher.

My father taught me to love work.
My father taught me to love writing.
My father taught me to believe that one person can make a difference.

"Writers," I said to the members of the group. "This is probably going to happen to you. You'll find that you have a great entry that doesn't really fit with the essay you'd planned to write. And if that happens, you have three choices. You could tweak the story so that it *does* align with one of your topic sentences. You could save the story for another time—another essay or another narrative. Or you could do what I want to do right now, and that is to rewrite your topic sentences so that it allows you to use your evidence in the essay.

"Specifically, I am thinking that maybe I could add a new folder, so my essay would shows four ways, not three, in which my father was my most important teacher. I am thinking that I could add a folder that says, 'My dad taught me that it is okay to be myself and not worry about fitting in.' I've got other information that could go in that folder too, and I'm willing to work hard to fill the folder! You, writers, could do similar work, if you wanted."

Teaching Our Topics

Remind students that talking through essay drafts can help writers organize their thoughts. Ask them to tell the first folder contents—the first paragraphs—of their essay to a small group.

"Writers, you'll remember that earlier this year, before you wrote your stories, you told versions of them to yourselves, to each other, to anyone who'd listen. You know stories get better when you rehearse them. Well, saying into the air the writing that you are soon going to do helps when writing essays, too. Earlier, when you rehearsed saying ideas in the air before you drafted, you weren't doing that work on the real ideas that undergird your essays. You didn't yet have those ideas. But now, the time has come to put all you've learned together, and that means you need to practice the hard work of making your essays strong in both form and content. It's like putting a cake together, it has to look great and taste great at the same time! Your essays have to be well structured *and* powerful.

"So I've put up the chart from Session 1." I uncovered the chart.

> (Thesis statement) because (reason 1), (reason 2), and most of all, because (reason 3).

- One reason that (thesis statement) is that (reason 1). For example, (evidence a), (evidence b), and (evidence c).
- Another reason that (thesis statement) is that (reason 2). For example, (evidence a), (evidence b), and (evidence c).
- Although (thesis statement) because (reason 1) and because (reason 2), especially (thesis statement) because (reason 3). For example, (evidence a), (evidence b), and (evidence c).

"Now you might have planned your essay using times or ways instead of reasons. So instead of saying 'One reason that,' you might say 'One time when . . .' and 'Another time when. . . .' Or 'One way that . . .' and 'Another way that. . . .'

"In a minute, Partner 1 will practice speaking like an essayist and rehearsing your essay by writing it in the air with your partner. Right now, choose one folder to start with and read over all the material that you have checked and organized. Get it into your mind. Look at the chart and practice writing the first body paragraph in your mind."

If children aren't stepping into professional roles, listen for a minute and then say, "Can I interrupt?" and for a minute press the rewind button on the course of study. Give the same lecture, only use your best professional tone, complete with the transition words that are part of this discourse. Then debrief, asking the child you displaced to try a new version of the lecture. The whole point of this is to step children into the role, the voice, of being a teacher.

As children did this work, I listened in. "Okay, Partner 2, now you practice writing *your* essay in the air. And Partner 1, be the best listener possible and give Partner 2 feedback on whether that paragraph feels convincing. Okay, get started."

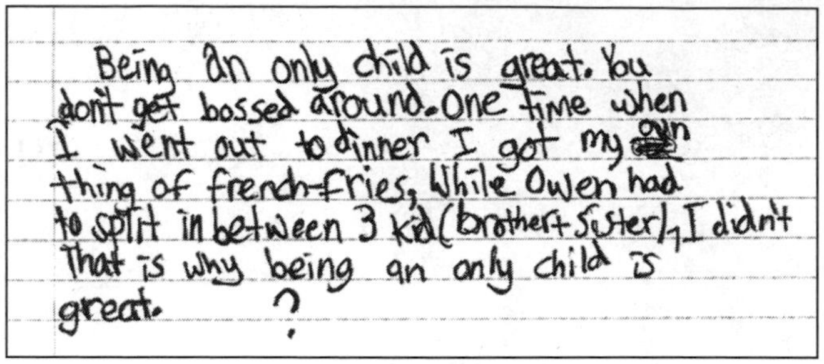
Being an only child is great. You don't get bossed around. One time when I went out to dinner I got my own thing of french-fries, While Owen had to split in between 3 kid(brother+sister), I didn't That is why being an only child is great. ?

FIG. 10–1 Sam's notebook entry

Emma pulled out all her materials for her first body paragraph. She turned to Fiona, "One reason my brother makes me feel like I am a big sister, not a little sister is because I can express myself." She pulled out one of her lists and continued. "I feel like a big sister because I can express myself when I am upset, and he can't. I can express myself when I am excited, and he can't. I can express myself when I am confused and he can't." Then she picked up a story. "For example there was one time when our parents accused us of breaking a vase that really the dog knocked over. My mom yelled, 'What were you two doing? That vase is so important to me.' My brother got red in the face, he tried to talk, but nothing that made sense came out. I took my mom's hand, 'Mom, it was Rosie. We were not even near the vase.' She realized I was right." Emma paused. "I can express myself and my brother can't."

After a few minutes, I stationed five children in different areas of the classroom and set each child up to sit before a small audience. In each circle, one child—the professor—sat on a chair, with other children grouped around. Then I asked the one child to teach a small class on his or her topic. When that child was done, the child selected someone to follow.

Debrief. Highlight what you hope students heard and did in their small groups.

"Writers," I said, "I just attended some lectures that were much more interesting than those I attend at the university! You are speaking with voices of authority, with clarity, and with precise, specific information—and that makes for some fabulous instruction. Sam's lecture (see Figure 10–1) went like this:

> Being an only child is great. You don't get bossed around. One time when I went out to dinner I got my own thing of French fries, while Owen had to split in between 3 kids (brother + sister). I didn't. This is why being an only child is great.

"As you taught others about your topics, I have a hunch that some parts of your teaching felt especially vital, especially alive. Remember those sections when you go to draft your essays, because you'll add to these when you write your final draft. On the other hand, some parts of your lecture may have felt hollow or wooden or irrelevant. When you go to write your final draft, you'll want to trust your own intuitions! If some sections of your lecture didn't work, when you go to write those sections you'll want to teach them differently. But above all, remember the teaching voice you used today, because when you write an essay you are teaching a course!"

ORGANIZING FOR DRAFTING

Fast and Furious Flash-Drafting

Writers, tonight is another night when you will set your clocks and timers and give yourself forty minutes or so to flash-draft an essay. Remember that you want to make each piece your best work, so you'll want to bring along your Opinion Writing Checklist and remind yourself of your goals before you start. And I also know that you'll want to take some time to recall all the new learning we've done about how to write essays—and make sure your piece shows that new learning. Write on a different topic than your larger piece and think of tonight as a dress rehearsal—a chance to practice essay writing before the final show.

Building a Cohesive Draft

IN THIS SESSION, you'll teach children that writers create cohesion with logically sequenced information, transition words, and repeated phrases.

GETTING READY

✔ Your materials for your essay including all the pieces of evidence from one of your folders that you can demonstrate ordering in different ways (see Teaching)

✔ Chart paper

✔ Tape and/or staples to order evidence

✔ Students' essay materials including their folders stuffed with evidence and their writer's notebooks, to be brought to the meeting area

✔ Mentor student essays (see Conferring)

✔ "Questions to Ask of Writing Before You Draft" chart from Session 10 (see Conferring)

✔ Several of your own mini-stories that can be used as mentors (see Mid-Workshop Teaching)

✔ "Essay Frame" chart from Session 1 (see Share)

✔ Chart of transition words organized by category

✔ Your first body paragraph for your draft that you are prepared to write in front of your students (see Share)

YOU'VE TAUGHT CHILDREN that essay writers combine different materials to lend more power to their claims and more artistry to their writing. You've supported your students in building folders full of evidence to support their reasons and claims, a skill they will increasingly rely on as the Common Core State Standards' expectations for opinion/argument writing escalate in the years ahead. In one essay, then, a writer may piece together an anecdote, a list, a statistic, an observation, a generalization—and a variety of other forms of writing as well! It's no surprise, then, that one of the challenges a writer faces when building a draft is the need to arrange these diverse materials into a single, cohesive whole. Ideas do not in themselves take a form in space or time; they do not lay themselves flat or set themselves up in three dimensions. The forms they take in words and on paper are completely up to the writer. Of course, many, many writers and essayists have taken up this challenge, and you can learn from the ways of communicating ideas that they have created.

In this session you'll teach children that essay writers often organize their ideas to create unity in their assemblage of pieces of writing. You'll also teach them to use special transition words that indicate certain types of relationships between ideas. Also, you will explain that essayists often repeat crucial words from their thesis statement in each supporting paragraph so the reader hears the message again and again and knows those words are the key to understanding the essay. These repeated words become a unifying refrain that creates cohesion in the writing. All three of these suggestions, combined, should help students get off to a strong start, turning the collections of writing in their folders into whole, unified, cohesive drafts.

COMMON CORE STATE STANDARDS: W.4.1.a,b,c; W.4.5, RI.4.2, SL.4.1, L.4.1, L.4.2, L.4.3.a

Building a Cohesive Draft

CONNECTION

Restate the building metaphor to help students imagine their essays as materials arranged in a structure. Tell students that today they'll learn to assemble these materials together.

"Writers, you know that building being built on my block? Well, it's almost finished. For weeks when I walked past that site, I saw construction going on and materials piled everywhere. It just sort of seemed like a big ol' mess. But then, this morning, I walked past it and I stopped. I had to walk back to take another look. All those materials that were gathered are being put in place. The walls are up, the windows are in. It's not a mess anymore. It's a building. It's like all the materials were put in place—and presto—there's a building! And seeing this building, nearly, almost finished, it reminded me that in essay writing, just as in building, the time comes to put everything together."

✤ Name the teaching point.

"Today, I'm going to teach you that writers put materials together by using a few techniques. First, they arrange their writing pieces in an order that they choose for a reason. Second, they use transitional words, like cement between bricks, holding one bit of material onto the next. And third, they repeat key words from their thesis statement or their topic sentence."

TEACHING

Demonstrate that you chose a logical way to sequence materials within a single category.

"I want you to watch while I decide what order I'll put the material into from one folder and start piecing my draft together. Research what steps I take, and then you'll try. Watch closely because this is challenging work."

◆ COACHING

This information can be said quickly, but it is complicated, provocative, and important. Whenever my teaching point is especially important, I try to speak clearly and slowly to show that the words are carrying a heavy cargo of meaning. I find that if I consciously think about the significance of my words as I speak, my tone helps children to listen carefully.

Notice the way that the concrete visual materials help to accentuate the structure of my essay. The thesis is written on a colored file, and the topic sentences are written on manila files that are contained within the thesis file. Incorporating the color-coded files into my demonstration teaching serves as a way to subtly remind children of the text structures that I'm assuming they recall.

"I'll work with this reason: my father taught me to love work. First I'll lay out all of the evidence from this folder." As I said these words, I taped each piece of material from one folder separately onto a big piece of chart paper so it looked like this:

My father taught me to love work.

At the end of summer my father took me sailing. I was sad that vacation was over but Dad seemed happy. He whistled as we got back to the harbor as the sun was setting. "I'm glad vacation is over," he told me. "Why?" I was shocked. "I miss work," he said. Seeing him so happy to go to work made me realize that work could be wonderful.

Every Christmas morning, my dad set off for the hospital carrying a waffle iron, ready to make waffles for all the doctors and patients. Dad wasn't sad to go. I asked him why he didn't send someone else and he admitted he liked going to work. "It's my hobby," he said. I wanted to grow up and find work that I loved as much as he loved his.

"Okay, so I need to decide what order to put these pieces of evidence in. So let me think about a common way that writers order evidence and see if it works for me here. So one way writers order evidence is chronological. That means they put the evidence in the order of what happened first, next, and last. Let me see if that helps. So the story of my dad making waffles on Christmas and telling me his work was his hobby happened when I was a little kid, so that would go first." I unstuck the Christmas waffles story and retaped it so it was near the top. Now the chart looked like this:

My father taught me to love work.

Every Christmas morning, my dad set off for the hospital carrying a waffle iron, ready to make waffles for all the doctors and patients. Dad wasn't sad to go. I asked him why he didn't send someone else and he admitted he liked going to work. "It's my hobby," he said. I wanted to grow up and find work that I loved as much as he loved his.

At the end of summer my father took me sailing. I was sad that vacation was over but Dad seemed happy. He whistled as we got back to the harbor as the sun was setting. "I'm glad vacation is over," he told me. "Why?" I was shocked. "I miss work," he said. Seeing him so happy to go to work made me realize that work could be wonderful.

ACTIVE ENGAGEMENT

Debrief quickly and then set writers up to try arranging material from their folder in chronological order.

"Writers, do you notice the way I lay out all of my material from one folder and ask myself what order makes sense for my evidence? Then I tried out one way—chronologically—and put the evidence in order of what happened first and next. If I had more stories I would put all three in order. In just a moment you'll get a chance to practice this work with

The use of "parenthetical" comments, or asides, in the midst of a demonstration is important. This is how I keep two tracks going. On the one side, I am being a writer, working publicly. On the other side, I am being a teacher, explicitly explaining to children what the writer under scrutiny (also me) is doing. I encourage teachers to use parenthetical comments when working with small groups, too, because these comments allow us to explicitly name the transferable processes one child is learning that every child can use.

I have deliberately chosen to model organizing two pieces of text evidence rather than more because I want to support the students in creating tight, focused body paragraphs. At this early stage of just beginning to write essays, organizing numerous pieces of evidence can feel unwieldy. Later, students will be pushed to write paragraphs chock-full of evidence, but for now my goal is to help them get that first essay under their belts.

one of your folders. Right now, take out the material from your first folder. Lay it out and try to order it chronologically. See if that order feels right to you." I gave them a minute to do this work.

TEACHING

Continue demonstrating ordering your evidence another way—least to most powerful.

"Writers, I am going to try a different order for my evidence. Watch, and then you'll get a chance to try this too. Another common way to order is by rank, from least to most powerful. That means I will order my evidence by what is least powerful or emotional or surprising to what is the most powerful or emotional or surprising. It's like my last piece of evidence packs a little punch for my reader! Okay, so let me try that. So which is the most surprising?" I studied the enlarged pieces of evidence before me. "Hmm, . . . Dad being sad vacation is over is pretty surprising. Maybe that should go last." I moved my hand as if to tape this, then paused. "But wait—Dad enjoying being at work on *Christmas* is *really* surprising and emotional and powerful. I'll definitely put that last. That means the sailing story will come first." I taped the pieces of evidence into a new sequence, with the evidence ordered from least to most powerful.

Debrief quickly, pointing out the replicable steps you have taken that you want writers to try.

"Writers, do you notice the way I tried out another way of ordering my evidence—from least to most powerful? That way seems really right to me. I think I'm going to use that order."

ACTIVE ENGAGEMENT

Set writers up to practice ordering their own evidence from least to most powerful.

"Now you try out ordering the evidence you have in your first folder from least to most powerful. Just like I did, you'll ask yourself what evidence is least powerful or surprising and which is the most powerful or surprising? Go."

Have writers turn and talk to discuss which system feels more right for their evidence.

"Writers, share your thoughts about how to order your evidence with your partner. Discuss which way of ordering feels more right for your evidence and why."

LINK

Send writers off to order their evidence and tape material together.

"Writers, you're starting to assemble your essays. Spend today deciding how you want to organize your evidence and start assembling it. Don't waste time recopying. You can use tape or staples, if you like. You have a ton to do today. Off you go!"

I have chosen to demonstrate this method second, as it requires more deliberation than chronological order.

You'll notice the structure of this minilesson is different than others. This structure is a double-decker minilesson with two active engagements. This structure allows students to have more time to practice the strategies you are demonstrating.

Helping Students Make Decisions

TODAY AS YOU CIRCLE THE ROOM, you will notice many children with bulging folders, having difficulty deciding what goes and what stays in the essay. Part of your job today will be to help students make decisions.

When I pulled up next to Olivia, she was struggling between two stories. I quickly gathered a group of other children who I had noticed were facing the same issue and asked them to watch while I worked with Olivia.

"Let's help Olivia," I said. "She's written a few different stories, and although it's possible that she could bring all of these stories into her essay, she will probably need to decide which one better illustrates her topic sentence, which is, 'Sometimes I hurt people's feelings to fit in.' Let's listen to one of her stories and think about the 'Questions to Ask of Writing Before You Draft' to decide if this shows her reason and then she can try this same work later with the other stories."

I taped up the chart "Questions to Ask of Writing Before You Draft."

Questions to Ask of Writing Before You Draft

Does each bit of material develop the thesis statement and reason?

Are the different bits distinct—based on different information—or do they overlap?

I read one of Olivia's stories aloud (see Figure 11–1).

I turned to the group. "What do you think?"

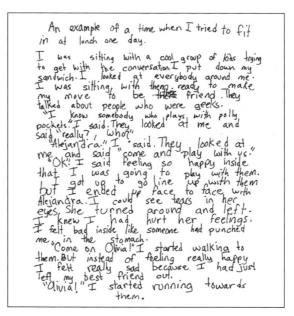

FIG. 11–1   The small group weighs whether this story is angled to support the topic sentence, the reason.

"I think it works. It shows Olivia's reason," David said, and he pointed to the words "trying to get with the conversation." "That shows you are trying to fit in."

In the same way, other children pointed to passages that supported her topic sentence.

When I asked what their advice was to Olivia, they agreed she should keep the story. I said, "So now, will you look at one of your stories the same way you looked at Olivia's? Does your story match your reason right from the start like Olivia's does?" I interjected. "If not, decide if you should revise or cut. Make some tough decisions!" I left them to work with another group, making notes to check back.

"Writers, can I have your eyes and attention? I have something very important to tell you. Not only do you need to put your evidence in order, but you also need to put your reasons in order." I held up my three folders. "That means you need to look at your plan and decide how to order your reasons.

"Watch me try out a few ways of ordering my reasons. I'm going to try out the ways we learned for ordering evidence and see if those ways work for my reasons. So here are my reasons," I said, and uncovered a chart.

> My father is my most important teacher

- My father taught me to love work.
- My father taught me that one person can make a difference.
- My father taught me to love writing.

"So first, I'll see if I should order my reasons chronologically. Should I put my reasons in order of what came first, next, and last?" I studied my chart for a moment and then shook my head. "No, I don't think that will work. My dad sort of taught me all these things at the same time. So let me try ordering from least to most powerful. Okay, let me ask myself which reason is the least powerful, emotional, and surprising.

Maybe my father taught me to love writing? Then which is most powerful? Which is most surprising? Hmm, . . . Maybe my father teaching me to love work is surprising, but really, my father teaching me that one person can make a difference is way more powerful than anything else. So let me try that order."

> My father is my most important teacher

- My father taught me to love writing.
- My father taught me to love work.
- My father taught me that one person can make a difference.

"I showed you two common ways to order your reasons—chronologically and by least to most powerful.

"Those same ways can work for your reasons too. Right now, think in your mind about how your reasons might go." I gave them a minute to do this. "Okay, so as you are ordering your evidence and reasons, you might decide that your third bullet is most powerful and will come third, or you might decide you need to put it first. If that's the case, put that folder first. What matters is that you choose an order that makes sense for you! Keep working and assembling your draft!"

Selecting Words to Make the Organization Strong

Tell students that writers cement their pieces together using transition words that match their organizational plan. They also repeat key words to help readers understand the most important parts of the essay.

"Writers, you've done a great job deciding on your organizational structures. How many of you think you'll organize the content of this first folder into chronological order? Thumbs up. How many of you think you'll organize your material from least to most powerful? Thumbs up.

"The next thing I want to teach you is this. When you actually recopy and combine your material, you need to cement it together. One way you can do this is through transition words." I put up the "Essay Frame" chart. "Remember this chart? It can help us organize and cement the different sections of our essay together. Each time we come to a new section of our essay we can use transition words to let readers know that it's a new section. If you used ways or times, instead of reasons, you can change the word *reason* to *way* or *time*. There are other transition words that can help us cement together the evidence inside a paragraph. I'll put some of those words up as well."

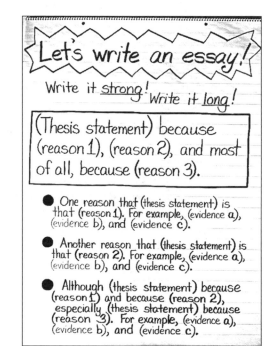

FIG. 11–2

When You Want to Give An Example Reason: Transition Words
One example that shows this is . . .
For instance . . .
One time . . .

When You Want to Add On . . .
Another example that shows this is . . .
Also, . . .
In addition to . . .

"So now watch me use these words and write my first body paragraph in the air. Here's how my essay looks so far."

My father is my most important teacher because he taught me to love work.

My father took me sailing at the end of summer and told me he was happy vacation was ending. When I asked him why, he said, "I miss work." I saw you could love your work more than vacation.

Every Christmas morning, my dad set off for the hospital carrying a waffle iron, ready to make waffles for all the doctors and patients. Dad wasn't sad to go. I asked him why he didn't send someone else and he admitted he liked going to work. "It's my hobby," he said. I wanted to grow up and find work that I loved as much as he loved his.

"Now I'm going to cement it together. I'll use the chart when I want to give an example and when I want to add on to my point. When you hear me use transition words from the chart, put a thumb up."

<u>One reason my father is my most important teacher</u> is because he taught me to love work, <u>for example</u>, he took me sailing at the end of summer and told me he was happy vacation was ending. When I asked him why, he said, "I miss work." Seeing him so happy to go to work made me realize that work can be wonderful. <u>Another example that shows this is</u> every Christmas morning, my dad set off for the hospital carrying a waffle iron, ready to make waffles for all the doctors and patients. Dad wasn't sad to go.

Debrief and set writers up to practice rehearsing and then drafting their first body paragraphs in the air.

"Writers, did you notice the way I used transition words from the chart to cement the pieces of my essay together? Now you can practice this. Look over all of the material in your first folder and use the chart to rehearse your first paragraph in your head. While you do that, I'm going to quickly jot down the transition words in my paragraph." I gave them a few minutes to do this work, and while they did this, I quickly jotted the transitions into my paragraph in a different color to serve as a model. Then I said, "Okay writers, practice writing your paragraph in the air with a neighbor. Help each other use the chart and make your drafts sound cohesive and flow smoothly. After you finish rehearsing, quickly jot down some of the transitions you used so you have a full draft assembled. Okay, go to it!"

BUILDING A COHESIVE DRAFT

Raising the Level of Flash-Drafting

Writers, think of all you learned about essay writing today! Ordering evidence logically, making all parts connect—wow, we've done some key work today. And I know you're probably thinking about that flash-draft piece you did last night and already getting some ideas for how you could make it better. So, tonight, it's time for another mission—write a *way* better essay than you did last night. You might decide to write a brand-new *way* better essay on a different topic, or you might decide to re-draft last night's essay and make it *way* better. Think of all the resources that can help you—the Opinion Writing Checklist, the mentor student work you've looked at across this unit. Think of what you'll bring home with you tonight to help you raise the level of your work.

Becoming Our Own Job Captains

IN THIS SESSION, you'll teach children that writers solve their own problems, taking ownership of the writing process by developing their own systems.

GETTING READY

✔ Your folders and draft for your essay

✔ Chart paper to create a "To-Do" list with your students to model how you will take yourself through the essay writing process (see Teaching)

✔ Students' essay materials including their folders, writers notebooks, and drafts

✔ Your example of a paragraph that is unfocused and a little unclear that you can involve writers in revising (see Conferring)

✔ "Guidelines for Writing Supporting Stories for Essays" chart from Session 8 (see Share)

O VER DECADES of teaching writing, I've found time and again that if students feel as if they are the authors of their own writerly lives, they step into this role with enormous seriousness. So I encourage you to create some fanfare around this upcoming part of the unit. Starting today, you are putting children in charge of their own writing lives—giving them the responsibility of taking themselves through the process of gathering evidence, organizing, and drafting. They'll do this in order to write their third folder, their third reason. You will hold each writer accountable for meeting a deadline and developing a system that is best for him or her. Act as if it is a very big deal that students will be deciding on their own work flow, moving themselves through the process. Celebrate their progress and growth as writers while inviting them to take up these new challenges.

There are times when you don't see your teaching "sticking." You don't see students drawing on all they have learned as they move forward. Today's work is aimed directly at counteracting that trend and ensuring transference. You'll provide a deadline (in this case two writing workshops) for your students to finish taking themselves through the process of developing a third body paragraph. You'll be teaching students to draw on the charts that you have made together, the strategies that you have learned together, as they progress along through the process of writing. During the rest of the unit, you will continue to remind students to use all they know and provide opportunities for repeated practice while ratcheting up the level of their work. The goal is always for them to outgrow what they can already do.

COMMON CORE STATE STANDARDS: W.4.1.a,c; W.4.2.a, W.4.5, W.4.10, RI.4.2, SL.4.1, L.4.1, L.4.2, L.4.3

Becoming Our Own Job Captains

CONNECTION

Celebrate your writers' rough drafts

"Writers, while you were at art this morning, I read through your rough drafts. I got so excited as I started reading them because they showed me that you have become essayists. Your essays are strong in form and in content. And so, I want to congratulate you. Give yourself a part on the back or a mental high five." The students did so, grinning and after one quick minute, I stopped them. "And so now I want to tell you, that as essayists, I think you are ready to take the next big step.

Remember the cakes that were all form and no content? By harkening back to them, the unit becomes more cohesive.

"I know that many of you have been wondering about that third reason—the one you didn't make a folder for. Well, today we are going to discuss that part of your essays. Until now, I've been taking you through this process step by step, saying, 'Today we'll do this . . . and now we'll do this. . . .'

"But writers don't have a teacher who says, 'Now we'll do this. Now we'll do that.' Writers have to be their own teacher, to give themselves their own self-assignment. You know this already. Remember last year when you worked to become job captains of your own writing and made work plans that helped you meet deadlines?" The students nodded. "And in the last unit in fiction, you also took charge of your writing in the middle of the unit? So now, you're going to take charge of your writing again. You will decide on your own system for writing that third reason. I'm not going to tell you what to do. But what I *am* going to tell you is that you will have two days to work on this final part of your essays, and on finishing up all you have been working on so far today and tomorrow. By the end of tomorrow, you will each have the entire body of your essays drafted."

When giving your students lots of free choice over what the work is they're doing, you limit any risk by curtailing the time they have for this freelancing.

❧ Name the teaching point.

"Today, I want to teach you that one way writers figure out plans for getting parts of their writing done is they think back over everything they know how to do and make a work plan for the upcoming parts of their writing. Writers sometimes use charts and their own writing to remind them of stuff they know how to do."

Teachers across the United States are asking, "How can I dramatically ramp up the level of my students' work?" We believe that teaching for transference is one of the most important ways available to you for doing this.

TEACHING

Highlight examples of two different systems that two different writers have used.

"When figuring out plans for getting an essay written, you can always decide to use the system that we've taught you so far in this unit. For example, last year a boy just your age named Andy collected for his first two folders and wrote them up, then he did that whole cycle super quickly with his third body paragraph. He collected stories, lists, and other kinds of writing—quickly—then pieced some of them together to make a great body paragraph.

"Another writer I know, Miles, has a different system. For instance, to write the third paragraph, he got out a sheet of notebook paper and wrote the topic sentence. Then he wrote, 'For example, one day . . .' and he could have just written a story, right there, but he actually first tried a story in his notebook, revising it a bit before copying it over onto his notebook paper, and shifting to writing a list."

Demonstrate creating your own work plan by thinking back on all you know about essay writing and your own writing.

"Research how I create a work plan for my third reason, and then in a minute, you can start creating your own work plan with your partner.

"Okay, so the first thing I do when I'm creating a work plan is to make a 'To-Do' list. It helps me stay organized. So let me think back on all I know about essay writing to make a To-Do list. As I do that, in your heads think back on all you know about essay writing and make your own To-Do list. Then you can see if yours is similar to mine." I was quiet, using my fingers to list my To-Do items.

Then I said, "As I read off my To-Do list, when I record an item that was on your list as well, put a thumb up."

_____ set up a place to gather evidence
_____ list true stories that match my reason
_____ draft just the part of each story that matches (1 or 2)
_____ gather lists
_____ choose the best evidence
_____ check, revise, and order my evidence
_____ rehearse with a partner
_____ draft

Continue to demonstrate creating your own work plan.

"Okay, it seems like most of us have similar To-Do lists. I just need to decide if I want to do all this on bits of paper, collected in a folder, or if I want to do a draft of these essay components in my notebook, or if I want to get my final essay paper and use a page or two for the final body paragraphing, writing right onto that paper. I'm going to return to my notebook, but you could choose differently."

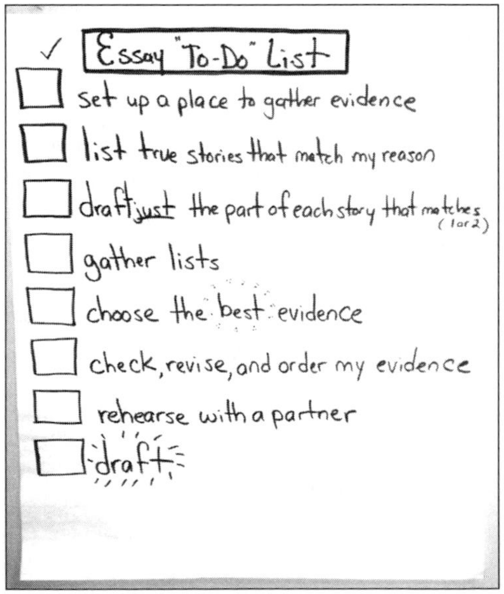

✓ Essay "To-Do" List
☐ set up a place to gather evidence
☐ list true stories that match my reason
☐ draft just the part of each story that matches (1 or 2)
☐ gather lists
☐ choose the best evidence
☐ check, revise, and order my evidence
☐ rehearse with a partner
☐ draft

FIG. 12–1

ACTIVE ENGAGEMENT

Set writers up to begin developing their own work plans by thinking about what they know about themselves as writers.

"Think about whether you want to write on bits of paper, collected in a folder, or you prefer to try using your notebook for this third body paragraph. Then again, you might want to write right onto final draft essay paper.

"Those who will work in folders, get started," I said. After those children left the meeting area I said, "Those who will work in notebooks, get started." After they'd settled, I sent the rest off to work.

LINK

In a voiceover, emphasize that writers make choices that work for them, so the students need to be sure that the plan they've chosen supports productivity.

"Essayists, as you get started, I want to tell you one final thing, and it is a *huge* deal. Writers decide on their own ways to work, but the point is that these ways are ones that work for the writers. You've made your own decisions because this will allow you to get a lot of writing done. So you have a huge responsibility today. You need to be in charge of your writing life, and you need to make sure your plan works for you. If not, you need to find one that does.

"Writers work on deadlines, so I want to remind you that this body paragraph must be finished by the end of writing workshop *tomorrow*. Think in your head right now of what you want to accomplish by the end of today." I gave them one minute to think and then eyed them seriously. "I expect you to work like the dickens to make sure you reach your goal. Go to it."

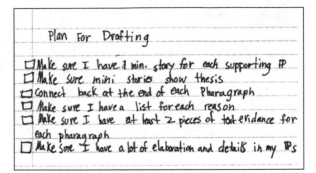

FIG. 12–2 Emma's plan for drafting

> My plan for drafting
>
> Look at all my minor small stories pick the ones that really show, what I feel!
>
> Make more lists.
>
> Make sure my mini stories fit my topic sentences.

FIG. 12–3 Fiona's plan for drafting

Small-Group Work on Paragraphing, Using Transition Words, and Revising

YOU HAVE SET YOUR WRITERS UP to go through the process independently, and while they are busily engaged in writing stories and lists, you can pull small groups to do intensive work in revision and editing.

In looking over your students' drafts so far, you may notice that some are still not paragraphing, and this is cause for an emergency group session. You will want to tell students that this is an emergency. You taught this earlier, so it is utterly inconceivable to you that they wouldn't be paragraphing. The subtext, then, is that learning to write involves a cumulative process. For writers to get better, they need to hold onto all they have learned so far, not leaving one day's instruction behind as they move to the next. You may also want to note that paragraphing helps readers understand a piece and provides readers with space to process what they have just read before coming to a new thought. "It's not kind to your reader to have huge chunks of text with no space in which they can think," you might tell your students before giving them a chance

---

MID-WORKSHOP TEACHING   Solve Your Own Problems

"Writers, I need your eyes and attention." My tone was urgent, worried. The students all looked at me. "Writers, we are facing a crisis. Some of you are waiting around for me to help you. This is not taking charge of your writing. I need to tell you, writers, that when you develop your own systems and take charge of your writing, you do not wait for someone to come by and solve your problem. You solve your *own* problems.

"To solve your own problems, you remember everything you have learned, and you use everything in the room and even each other to help you figure out what to do. That's how you take charge of your writing life.

"Let's try it. In a minute, will one of you ask a question or say a problem that you are having? Tell the class. I am not going to solve it. The rest of you will. Who has a question or problem?"

I saw Tyrone's hand go up. "I don't know if this is a good story for my reason or not."

I raised my eyebrows at the class, indicating they should jump in with responses. Allison raised her hand. I did not call on her, but looked at Tyrone and motioned that he should call on Allison. "Allison," he said.

"Maybe you could use the chart 'Guidelines for Writing Supporting Stories,'" she said. "Make it like a checklist. If your story meets everything, it's good."

"Or you could have a partner help you check it," David added.

"Or you could check that all the parts match your reason," Maya chimed in.

I spread my arms wide. "See writers? That wasn't one, but three different solutions to a problem and you *had those solutions.* All you had to do was remember what you learned and think about what in the room could help you.

"Writers, you are never going to sit and wait for someone to solve your problems for you again. After today, you will always know that you are in charge of your writing life and you can solve your own problems. Now, let's get back to writing. You have a deadline to meet!"

to practice finding possible paragraphs in drafts of essays. If students are given the chance to decide on paragraphs collaboratively, they can meanwhile create a joint sheet titled, "Guidelines for Paragraphing." This sheet, then, could help other students create their own paragraphs and check those of their partners.

In the meantime, you might convene another small group, perhaps this one on transition words. For example, you might challenge these writers to think about whether there are specific transition words that are most apt to be used when a text is ordered chronologically or by ranking or by some other system. Push them to consider phrases like, "but the most important reason . . ." or "especially . . ." when they are working to show that they have logically ordered their evidence from least to most powerful, for example.

Then, too, you may pull a group to teach them to revise. To do this, you may want to study their drafts and create your own rough draft of an essay, making sure your writing has exaggerated versions of the problems you found in theirs. Then you can engage them in helping you revise your draft before sending them off to revise their own. To create your "mirror" drafts, consider what trends you are noticing that are problematic. One trend that you probably see, for example, is that many writers allow a story to swamp the paragraph, obscuring rather than supporting the reason. If that is the case, you might want to create a body paragraph where your own story swamps the writing, and then rally students to help you cut extraneous details.

Then too, you might notice the trend of making fuzzy unclear points. As writers try to reach for words to grapple with large concepts, they may have difficulty finding ways to say exactly what they mean. Rereading for clarity is one of the most important and most difficult revision strategies to learn, you may tell them, before showing them your second body paragraph that you will have purposefully created so that it is not clear, perhaps not stating exactly what *you* mean. This is an example of one such unclear paragraph that I wrote for these purposes:

> My father is my most important teacher because he taught me that one person can make a difference. One person is not just a person. One person can be more. One example of this is my dad adopting orphans. Another example of this is my dad works at a soup kitchen. And once he got arrested for protesting!

Ask students to identify the fuzzy or unclear parts of this paragraph, underlining them as they point them out. Then rally writers to work with partners to offer more precise wording for the unclear concepts. They might suggest changing "One person is not just a person" to "One person can do the work of many people." Or, they may suggest deleting "And once he got arrested for protesting" and replacing it with how he, as one person, made a difference *by* protesting.

Qualities of Good Writing

Remind writers to check their work for evidence that they are following the "Guidelines for Writing Supporting Stories for Essays."

"Writers, after our conversation, I was so pleased to see you all making responsible decisions. You've been gathering a variety of evidence without me having to remind you. You've also been gathering evidence more quickly for this reason than you did for your first two. *But* some of you have forgotten the 'Guidelines for Writing Supporting Stories for Essays' chart. Right now, take out your assembled draft. I'm going to read off our guidelines chart, and after I read each item on the chart, give me *two* thumbs up if your first body paragraph *and* your most recent one both show you followed this guideline, and one thumb up if you followed the guideline in one of your body paragraphs and not the other." I read each of the items on the chart, pausing at the end of each bullet for the children to signal yea or nay.

Most children had followed most of the guidelines while creating their first body paragraph, and many had not followed the guidelines when writing with more independence. "Guys, most of you have followed the guidelines in the first part of your essay, so that is terrific. But here is the problem. What I noticed today is that a lot of you did *not* do those things in the writing you did today. I know that is hard to believe because we just established you can do this work. But let me read the items on the chart again, and you look at your most recent writing, the writing you did on your own, and look with honest eyes. Signal yes, no, or maybe." I adjusted my thumb to illustrate each signal. I again read off the items in the chart.

Guidelines for Writing Supporting Stories for Essays

- Writers usually include a transition into the story.
- The story needs to have a beginning, middle, and end.
- The story needs to be told to especially reveal the part of it that illustrates the thesis statement and bullet points.
- At the end of the story, it is usually wise to include a sentence that refers back to or repeats the main idea of that paragraph.

When many writers admitted to not having done the things we'd charted, I acted baffled. "So, writers, I have to say this really confuses me. You know how to include transition words and refer back to the main idea of the paragraph. You know how to check and revise your mini-stories so that each bit matches your reason. So what is keeping you from doing these things in your independent writing?"

I let the room grow quiet. "Talk with your partner. Talk about which of the guidelines of good writing you didn't remember, and talk about what your work plans will be for tomorrow. My hunch is that many of you are going to begin by rewriting some of your entries—if you like them—so that your notebook doesn't contain work that is so much below the best that you can do, but that, of course, will be up to you."

The room erupted into talk and I circled the desks, listening in to conversations, taking notes on what I heard and considering what small-group work might be needed in the next few days.

BECOMING OUR OWN JOB CAPTAINS

Making Choices About What to Practice to Get Stronger

Writers, since you are becoming so independent, I'm going to give you the responsibility of creating your own homework assignment tonight. The only thing I will tell you is that your assignment to yourself must let you practice work that will push you to get stronger. So probably you'll want to be looking at your goal sheets and thinking about what kind of work you want to practice.

I'm sure a lot of you will choose to flash-draft a new entire essay to practice work that will help you reach your goal, but maybe some of you think you really need to practice writing angled stories most and so tonight you'll write a bunch of angled stories. Decide right now what work you will assign yourself and open up your notebook. Draw a box and give yourself a big assignment that is just right for you tonight!

Writing Introductions and Conclusions

IN THIS SESSION, you'll teach children the different ways writers commonly open and close essays, and that writers try out multiple leads and conclusions before deciding which work best for their essays.

GETTING READY

✔ "Ways to Start an Essay" chart (see Teaching)

✔ Your list of possible introductions using your draft (see Teaching)

✔ Students' essay materials including their drafts and folders

✔ Sample introductions from you or a student (see Teaching)

✔ Samples from you or students of a list of possible introductions (see Mid-Workshop Teaching)

✔ "Ways to End an Essay" chart (see Share)

✔ Your sample conclusions using your draft (see Share)

COMMON CORE STATE STANDARDS: W.4.1.a,d; W.5.1.a,d; W.4.5, RI.4.2, SL.4.2, L.4.1, L.4.2, L.4.3

120

WHEN CHILDREN WRITE STORIES, you hand story language over to them that can cast magical spells over their narrative accounts, turning plain-Jane recounts into stories that pull listeners close, giving them goose bumps. You do not hesitate to suggest to a child that he or she start a story with phrases like "On a dark and stormy night" or "Once, long, long ago, I . . . ."

It is just as important that you also hand over language that essayists use, allowing youngsters to feel the persuasive power that special sets of words can have on listeners. It will not be a surprise that the Common Core State Standards place special emphasis on introductions and conclusions for opinion writing, expecting fourth- and fifth-graders to "Introduce a topic or text clearly, state an opinion, and create an organizational structure" (W.4.1a; W.5.1a) and to "Provide a concluding statement or section related to the opinion presented" (W.4.1d; W.5.1d). In this session, then, I am direct. "Try these phrases on for size," I say, and hand over some of the language that I know will work for these youngsters' essays.

The results are once again magical. Try this with your own writing. Use these phrases when you address your children's parents in open-house meetings. Notice how the words work, just as the start of a story works, to cast a spell, to set the stage, to invite listeners to draw close, to lean in. Notice also how the words work on you, not just your listeners. As you say the words, essay-like language and structure flow from you more easily, evoked by tone and expectations you associate with those "expository" phrases.

I used to think each writer always needed to use brand-new words—words written for the occasion that come from the heart. But I've come to realize that for generations, people have begun stories, "Once upon a time, long, long ago" and not felt abashed to do so. Why not, in a similar way, borrow from the language of essayists and orators? I've done so in this paragraph, in fact, using borrowed phrases to frame my sentences. Try doing the same! Some people begin their speeches awkwardly, hemming and hawing, but if you draw from great orators or writers, you will have words that you can rely on whenever you want to teach listeners something important.

Writing Introductions and Conclusions

CONNECTION

Remind writers of the work they've done so far in this unit—the process that essayists use.

"Writers, I know you'll want to spend today continuing to work on the system that is best for you to get your body paragraphs drafted. You know that by the end of workshop you must have your draft completed. Take a minute and think right now about how your work on that last reason is coming along. Now think about what you need to do next today. Turn and tell someone near you quickly what your next steps will be when you go off to work."

"I've got stories gathered," Tanya said eagerly to David. "I need some lists."

"I have some stories, too," David said back. "I think I'm going to start putting it all together and using transition words."

"Writers, you all know what you need to do to get your body paragraphs drafted. As your body starts to take shape, I know you will also want to learn a bit about how essayists write introductions to essays so you can start working on those. Last year, you learned a little about how to hook your reader right from the start. Now you're going to do some of the work but you're not just going to hook the reader and get the reader to want to read the piece, you're also going to get the reader to start to care deeply about the ideas in the essay."

Name the teaching point.

"Today, I want to teach you that essay writers often use the beginning of an essay as a place to convey to readers that the ideas in the essay are important. The beginning is the place where essayists *get readers to care about their ideas and place them in context*."

TEACHING

Tell writers that at the beginning of essays, essayists often rely on some common ways to say, "This is important!"

"I am ready to start writing my introduction, so I've been studying other people's essays and, in particular, looking closely at the way they begin their essays. I've been asking myself, 'How do essayists introduce topics clearly?'

You'll recall that in order to teach children to write leads and endings to narratives, I invited them to pore over texts by authors they love. I invited them to find patterns in those leads and endings. As you realize by now, the truth is that I do not have a vast storehouse of exemplar essays that are simple enough for children to study and emulate. That explains why I've been the one to do this research and extrapolate these patterns, rather than sending children off to search through the essays they love, noticing how authors began and ended those essays. If you discover enough texts, you could structure a minilesson in which children extract for themselves a host of ways to start and finish an essay.

"I've learned that essayists do a couple of things when introducing topics clearly: they provide a little bit of background to get the reader's mind revved up and let the reader know that this essay is *important*!

"But essayists don't write, '*This essay is important! Listen up!*' They want their readers to take them seriously, and so they use a serious tone. Instead of writing, '*You should read my essay,*' they have more formal, or serious, ways of saying this. I've made a list of some common ways that essayists begin essays. Each of these ways to introduce an essay clearly tells readers the topic, and each way conveys that this essay is important."

Ways to Start an Essay

- What people need to know is that . . .
- Many people (don't know, don't think, don't realize) but I've come to (know, think it's important) . . .
- Sometimes in life . . .
- I have found . . .
- Sometimes people ask . . . Well, I have found . . .

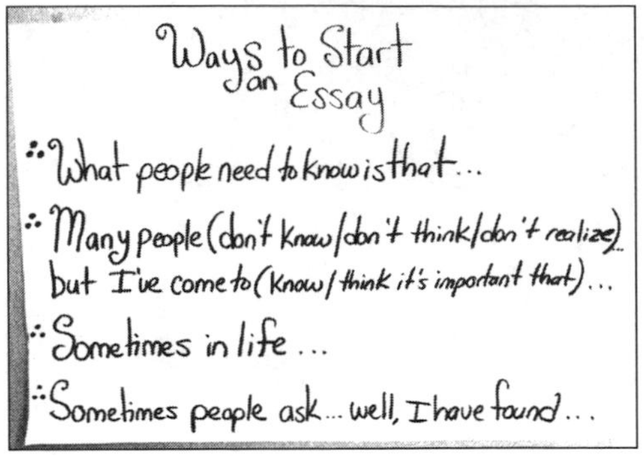

FIG. 13–1

These lead sentence templates can have a dramatic effect on children's essays. Just as starting with "Once upon a time" can lift the level of a story, these leads can wrap children's rather pedestrian paragraphs in an aura of drama. Be sure to emphasize that writers need to try them on for size, to revise the set phrases a bit so they fit exactly with each essay.

Set students up to be researchers and watch as you demonstrate using the phrases to try out a few ways your introduction might go.

"Be researchers and watch the way I take these phrases and see if they might work for my essay on 'My father's been my most important teacher.' Notice that some work for me, some don't. They never work exactly, so I change the wording around a bit to fit what I want to say. And I often write beginnings that don't use these templates. I usually list a couple of possible introductions and then choose one."

Looking at the list, I read the first item aloud. "'What people need to know is that . . .' Hmm, . . . Who will *need* to know that my father is my most important teacher? That's a big question, now that I think about it. Who *will* want to read this essay? Maybe my father? Or people who want to know him? Or parents who need to realize they could be the important teachers for their children? That's the best idea."

> What parents need to know is that the schools their children attend and the teachers they have are nowhere near as important as the education that children receive at home. My father has been my most important teacher. He's taught me to love work, to love writing, and to believe one person can make a difference. I tell her not to worry; what she needs to know is that she and her husband will be her child's most important teachers.

I said, "You see how I started with the first idea on the chart and wrote a sentence or two about that. Then I added in my claim and my reasons—my thesis.

"Let me go back to the list. I'll see if this next one could work: 'I used to think . . . but now I realize . . .' Let's see. I don't want to say, 'I used to think my father wasn't a good teacher' because that's not true. How about this":

> I used to think that the teachers my children have in school would make or break them. I'd worry frantically if one of them had a teacher who wasn't superb. But I've come to realize that the teachers who matter most aren't always the official ones children have in school. In my life, my father is my most important teacher. He taught me . . .

"That one works too, doesn't it?"

ACTIVE ENGAGEMENT

Ask students to try some of the introductory phrases to frame their own essays.

"Right now, work with your partner to see if one of these starting phrases might work for your essay. Partner 1 and Partner 2, work together on Partner 1's essay first. Could Partner 1 use a lead that shows that this essay is the answer to someone's concerns? If so, try the first lead idea. Talk about who the reader is and how this essay could fit with the reader's questions and concerns. If you think it would be better to start with a 'Have you ever wondered . . .' question, try that. Try more than one way for Partner 1, then switch and work on Partner 2's essay."

LINK

Restate the teaching point. Remind students that writers use introductions to help readers grasp the importance of the essay's thesis.

"So writers, I know that today you will be sifting through materials, lining them up in your minds and revising them as needed to finalize your supporting paragraphs, and then connecting all your materials into a draft. Once you have done that, write a few possible introductions. Then choose the one that best makes your case that your thesis is important and should be listened to. This is your final day to draft. By the end of the workshop today, you must have a completed draft. Tomorrow we'll spend time self-assessing and revising. So today is crunch time. Work like the wind! Go writers!"

I don't try out every single possible way to start an essay, because by now children should grasp my point—and be eager to try this themselves.

You may well decide to ask children to do this on their own, jotting possible introductions in their notebooks, as this uses the minilesson to get more writing accomplished. You decide.

Whenever I link the minilesson, I try to make sure that the students understand that their work for the day is not just the work of the minilesson. Notice that I said they are drafting and trying out introductions. If the minilesson alone is the work for the day, then this session becomes an activity instead of a workshop. Workshop teaching means that there is always something to work on.

Turning Scraps of Paper into an Outline

YOU WILL PROBABLY FIND a small group of writers who are having trouble turning their materials into a draft, even when those materials are already lined up, revised, and ready to go, and even though you've coached them through this process before. When I encountered this situation I handled it like this: "Writers, come and gather in a circle around Diego and me because I'm going to show you how Diego goes from having all these bits and pieces to having a whole rough draft of an essay.

"You'll notice that Diego has a stack of blank notebook paper and scissors and tape. Now watch." Turning to Diego, I said, "I'll coach you, telling you what I'd probably do to make an essay, and then you do it while all of us watch and learn, okay?"

"First, Diego, I'd look over your folders, and sort through your material, paper-clipping the stories or lists you aren't going to use to set them out of eyesight, and then deciding on the order for the material you will use." As Diego started to work, I channeled the other students to do the same.

"Next, Diego, I'd decide on the sequence of your folders, your body paragraphs. Does one somehow seem like it belongs earlier or later? If you have no other way to sequence them, put your most convincing reason last so you can start that paragraph saying something like, 'But most of all . . .' ." Diego shuffled through his folders, rearranging them so his most important idea was last. Again, the children in the group did the same.

"Now take your first folder and your first sheet of notebook paper. Copy your topic sentence onto the top of the notebook paper. It will be the start of a paragraph, so indent." Diego did this, copying "Friendship dies when there's new friends" onto the top of his paper.

"Now you need to tape the bits you'll use in the order you decided onto this page. I see you put numbers, right? That's a great idea." Diego did this. "Now, tell me which kind of order you have planned for this, Diego. Okay, chronological, great. So now, Diego, read your essay aloud, but add in some words. You'll be using the transition words that

---

MID-WORKSHOP TEACHING   Revising Introductions

"Writers, listen to the three different drafts Mimi has written of her introduction. You'll see she's taken ideas from our chart but switched them around so they work for her opinion statement, which is 'School is important because you learn to work with people who are different from you, you make friends who help you feel less alone, and you learn skills that will be important for life.'

"These are her first drafts of an introduction."

1. Recently I have known people to think that school is just not important and a waste of time. But I think differently. I think that school is as valuable as gold.

2. Other people have a theory that school isn't important. But lately, I couldn't disagree more. I think school is important.

3. When people talk about wishing to miss school, I just don't understand it. I think it is wrong. They should find school extremely important.

"I hope hearing what Mimi has done helps you with the work you are doing with your introduction. You can try making a list of possibilities like she did!"

---

go with chronological essays, right? So you can add in words like *first* and *then* and *next*? Okay, read/talk this last part of your essay."

Turning to the rest of the group, I said, "When you have sorted through your folders, you'll want to assemble a first draft of your essay just like Diego has done, revising as you go to make the pieces fit." While I was working with that small group, other students had relied on the teaching of the minilesson to draft introductions.

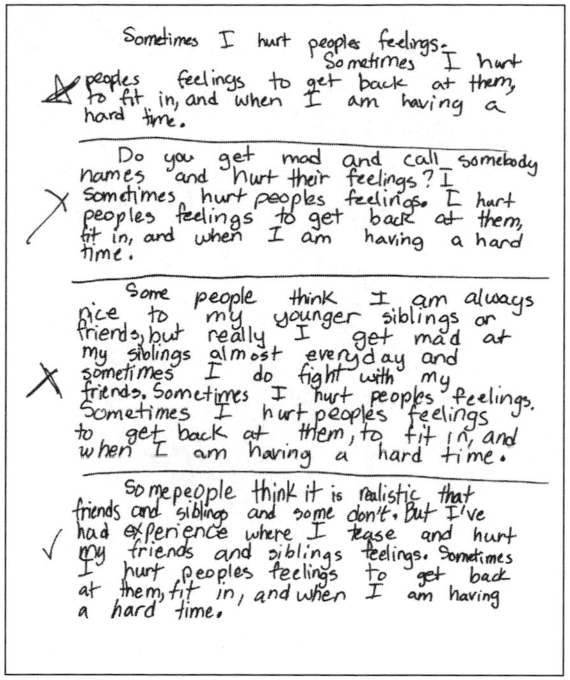

Sometimes I hurt peoples feelings.
Sometimes I hurt
peoples feelings to get back at them,
to fit in, and when I am having a
hard time.

Do you get mad and call somebody
names and hurt their feelings? I
Sometimes hurt peoples feelings. I hurt
peoples feelings to get back at them,
fit in, and when I am having a hard
time.

Some people think I am always
nice to my younger siblings or
friends, but really I get mad at
my siblings almost everyday and
sometimes I do fight with my
friends. Sometimes I hurt peoples feelings.
Sometimes I hurt peoples feelings
to get back at them, to fit in, and
when I am having a hard time.

Some people think it is realistic that
friends and siblings and some don't. But I've
had experience where I tease and hurt
my friends and siblings feelings. Sometimes
I hurt peoples feelings to get back
at them, fit in, and when I am having
a hard time.

FIG. 13–2   Olivia's introductions

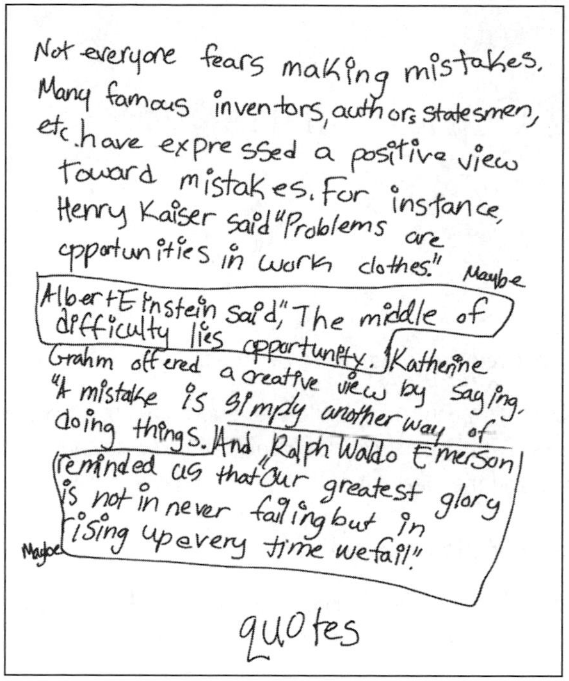

Not everyone fears making mistakes.
Many famous inventors, authors statesmen,
etc. have expressed a positive view
toward mistakes. For instance,
Henry Kaiser said "Problems are
opportunities in work clothes." Maybe
Albert Einstein said, "The middle of
difficulty lies opportunity." Katherine
Grahm offered a creative view by saying,
"A mistake is simply another way of
doing things. And Ralph Waldo Emerson
reminded us that "our greatest glory
is not in never failing but in
rising up every time we fail!"
Maybe

quotes

FIG. 13–3   Rie's introductions

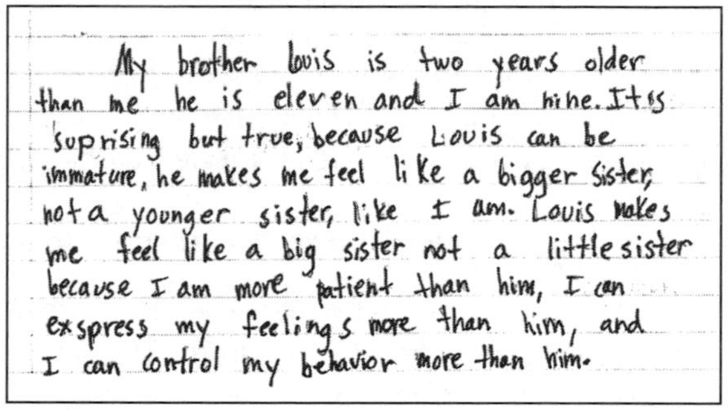

My brother Louis is two years older
than me he is eleven and I am nine. It is
surprising but true, because Louis can be
immature, he makes me feel like a bigger sister,
not a younger sister, like I am. Louis makes
me feel like a big sister not a little sister
because I am more patient than him, I can
exspress my feelings more than him, and
I can control my behavior more than him.

FIG. 13–4   Emma tries out surprising the reader as a way to introduce her piece.

Writing Conclusions

Tell writers that the end of an essay is another place to convey the importance of ideas.

"Writers, can I have your eyes and attention? I want to tell you that the introduction to your essay is not the only place where you will want to convey the importance of your ideas. Essayists use the conclusion of their essays to convey that their ideas are important and to make sure readers will understand the meaning of their essay and why it matters."

Explain that one way to convey importance is to use common phrases to end an essay.

"At the end of essays, writers want their readers to know that they have realized something and now will act differently or think other people should act differently. One way they do this is by using common phrases or sentence starters to help them." I uncovered a chart.

Ways to End an Essay

- I realize that . . .
- This makes me think . . .
- I realize that when I . . . , I feel . . .
- Other people should care about this because . . .
- This is important because . . .
- (My thesis statement) is true. Because this is true, isn't it also true that . . .

Demonstrate using common phrases to help you try out a few endings for your essay.

"Watch while I use some of these phrases to help me try out a few endings for my essay. Then you'll have a chance to try out some endings for your essay.

"So I want to show that my ideas are important and that I have realized something and will act differently. Let me try using 'I realize that. . . .'"

> I realize that parents have a big responsibility. They are important teachers for their children even when they may not realize they are teaching. This makes me wonder what my own children will say I have taught them. I hope I have been as good a teacher for them as my father was for me.

"Now, writers, in a minute you will try this. Right now, to practice, just pick one of the phrases from the chart, and in your head, try out a possible ending for your essay. Thumbs up when you've done this." I waited until the majority of thumbs popped up. "Okay, writers, now just choose another phrase and try out a different possible ending in your head. Thumbs up when you've done that." Again, I gave them a moment to do this work. "Okay, now think of which possible ending you like better for your essay and turn to a partner and share that one.

"Writers, you'll want to make sure your essay conveys to readers that your ideas are important. Spend the rest of today making sure that you have done that. You might need to keep trying out introductions and conclusions. Help each other. Go to it!" (See Olivia and Rie's conclusions in Figures 13–5 and 13–6.)

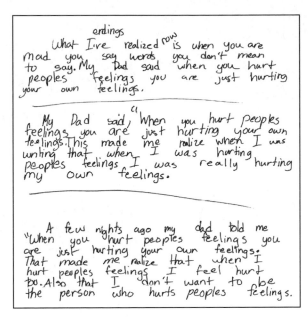

FIG. 13–5   Olivia's conclusions

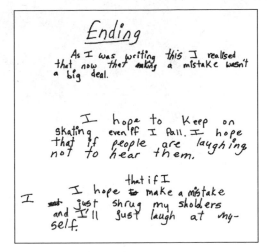

FIG. 13–6   Rie's conclusions

WRITING INTRODUCTIONS AND CONCLUSIONS

Writers, we're about at the middle of this unit. This is a great time for you to see how much stronger you've gotten so tonight, you will do another on-demand piece. Set your clock for a half hour or forty minutes and write fast and furiously to support a strong thesis. Then bring that piece into class tomorrow because you'll get the chance to assess it and reflect on your goals. You might remind yourself of your goals before you start writing so you can hold yourself accountable to meeting them. Sometimes I even make myself a self-assignment box on the top of my paper with a goal or two written down so I can hold them in my mind as I write. You might try that as well.

Revising Our Work with Goals in Mind

IN THIS SESSION, you'll again teach students to self-assess their writing, using the Opinion Writing Checklist. You will support your writers in creating a brand-new, revised draft.

GETTING READY

✓ Chart-sized version of the Opinion Writing Checklist, Grades 4 and 5, and small copies, one for each student (see Connection and Teaching)

✓ Students' on-demand pieces taped in their notebooks (both unrevised and revised), along with the Opinion Writing Checklist they used to check this writing in Session 7, to be brought to the meeting area

✓ Students' drafts of their essays from yesterday, to be brought to the meeting area

✓ Students' personal goals, to be brought to the meeting area

COMMON CORE STATE STANDARDS: W.4.1, W.4.5, RFS.4.4, SL.4.1, L.4.1, L.4.2, L.4.3, L.4.5

WHEN WE ASSESS STUDENTS we make decisions about what we feel they can do and where they are along a trajectory of work that leads toward goals we have created for each child, and we become clear in our own minds about what we need to do as teachers to help them make progress along this trajectory. When we assess students we create the instruction that must necessarily follow, we become accountable for where they need to be—responsible owners of students' education. Yet if we do not involve students in the assessment process, we deny *them* the chance to play these same roles in their own education, the chance to become responsible owners of their progress, aware of where they want to be and how to get there, accountable for their growth. If we deny our students the opportunity to internalize their own learning for their own purposes and transfer and apply that learning, and we are the only ones who hold the assessment tools, the criteria for success becomes a mystery and worse, largely purposeless to students. Our students need assessment that is transparent and is a joint project so that they have internalized accountability to themselves and to learning, not just to us. Only then will they truly be independent.

There is little that is more important in building a sense of investment in students than saying to each child, "You are in charge of your own learning life." Offering students a feeling of control and choice is the way to create lifelong learning.

This lesson works to imbue your writers with a sense of urgency and a feeling that every piece of writing should reflect their best work. Writers will begin to redraft their entire essay with their goals in mind, ensuring that the piece shows they are making progress, and they will also go back to look at drafts from earlier in the unit and revise these, learning that a piece is never fully done and good work can always get stronger.

In a few days, students will begin a second piece; today's lesson serves as a chance to assess their current draft and revise with goals in mind as well as charge students with keeping those goals in mind while writing their next piece, work that is of high cognitive demand. As the unit moves toward its final bend, the complexity of work and the cognitive demand increases as students are pushed to analyze and apply what they have learned.

Revising Our Work with Goals in Mind

CONNECTION

Let writers know that today they will have the opportunity to again assess their work.

"Writers, when you come to the meeting area you'll see that there is a new copy of the Opinion Writing Checklist waiting for you." I pointed to the chart-sized version I had in the meeting area.

"Remember, that you are always aiming to outgrow what you can already do. And to do that, it helps to keep checking on your progress. Now that you have your essay drafted, you will look to see if your work shows that you are getting stronger as an opinion writer. So, today you are going to take stock of your writing again. You are going to hold yourselves accountable to all that you've learned and hoped and planned to do so far in this unit."

❖ **Name the teaching point.**

"Today, I want to remind you that it helps to pause sometimes and to look back at your progress as writers, asking, 'Am I living up to the goals I set for myself? Am I getting better?' And 'What should I work on next?' You can use checklists, charts, even personal goals to help you do this."

Opinion Writing Checklist

	Grade 4	NOT YET	STARTING TO	YES!	Grade 5	NOT YET	STARTING TO	YES!
	Structure				**Structure**			
Overall	I made a claim about a topic or a text and tried to support my reasons.	☐	☐	☐	I made a claim or thesis on a topic or text, supported it with reasons, and provided a variety of evidence for each reason.	☐	☐	☐
Lead	I wrote a few sentences to hook my readers, perhaps by asking a question, explaining why the topic mattered, telling a surprising fact, or giving background information.	☐	☐	☐	I wrote an introduction that led to a claim or thesis and got my readers to care about my opinion. I got my readers to care by not only including a cool fact or jazzy question, but also figuring out was significant in or around the topic and giving readers information about what was significant about the topic.	☐	☐	☐
	I stated my claim.				I worked to find the precise words to state my claim; I let readers know the reasons I would develop later.	☐	☐	☐
Transitions	I used words and phrases to glue parts of my piece together. I used phrases such as *for example, another example, one time,* and *for instance* to show when I was shifting from saying reasons to giving evidence and *in addition to, also,* and *another* to show when I wanted to make a new point.	☐	☐	☐	I used transition words and phrases to connect evidence back to my reasons using phrases such as *this shows that. . . .*	☐	☐	☐
					I helped readers follow my thinking with phrases such as *another reason* and *the most important reason.* I used phrases such as *consequently* and *because of* to show what happened.	☐	☐	☐
					I used words such as *specifically* and *in particular* in order to be more precise.	☐	☐	☐

TEACHING and ACTIVE ENGAGEMENT

Help children to assess their own writing using the checklist and their personal goal sheet.

"We're going to use the Opinion Writing Checklist to assess your latest draft and make sure it is *eons* above your last on-demand piece. *If it is not, that is an emergency.* You have learned a tremendous amount of new things since you wrote that on-demand and your new learning should be showing up in your draft. Every piece you write should be better than the last. So, today we'll make sure that's true for you. You'll revise your work using all you know to do. First, get your personal goals into your mind so you remember what you have been striving to achieve as an opinion writer."

I asked the children to lay out their materials, setting their personal goals chart, their copy of the Opinion Writing Checklist, and their fast draft from yesterday in a row before them. "Right now, will you reread your draft from yesterday and give yourself a check for each of the qualities of good opinion writing on the checklist? After you are finished, I want you to compare your checklist today with the checklist you filled out for your on-demand writing a couple weeks ago. You should have it in your writer's notebook."

I gave the children some time to work, moving around the meeting area to coach and support them as they did. "If it felt right to do so, I made deliberate word choices to convince my reader, maybe by emphasizing or repeating words that would make my readers feel emotions. Hmm, is there a part of your essay where you really work to draw your reader into your topic?" And "Maybe you could circle the parts where you feel you made really precise word choices and see if there is more than one place where you did that work." As children wrapped up, I called for their attention again.

"Writers, many of you are noticing all the growth you've made this year. Some of you are even saying that you feel you have met some of your goals. Hooray! Remember that you want to have evidence of lots of places where you can see yourself doing that work before you can say you have met a goal. And, even more importantly, many of you are still noticing that you are not quite at your goal yet and so you are figuring out next steps for what you'd like to do when you revise this essay today. Having an action plan is the most important thing you can have! Before you forget, take a minute to jot down some of your new goals on your personal goal sheet. If it's an especially important goal, you might even choose to put stars or fireworks around it."

LINK

Send students off with at least one personal goal to help them write the second drafts of their essays.

"Here's the thing, writers. Goals are only helpful if you actually try to meet them! We're going to spend time today ratcheting up the level of your draft by making sure that your piece meets all of the goals on the fourth-grade side of the Opinion Writing Checklist. Will you take a second right now to read over your goals? What will be the big work you do in this second draft? Think of one way you will completely rework this piece. Point to a section that you know needs extra attention. Put your finger on that place right now. Of course, you should also feel more than welcome to push your piece to meet the fifth-grade side of the checklist, as well! When you're ready, head right back to your seat and start redrafting!"

Keeping Writers Focused on Their Goals as They Work

DURING TODAY'S WORKSHOP, you will want to be careful not to pull writers away from the work of writing fast and furiously. You have set out the task of revising their drafts and making them better in one day's writing time, and you want your writers to feel success at having accomplished that work. Instead of pulling them into small groups, you will want to spend time today doing some quick, targeted pushing in to help your writers raise the level of the work they are doing by helping them to stay focused on their goals.

You will want to use a combination of table compliments and quick voiceovers to remind children of goals and urge them on. You might see one child glance quickly at a chart and suddenly rush over to her. "Francesca, I love the way you just checked the chart on transition phrases and linking words. You are really using all the resources in the room to make this piece the best piece you have ever written in your life. I think that *everyone* should learn how to make use of all the resources in the room the way

---

MID-WORKSHOP TEACHING **Voice Over So as Not to Stop Momentum**

"Writers, keep working but listen to what David did. He circled one of the goals on his sheet, and when I asked him why, he said, 'I'm not really sure I did that in a great way. I'm going to ask my partner about it.' Isn't that smart of him to be thinking about how to use his partner to help him meet his goals? As you keep working, if you come to a goal that you want to talk to your partner more about, you might try doing what David did.

"I'm noticing that a few of you are starting to finish up your drafts. Remember, there are always ways to make your writing stronger. If you do finish, try looking at your piece against the Opinion Writing Checklist again and see what you may have forgotten to do in your new, second draft. Or even better, meet up with someone else who is done and swap pieces. You'll have to do this silently so as not to disturb other writers, but sometimes other readers can spot things that you didn't notice."

> I was sitting on the front steps feeling sad because I teased in school. The kids where saying that I was horrible at sports and I was dumb. It felt like the worst day ever. Then down I saw my step sister walking towards me. Just seeing her made me feel much better. As you can see, my step sister is important to me. She is important to me because, she helps me, she makes me feel good when i'm sad, and she makes me laugh.

> In the beginning of the essay I hooked in my reader by making a cool miny story showing why having a sister is an advantage. I tried to tell the reader about my sister.

FIG. 14–1   Andrew reflects on writing goals as he drafts his personal essay.

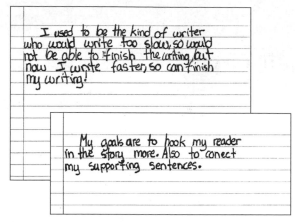

FIG. 14–2   Andrew's pages where he reflects on himself as a writer and sets goals for his writing

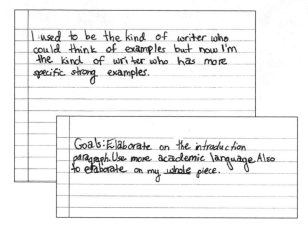

FIG. 14–3   Hannah's three pages where she reflects on herself as a writer and sets goals for her writing

you did." Likely, as soon as you say this, you will notice all eyes nearby go to the chart. "That's so brave," you might tell another child. "You are not just adding a word or two to your introduction. No, you are the kind of writer who is brave enough to cover up your first try and start all over again from scratch. That is truly courageous work."

You may have writers who finish revising quickly and you may have longer conferences with these writers. Read their work closely. Over and over when teaching this unit, I have found that skills and strategies that sound simple when I talk about them in minilessons prove to be vastly more complicated than I'd ever dreamed possible when a child actually tries to do the work. Don't just scan a child's words. Take them in. Think, "What is this child trying to say and do?" Ask, "Is this writing basically working? What has the child done that I can name in a fashion that will transfer to other pieces? What isn't working? How can I equip the writer to handle this area of difficulty in this piece and in future pieces?" Consider this section of Estefan's piece with these questions in mind.

My dad is important to me because I have fun when he teaches me baseball. One time my dad woke me up to tell me if I want to go play baseball. I said, "Ok, I'll get ready." When I washed up and got ready we went to the baseball field. There we got out the baseball bats and balls. At the baseball field, my dad was throwing fastballs, so I telled him to slow down. My dad said, "Alright, but you got to get used to fastballs." I said, "Ok, I will."

There are many things Estefan has done well:

Estefan has adroitly shifted from stating a big idea (My dad is important to me) to telling a specific story, and he's done so using the transitional phrase "one time."

Estefan has transferred what he knows about writing stories to this new work with essays. His story is told in a step-by-step chronological way, and as a reader I can reexperience it. He includes dialogue and details.

Estefan's story is generally about the idea he wants to convey. The part of the story that he has elaborated upon (his father's efforts to instruct Estefan) is the part that matches his idea.

In a conference with Estefan I'd probably choose just one or two of these points to compliment. In this case, because of what I know I will soon teach, I created a compliment by combining the second two points. "Estefan," I said, "I absolutely love the fact that you brought all you know about stories to bear on the miniature story you tell inside this essay! And, more than that, you knew to elaborate with precise details."

There are a number of qualities and strategies I could teach Estefan. Most important, I'd want him to realize that although it's great that he used all he knows about stories to write this one, we place special demands on the stories that we embed into essays. These stories need to efficiently and directly address the main idea of the essay. I'd teach Estefan that I reread the stories I write within nonfiction texts, pausing after almost every line of the story to ask, "Does this go with my main idea?"

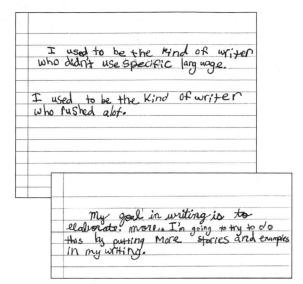

I used to be the kind of writer who didn't use specific language.

I used to be the kind of writer who rushed alot.

My goal in writing is to elaborate more. I'm going to try to do this by putting more stories and examples in my writing.

FIG. 14–4   Jessie's pages where she reflects on herself as a writer and sets goals for her writing

When Estefan read his first sentence, asking, "Does this go with my main idea?" the answer was yes. It is really smart of Estefan to not just say that his dad woke him, but to say that his dad asked about baseball. I didn't point out to Estefan that he could have done even more to highlight the role baseball played in waking up. For example, he could have written, "I lay in bed and thought about how much fun it is to play baseball with my father. Even though it was early, I raced out of bed. I didn't want to miss this chance." I didn't bring out this point because I felt it wasn't something that Estefan could learn to do on his own just yet—and because I had less subtle instruction in mind. Estefan and I noted that yes, his first sentence pertained to his main idea. But as Estefan read on, pausing after each sentence to ask, "Does this further my main idea?" he realized that none of the next details—that he got ready, woke up, and traveled to the field—advanced his main idea. I taught him that he had choices. He could include the fact that he washed up *if* (and only if) he could find a way to integrate his father teaching him baseball into washing up. (This might seem like a ridiculous suggestion, but of course all Estefan would need to do is to scrub his face, thinking as he did so about the upcoming game.) Alternatively, Estefan could fast-forward his story, skipping past events that didn't relate to his main idea, which is what he in fact decided to do.

My larger point is that we need to read our children's pieces with care, expecting that they'll struggle with aspects of this work. Be prepared to compliment them on what works, to teach skills they need to know—and to learn volumes in the process.

Transferring Revision Plans to Earlier Drafts

Recruit writers to revise not just their current draft, but also their on-demand pieces.

"Writers, you have learned so many ways to make your writing stronger. When you learn how to raise up the quality of your writing, you do not just use that learning to make that one piece of writing stronger; rather, you look back at all of your previous writing to see how to raise the level of that writing too. For example, I could think about the new goals that I have set and look at my personal essay writing from the very beginning of the unit, or even last year, to see how to make sure that piece shows that I am meeting my goals. Writers do not just write pieces and lay them aside. They constantly think about how to take what they are learning and apply it. So, right now, will you take out all of the essays you have done so far for this unit—the on-demand pieces you have written and even your revised on-demand pieces—and lay them out and look across them? You can use all you know about effective opinion writing and revise *all* of your previous work. Help each other. Tonight for homework, you can continue to do this and come in tomorrow with essays that all represent your latest learning and all that you know to do."

REVISING OUR WORK WITH GOALS IN MIND

Fast and Furious Flash-Drafting

Writers, you want to be the kind of people who are always pushing yourselves, the kind of people who are not content with anything less than your best. Tonight, you will spend time bringing all of your pieces across this unit up to the level of your best. By now, you have learned a ton of ways to develop a strong essay and you have worked in ways that are not just fourth-grade level but also fifth-grade level. Tonight take your pieces and give yourself a challenge or a mission. I hummed a few bars of the *Mission Impossible* theme song. Your mission: Make all of these pieces meet fourth- and fifth-grade level goals. You'll probably decide to take a brand new piece of loose leaf and completely redraft at least one of your pieces and maybe more than one. You can do it!

Session 15

Correcting Run-On Sentences and Sentence Fragments

ear Teachers,

Today is the day when you'll help children wrap up their revision work and move to editing—fixing their spelling, punctuation, and grammar so others can read their work and grasp the intended meaning. In this letter, we will help you imagine the teaching you might do today.

MINILESSON

We suggest you begin with a connection that reminds your students of all they already know about editing to make their work clear to readers. During your connection you might ask students to think of one way that they already know to edit work and put a thumb up when they have it in mind, then quickly turn and share. You might jot two or three items that you heard mentioned (or that you already have in mind), such as the following:

- ☐ Reread for sense and missing words.

- ☐ Edit for punctuation.

- ☐ Check for capital letters at the beginning of new sentences, when using proper nouns, or when giving someone's title.

- ☐ Check that known, high-frequency words are spelled correctly.

You might then remind children that they *already* know to edit by relying on an editing checklist. They have already learned to read a piece multiple times, each time through a different lens. Then you might tell them that you are going to add one new item to their editing checklist, one new way of editing to their repertoire of strategies, saying, "Today, I want to teach you another way that writers edit their work: they check that each sentence is complete, and they correct run-on sentences and sentence fragments."

COMMON CORE STATE STANDARDS: W.4.1, W.4.5, RFS.4.4, SL.4.1, L.4.1, L.4.2, L.4.3

Then, in your teaching, you can model editing some of your own writing or an anonymous student's writing (riddled with a variety of sentence fragments and run-on sentences, of course). You might show students that, for this editing lens, it always helps you to read aloud, listening for where you finish a complete thought. You might tell students that you want to make sure that you do not place ending punctuation too early, thus leaving a fragment, or too late, thus leaving a run-on sentence.

For the active engagement, you'll want to give children an opportunity to practice checking for complete sentences on a bit of their own writing, perhaps asking Partner 1 to read aloud to Partner 2 so the two can decide where the ending punctuation should go. At the end of the lesson, add "Read work aloud to check for fragments and run-on sentences" to the class editing checklist and send each child off with a copy of the checklist to continue this work on his or her own. The Editing Checklist can be found on the CD-ROM.

CONFERRING AND SMALL-GROUP WORK

During the day's time for conferring and small-group work, you'll want to continue to support your writers in mastering conventions. You might consider sorting children into clusters based only on their issues around the conventions of written language. One way you might group children is around some common types of issues with conventions, as follows:

1. Children in the first group are so swamped with problems that you hardly know where to begin. They have problems with spelling, handwriting, punctuation, stamina, syntax, making sense, length—the works.

2. Children in the next group write quickly and generally write with 90% accuracy (although at first you thought they were worse because their errors stand out). These children make all the common mistakes that many kids do: mixing up *to*, *too*, and *two*, forgetting to double consonants when they add endings, and so forth.

3. Children in this group are English language learners who are literate in another language and use their knowledge of that other language to help them write in English. While this has helped them in some ways, it also creates its own set of problems. For example, a fair percentage of the errors these children make in English result from relying on their knowledge of their first language in ways that don't work for English. These children sometimes put an adjective after the noun it modifies, mix up their gender-related pronouns, struggle with tenses other than the present, or spell phonetically.

4. Children in this group write with fairly correct conventions. They concern you not because they make errors, but because they are not using complex sentences or vocabulary. You worry that their zeal to be correct and in control has led them to cling to safe terrain. As a result, much of their writing reads as if it is a list. They don't seem at home with literary syntax, and they don't use a diversity of connectors, relying almost entirely on *and*, *so*, and *then*.

5. Children in this last group have an easy command of the conventions of written language. Some seem to be trying new things and pushing themselves to experiment, to create effects on the page, to use mentor texts as models; others do not, but all of these children seem to have this aspect of writing well under control and avoid making errors.

You'll want to look closely at the work of at least one representative child from each group. Consider whether that one child's progress (or lack thereof) is representative of the others from that group. Ask yourself, "What progress am I expecting from this group of children?" Based on your answer, you should be able to think about the most appropriate teaching you'll do with this group, on this day.

You can look at the Common Core Language Standards to decide where your teaching needs to begin. For example, for the group of students whose writing seems riddled with every type of error, you might decide you need to take a triage approach. That is, when patients go to an emergency room, doctors handle the most serious emergencies first. Heart attacks before broken arms. So when deciding what emergencies in language are the most serious for your writers, you might look at the Common Core Language Standards across several grades. If you see writers not capitalizing names of people, for example, you know that this is a standard they were expected to meet by the end of first grade. Which means it is totally unacceptable for writers to not be doing that a full three grades later. Standards that are expected of primary writers should be emergencies, and you should be filled with a sense of urgency that these writers will grasp and meet these standards, *no matter what* this year.

Chances are extremely strong that writers have heard about these standards over and over again. So your teaching needs to not reteach them this same work yet again; rather, your teaching needs to remind them to draw upon what they already know to do and transfer it to new work. To assess quickly what writers already know to do but are not doing in their own work, you might hand them a piece of your own writing with mistakes that relate to standards of previous grades and ask students to find and correct the mistakes they notice. If they notice mistakes on yours and correct these but do not do the same work on their own, then you might note that these students need to be taught to transfer what they know to their own work. (If they do not find and correct mistakes on your work then you might decide they do need some teaching into this work.) Just as you would do with guided reading groups, you can coach into what each individual child needs. For example, in a group of five students you might notice that three can find and correct the majority of your mistakes, while one child is not noticing where you have made mistakes in using quotation marks and another has not corrected multiple mistakes of varying types. You might involve all of the five students in creating a checklist about what they already know to do based on what they are able to correct in your piece and then have them use this

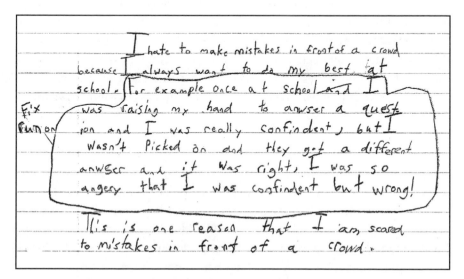

FIG. 15–1 Nora identifies a run-on sentence.

checklist as a lens to look over their own pieces. As they seem to show they can correct the work of others, assign them each a partner who will look over the corrected piece and circle any errors that still remain. It will be up to the writer to correct these.

In assessing another group of children, you might decide that instruction into verb tense is necessary, and then you might decide to convene a small group of writers around verb tense. Some of your writers may be writing essays in present tense (e.g., Parents are their children's most important teachers.) and needing to shift to past tense when incorporating anecdotes (e.g., For example, one summer my friend Natalie taught . . .). You might tell your writers that when they are checking their writing, they should pay attention to when time shifts so that they know what verb tense to use. You might model reading a piece of your writing and telling writers when you are reading a portion that is true for now and needs to be in present tense and when you are reading a portion that takes place in the past and needs to be in past tense. For many writers, you may find it helpful to involve them in guided practice, perhaps showing them a portion of a text with correct grammar, and then another section with mistakes and involving all in the group in helping to revise it.

You'll want to remember that your teaching on this one day will not solve all their problems, but instead will help them with one aspect of conventions. See today as one piece of a much larger sequence of work around conventions and editing.

MID-WORKSHOP TEACHING

For your mid-workshop teaching, you might remind writers that peers can be helpful editors, and then have writers exchange pieces with a neighbor to help each other catch final errors. This will be a quick mid-workshop teaching because you'll want to leave time for a longer than usual share. It may come as a surprise that tomorrow you begin Bend III and the children begin new pieces. Why wouldn't they publish these essays first, you might ask? The answer is twofold. First, you are teaching your young writers to cycle through the writing process faster and faster, raising the level of their work at each step, and second, taking a day to copy over their writing might bring that process to a grinding halt.

SHARE

You'll want to convey to children that they will soon be writing a new essay and make today celebratory. For today's share, we recommend you convene the class to do just that. You'll want to think about how you'd best like to celebrate their mammoth achievements. Perhaps you will inspire them with a quote about personal writing such as one from Maya Angelou: "I will write upon the pages of history what I want them to say. I will be myself. I will speak my own name." Or a quote from Byrd Baylor's *I'm in Charge of Celebrations* (1995). You might choose to tell students that in writing personal essays, they are putting their own lives on the paper and they are learning more about themselves, and that is something to be celebrated! You might then ask each student to think about one thing he or she has learned about him- or herself through writing the essay and write it down on a special piece of paper that you provide—perhaps a gold one. You might feel that a celebration of personal writing calls for silence, so after writing down one thing they have realized about themselves through writing this piece, students might participate in a silent celebration, one that consists of their moving in silence from desk to desk, reading a classmate's writing, and perhaps noting a respectful comment, letting the writer know how they have been affected by the piece.

Of course, you will want to put your own piece out as well and make it available for students to read. Let them see that you have been as invested in this process as they have and that you, too, have learned about yourself through writing. Make this day special for your children. Help them feel proud of all they've accomplished. And rally their energy for the next round of writing!

Good luck!

Lucy, Cory, and Kelly

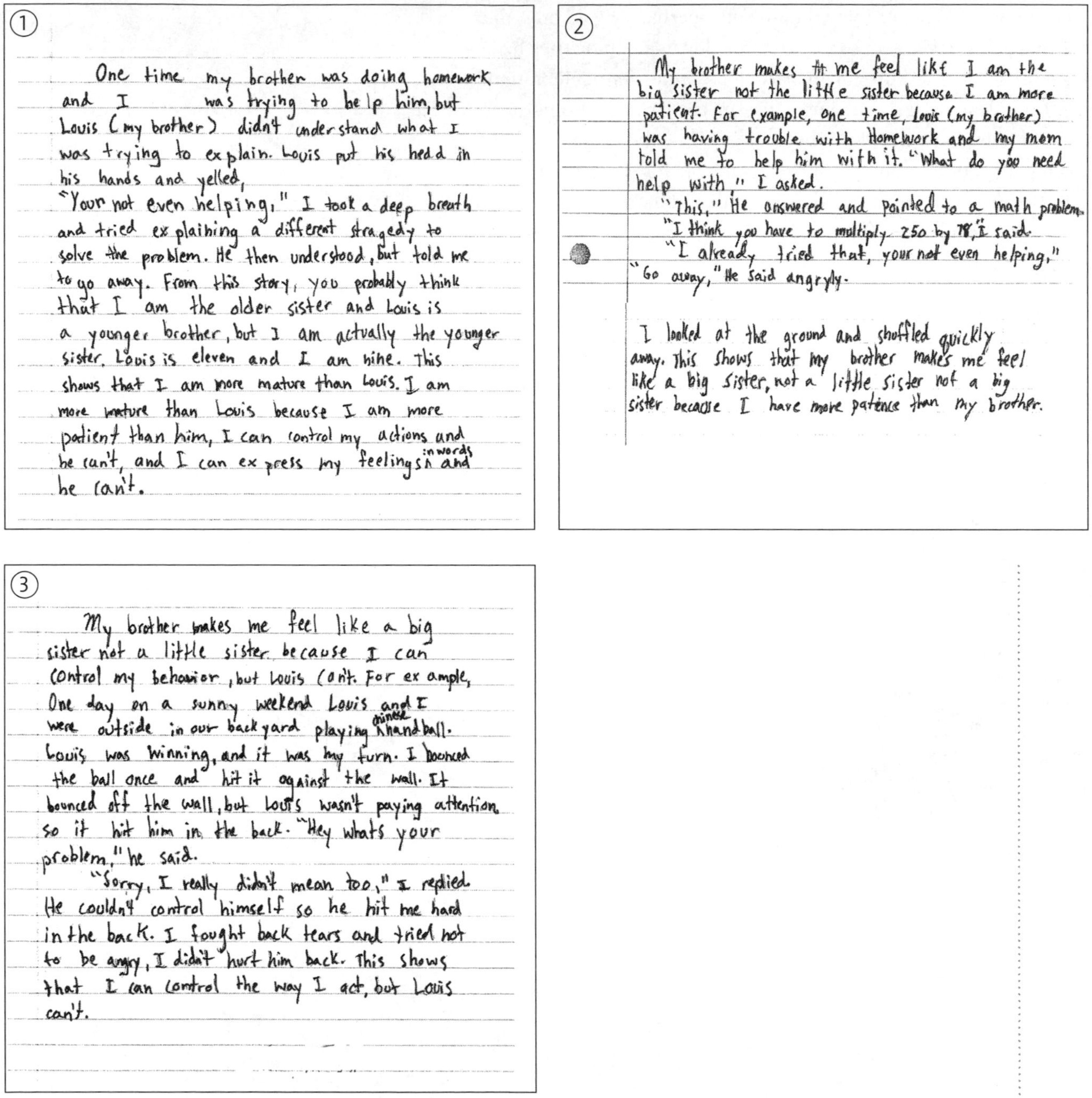

①

One time my brother was doing homework and I was trying to help him, but Louis (my brother) didn't understand what I was trying to explain. Louis put his head in his hands and yelled, "Your not even helping." I took a deep breath and tried explaining a different stragedy to solve the problem. He then understood, but told me to go away. From this story, you probably think that I am the older sister and Louis is a younger brother, but I am actually the younger sister. Louis is eleven and I am nine. This shows that I am more mature than Louis. I am more mature than Louis because I am more patient than him, I can control my actions and he can't, and I can express my feelings in words and he can't.

②

My brother makes me feel like I am the big sister not the little sister because I am more patient. For example, one time, Louis (my brother) was having trouble with Homework and my mom told me to help him with it. "What do you need help with," I asked.

"This," He answered and pointed to a math problem.

"I think you have to multiply 250 by 78," I said.

"I already tried that, your not even helping,"

"Go away," He said angryly.

I looked at the ground and shuffled quickly away. This shows that my brother makes me feel like a big sister, not a little sister not a big sister because I have more patience than my brother.

③

My brother makes me feel like a big sister not a little sister because I can control my behavior, but Louis can't. For example, One day on a sunny weekend Louis and I were outside in our backyard playing chinese handball. Louis was winning, and it was my turn. I bounced the ball once and hit it against the wall. It bounced off the wall, but Louis wasn't paying attention so it hit him in the back. "Hey whats your problem," he said.

"Sorry, I really didn't mean too," I replied He couldn't control himself so he hit me hard in the back. I fought back tears and tried not to be angry, I didn't hurt him back. This shows that I can control the way I act, but Louis can't.

FIG. 15–2 Emma's final essay across many pages

④

My brother makes me feel like a big sister not a little sister because I can express myself in words, but he can't. For example, one day, my brother was in a unusually bad mood. I tried to ask him why he was so upset, but when Louis tried to tell me, he gave up quickly in frustration. I told my mom that Louis was having a bad day. She walked over to where Louis was standing and said, "Hey Louis, whats going on? You seem a bit down."

"I don't know, well I do, but it's hard to explain," he replied. I could tell by the look on his face that he was trying really hard to explain his feelings. My mom and I kept trying to get him to say what was wrong, but he didn't. Eventually he got angry and yelled at me.

"Yelling doesn't help, it just makes feel bad," I said. Louis scowled and walked away. This shows that I can express my feelings in words, but Louis can't.

⑤

As you can see, my brother makes me feel like a big sister not a little sister. My brother makes me feel this way because I am more patient than my brother, I can control my actions and behavior better than my brother, and I can express the way I feel and my brother can't do this.

FIG. 15–2 (Continued)

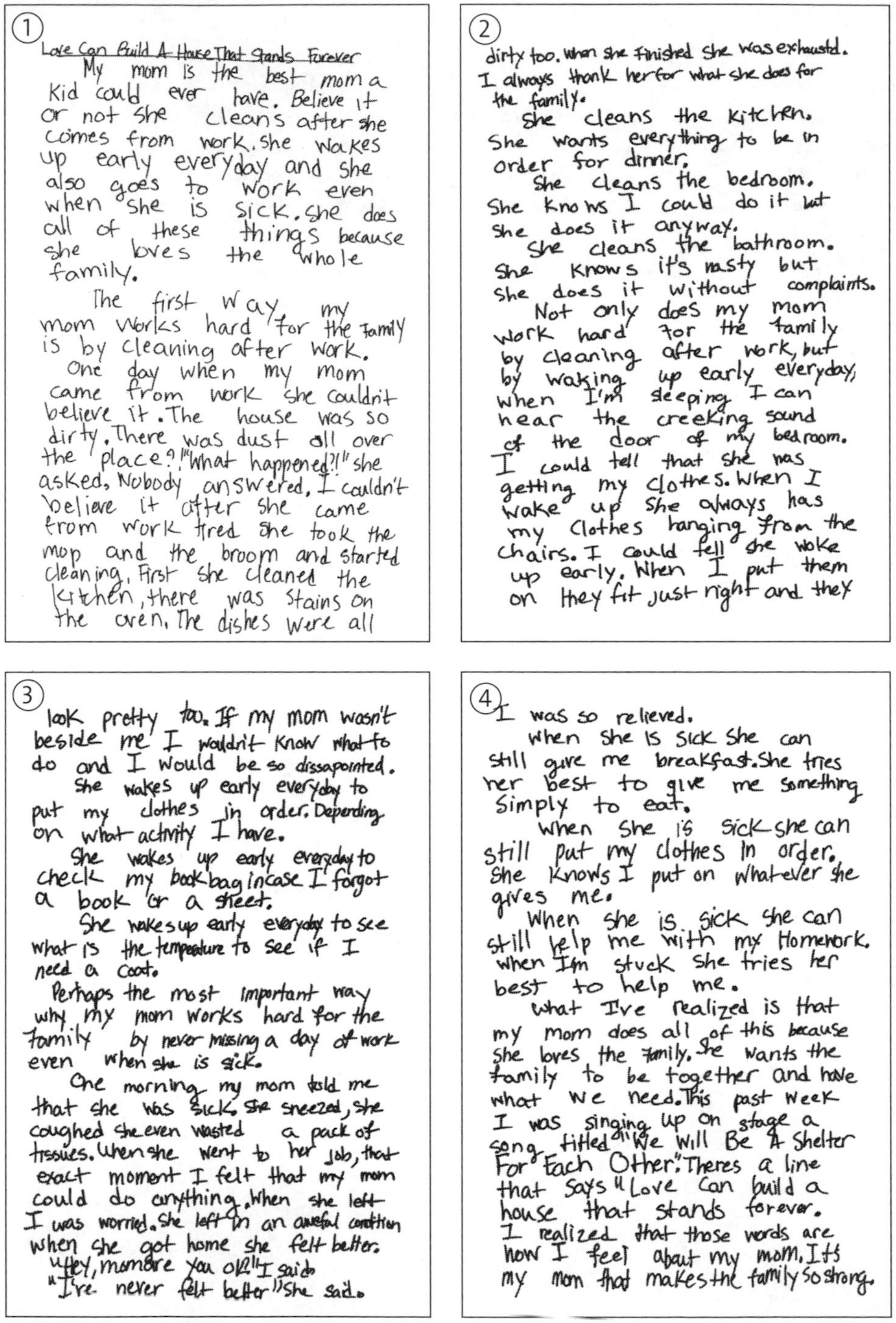

1

Love Can Build A House That Stands Forever

My mom is the best mom a kid could ever have. Believe it or not she cleans after she comes from work. she wakes up early everyday and she also goes to work even when she is sick. she does all of these things because she loves the whole family.

The first way my mom works hard for the family is by cleaning after work.

One day when my mom came from work she couldn't believe it. The house was so dirty. There was dust all over the place? "What happened?!" she asked. Nobody answered. I couldn't believe it after she came from work tired she took the mop and the broom and started cleaning. First she cleaned the kitchen, there was stains on the oven. The dishes were all

2

dirty too. When she finished she was exhausted. I always thank her for what she does for the family.

She cleans the kitchen. She wants everything to be in order for dinner.

She cleans the bedroom. She knows I could do it but she does it anyway.

She cleans the bathroom. She knows it's nasty but she does it without complaints.

Not only does my mom work hard for the family by cleaning after work, but by waking up early everyday. When I'm sleeping I can hear the creeking sound of the door of my bedroom. I could tell that she was getting my clothes. When I wake up she always has my clothes hanging from the chairs. I could tell she woke up early. When I put them on they fit just right and they

3

look pretty too. If my mom wasn't beside me I wouldn't know what to do and I would be so dissapointed.

She wakes up early everyday to put my clothes in order. Depending on what activity I have.

She wakes up early everyday to check my book bag in case I forgot a book or a sheet.

She wakes up early everyday to see what is the temperature to see if I need a coat.

Perhaps the most important way why my mom works hard for the family by never missing a day of work even when she is sick.

One morning my mom told me that she was sick. She sneezed, she coughed she even wasted a pack of tissues. When she went to her job, that exact moment I felt that my mom could do anything. When she left I was worried. She left in an aweful condition when she got home she felt better.

"Hey, mom are you ok?" I said

"I've never felt better." she said.

4

I was so relieved.

When she is sick she can still give me breakfast. She tries her best to give me something simply to eat.

When she is sick she can still put my clothes in order. She knows I put on whatever she gives me.

When she is sick she can still help me with my Homework. When I'm stuck she tries her best to help me.

What I've realized is that my mom does all of this because she loves the family. She wants the family to be together and have what we need. This past week I was singing up on stage a song titled on "We will Be A Shelter For Each Other." Theres a line that says "Love can build a house that stands forever.

I realized that those words are how I feel about my mom. It's my mom that makes the family so strong.

FIG. 15–3   William's personal essay

1

Love Is Missing Someone When He's Away

Everyone has someone who is special to them. Maybe its their best friends, their sisters or brothers. But to me that someone is my dad because he is so close to me. my dad goes on trips a lot. I miss my dad when he is away because we have so much fun together. He takes care of me when I am sick and because when I am afraid he makes me safe.

One reason why I miss my dad is because we had so much fun together.

During the weekend we enjoy jogging together. We run around lakes.

Afterschool we enjoy sitting at the computer. We play all

2

these different kind of games.

At midnight we enjoy sitting on the sofa. We tell stories and jokes.

But when he's not around I don't jog with anyone, I don't sit down on a chair and plays games with anybody and I don't stay at midnight and talk with anyone.

An example of this is when my dad went on a trip. I was lonley sitting by myself. My sister was doing homework and my mom was busying doing work. I was waiting to play with some body. "Lena could you play with me" I asked her. "I can't" she said. But all of sudden the door bell ring - Ring - Ring - Ring. "Hello?" I asked.

3

"Hello" a guy said back. "Daddy's coming" I yelled so that my family could hear me. I buzzed him in. I heard footsteps. "Daddy" I yell. I huged him and kissed him. "I love you" I said to him. "Me too" he said back.

My dad and I share good times together, but when he is away, I feel lonely and have no one to play with.

A other reason why I miss my dad is because he takes care of me when I am sick.

I miss the way he gives medicine and alway puts

4

a olive on the top.

I miss the way he plays cards with me and always lets me win.

I miss the way he told me stories. They make me feel really close to him.

But now I am sitting alone and medicine taste bad, nobody is playing with me no one is going to tell stories the way my dad did. Perhaps most important reason why I miss my dad is that he makes me safe when I am afraid.

An example of this is when I was afraid of the dark, he wasn't there to make me feel better.

5

If he was there he would be telling me some stories.

If he was there he would be singing a song to make me sleep.

If he was there he would be huging me and telling me that it was okay.

An example of this is one day when he was away I was afraid. I needed someone to be there My mom and my sisters was busy. But if my was there we would stay up, laughing at jokes or watching baseball.

I been thinking a lot about my idea. I read some books and I was thinking of it every where I go. One day I found this

6

quote, "Love is missing someone when even they're away." I like this quote because it connects my thesis I love him and miss him when he goes away. Many people, like me, agree with the quote. I know that my dad is always there for me no matter what. I am really thankful to have him as my dad!

FIG. 15-4 Fatmire's personal essay

① My Father is My Worst Enemy

Everyone deserves a good father. Everywhere I go I see kids spending time with their fathers, but not me. My father is my worst enemy. For example, he picks his wife over me, he makes me feel like a small kid next to big foot, and he made me into a person I don't want to be.

My father is my worst enemy because he picks my stepmother over me. He lets his wife dominate him like a toy. For example, one day I was supposed to go to their house to sleep over. I was ready to go when I get a call from my father. He said "Sorry but I can't pick you up because my wife is in the hospital." I hope she feels better, that's what I said. Then a

② short while later my mom calls me and says that my father was lying. My stepmother wasn't in the hospital. My step mother just didn't want me to come. It wasn't a real shock because my father has stood me up various times. I was so angry but the worst part is he couldn't even tell me the truth. Another time is when I was play fighting with my step brother because he wanted me to. Then I scratched him by mistake on his neck. He told his mom tha I scratched him on purpose. My stepmother came in the room and started yelling at me. My dad was right beside me and didn't even try to defend me. I got so mad I responded and said "he hit me too."

My father is my worst enemy. He makes me feel like a small kid next to big foot. I feel use less like when I was small or a younger child. I used to wait for my father to call me. Wishing the phone would ring, for him to take me to the movies or the park. He always

③ told me lies and excuses. I can't believe he never ran out of what to say. Everytime he let me down I'd get very upset. Even though I knew he would do it again it still would always hurt.

My father is my worst enemy. He made me into a person that I don't want to be. He made me angry and mean. I remember I used to be happy, friendly, and my friends used to call me "peppy." I wish I could tell him how much he hurt me and that he made me into a person I don't want to be. Like I used to be confident, now I'm insecure and can't make decisions on my own.

My father can be the worst father in the world but I bet there are worse. There's nothing I can do to change it, what's done is done. He will always be my dad even if I don't want him to. I guess I'll have to deal with it.

FIG. 15–5 Tanya's final draft

Moving from Personal to Persuasive

IN THIS SESSION, you'll teach writers to be brave and turn their personal essays into persuasive opinions. You will show them other strategies for generating ideas for persuasive essay writing.

GETTING READY

✔ A thesis for a personal essay from a past student and a new version of that thesis that is persuasive to show to students as an example of how to turn a personal thesis into a persuasive one (see Teaching)

✔ Your thesis from your personal essay and ideas for a new version of it that can be used to write a persuasive essay (see Active Engagement)

✔ Students' essay materials including their personal essay draft, their folders, and their writer's notebooks, to be brought to the meeting area

✔ Your thesis in box-and-bullets format, from Session 6

✔ Chart paper and markers, to write your new persuasive thesis in front of students and for the mid-workshop teaching

✔ Students' theses for their personal essays, in boxes and bullets

✔ "Persuasive Thesis Starters" chart (see Mid-Workshop Teaching)

COMMON CORE STATE STANDARDS: W.4.1, W.4.4, W.4.9, W.4.10, RI.4.2, RL.4.3, SL.4.1, SL.4.3, L.4.1, L.4.2, L.4.3, L.4.5

T HE ABILITY TO WRITE SOUND ARGUMENTS IS CRITICAL. Students who are able to reason thoughtfully, gather and weigh evidence, assess the validity of that evidence, and know how to use it are prepared not only to enter the world of academia and begin writing papers, but also to take on roles as active citizens in a democracy.

As citizens of a country that is founded on the principle that people can argue and protest against that which they find unjust, argument is not just a right; it is a necessity. Consider all that would be radically different if not for argument. Consider the Nineteenth Amendment and the stirring, passionate, and persuasive speeches heard at the first women's rights convention in Seneca Falls. Consider Thurgood Marshall fighting the case of *Brown v. Board of Education*, who helped to change the law concerning "separate but equal schools" by arguing against it. Inequalities and injustices do exist, and our children need to be capable of taking action where they see a need. If we want our children to be active citizens in this country, they must learn the art of argument.

The Common Core State Standards place special emphasis on the ability to write sound arguments. In the appendix of the document, the authors devote space and time to explaining why they have chosen to highlight argument writing across grades K–12, quoting authors such as Neil Postman, who calls argument, "the soul of an education" (Postman as cited in Common Core Appendix A 2010, 24) and asserting that argument plays a uniquely important role in both college and careers. The Common Core Standards make an important distinction between the kind of arguments where authors use strategies such as playing on an audience's emotions—trying to appeal to what an audience wants—and establishing themselves as an authority and "logical arguments" (24). As defined by the Common Core, logical arguments are those that "convince the audience because of the perceived merit and reasonableness of the claims and proofs offered rather than either the emotions the writer evokes in the audience or the character or credentials of the writer" (24). Logical arguments, then, require students to use evidence that is not solely lodged in their own personal experiences.

In this last bend of the unit, then, your students take the first steps away from personal opinions, which cannot truly be proven on the basis of evidence, to persuasive writing, in which the relevancy, sufficiency, and validity of the evidence is critical, and how you use the evidence an art. Soon, they will engage in research-based argument essays where they will quote sources and assess the relative validity of those sources, but for now they will take the beginning steps. Over the next few sessions you will help writers turn their personal thesis statements into persuasive opinions that consider their audience. You will involve them in gathering evidence, this time from outside sources, and unpacking that evidence to connect it to their reasons and claim to construct a tightly focused argument. And meanwhile, you will be holding them accountable for all they have already learned about essay writing, charging them with transferring all that they know and applying that learning to this new writing. You will also teach toward independence, watching your writers take themselves through the writing process and assessing where your teaching needs to go next.

In sum, you will support your students in moving toward more sophisticated opinion writing that will ready them to take the leap from opinion writing to argument writing next year.

"Over the next few sessions you will help writers turn their personal thesis statements into persuasive opinions that consider their audience."

Moving from Personal to Persuasive

CONNECTION

Celebrate the work your writers have done with their personal essays.

"Writers, I read over your personal essays this morning and I am totally thrilled for you. Remember earlier I said that writing essays was like baking a many-tiered cake when you had to keep both form and content in mind? Well, your essays show that you have done that difficult work of making your essays both well-structured and about topics that matter to you. Take one minute to give yourself a silent congratulations. You might pat yourself on the back or give yourself a mental high-five or a silent cheer. Ready? Okay go!" The room was filled with vigorous silent celebration.

After a minute I gave the signal to stop. I eyed the writers seriously. "And so your accomplishments show you are ready to take the next huge step forward."

Describe the differences between personal and persuasive essays, focusing on the reader.

"Up till now you have been writing about your own personal opinions, which no one can really disagree with. It's like each one of you making a cake and saying 'I love this cake.' No one can say, 'No way! That's not true!' In the same way, when you write a personal essay about your personal opinions no one can *really* argue against those personal opinions and say 'No way! That's not true!' If I say that my father is my most important teacher, no one can *really* tell me I'm wrong. That's how I feel so it's true for me.

"But now we are going to make the leap from writing personal opinions to writing persuasive opinions that you want everyone to believe are true about the world. It's kind of like you're going to go from saying, 'I love this cake,' to taking a risk and saying, 'This is the best cake in the entire world!' If you say, 'This is the best cake in the entire world' anyone could say, 'No way! That's not true!' There's risk involved when you declare something is true in general and not just true for you. That's how persuasive essay writing is. When you write persuasive essays, you are writing about opinions that you think are true about the world and trying to get other people to believe it too. And that means anyone could say, 'No way! That's not true!' to your persuasive essays."

◆ COACHING

You may be asking yourself, "Will my students really want to have a silent celebration? Will they really want to give themselves mental high-fives?" We suggest you try it. You may find that the chance to validate themselves and expend a little energy is just the thing to get your students engaged in the lesson and rallied for the work ahead, as well as, of course, reinforcing the idea to students that they should be proud of themselves.

"So today I want to teach you that when you are writing persuasive essays you need to be brave. You need to be willing to take risks and develop strong opinions that others could disagree with."

TEACHING

Provide more explanation about the process of turning a personal opinion into a persuasive opinion.

"You be researchers and watch while I show you how another student, Yvette, turned her personal opinion into a persuasive one. Pay careful attention to what Yvette did so that you'll be able to try this in a few minutes.

"So this was Yvette's personal essay thesis: 'It's hard for me to be a good friend.'" As I spoke I held up a piece of construction paper with Yvette's thesis written on it.

"So to make it a persuasive thesis, first she revised it so it could be one that lots of people could state, not just her. So she crossed off the part about herself." I crossed out the "for me" so now the statement read, "It's hard to be a good friend."

"Then Yvette asked herself if other people could disagree with her about that. And she thought that some people might disagree with her and say that it isn't hard to be a good friend. And then she asked herself if this was a thesis that she wanted other people to believe. And she realized she did. She *did* want people to think that it is hard to be a good friend. So she decided this was a good start for a persuasive thesis."

Debrief quickly, pointing out the replicable steps you have taken that you want all writers to follow.

"Writers, do you see how Yvette took out the parts of her thesis statement that were just about her and pictured lots of people saying the opinion to help her to make a thesis that could be stated by many people? Give me a nod if you noticed that." I watched the writers nod. "Then, do you notice how she made sure she had a brave statement by checking to see if others could disagree with it?" Again the writers nodded. "And did you notice that last she checked that this was a thesis she wanted others to believe?"

ACTIVE ENGAGEMENT

Involve writers in helping you turn your personal thesis into a persuasive one.

"Okay, so now you'll get a chance to try it. I'm hoping you can help me turn my personal essay thesis into a persuasive one.

"So here's my thesis:" (I held it up on a piece of construction paper).

My father is my most important teacher.

"Remember that first you'll want to help me to revise my personal opinion so that it's an opinion that could be stated by many people, not just me. Next you'll want to check that the opinion is persuasive by making sure that it is an opinion that others could disagree with. If not, keep working on it so it is a brave and bold thesis. And then make sure that opinion is one that you want other people to believe. So, will you study this for a minute and think about how you would revise it? You might even squeeze your brain to think of more than one way to revise it." I gave the writers a minute to look at my personal thesis statement and think.

"Thumbs up when you have a way. Okay, turn and tell your partner. Try to say the thesis a few different ways until it feels exactly right to you."

Convene writers and highlight what you heard, choosing to show an example that you want others to follow.

"Writers, will you turn back to me? I'm going to tell you one way I heard people revising this and if you and your partner did that please nod and put a thumb up.

"Okay, so first I heard people cross out words like *I, me, mine, my.*" I crossed out the word *my* each time it appeared in the thesis. "So then the thesis said 'father is most important teacher.' And then I saw some of you say the revised thesis could then be, 'Fathers are the most important teachers,' but then you were shaking your heads and saying that wasn't a thesis you wanted people to believe. And you were totally right to think that. So then Stephen told his partner Lilly that he thought maybe a good start for a persuasive thesis could be, 'Parents are the most important teachers.' Thumbs up if you were thinking something like that too."

LINK

Set kids up to develop persuasive thesis statements.

"Writers, you've given me some great help in turning my personal essay thesis into a persuasive one. Now you'll spend part of the workshop today doing that same work for your own personal essay thesis. Today will be a little different because you'll all stay here and work right in the meeting area to develop persuasive thesis statements. By the end of today, you'll start working to create your boxes-and-bullets plan for your persuasive essay and hand it in to me. So, one tip I want to give you as you are working today to turn your personal thesis statements to persuasive is that you will probably think of reasons to support your persuasive thesis as you try to develop one that feels just right. Most writers do this and it's another way to check that you have a strong persuasive thesis statement. Okay, let's get started turning our personal thesis statements into persuasive."

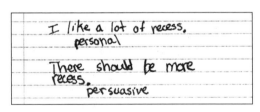

FIG. 16–1   Andrew's personal to persuasive opinion

Providing Children with Both Support and Enrichment

TODAY YOU'LL WANT TO SPEND a few minutes watching your students as they get started and taking careful note of who seems to be working productively and who might be stuck. If you have a group of writers who all seem to need a little extra support with this work, you can gather them into a section of the meeting area and let them know that sometimes you, too, get stuck when trying to develop a thesis. Then you might let them know that one strategy that helps you is to pull out the web you made of what you wanted to say about your topic and look it over again, and this time think about what you want to say about it that you want all people to believe. *(continues)*

MID-WORKSHOP TEACHING   **Strategies Writers Use to Generate Persuasive Opinion**

"Writers, can I have your eyes and attention? I want to give you another strategy for generating persuasive opinions. There are some common ways that writers state their theses, and trying out these ways can help you state strong opinions. I made a list of ways that I have noticed."

Persuasive Thesis Starters

People should/should not . . .

_____ are the best/worst _____

It is important that . . .

Some people think . . . but I think . . .

"I want you to watch me try out some of these ways and come up with a quick list of persuasive theses. I'm going to stay on my topic and keep thinking about parents as teachers. So, for the first sentence starter on our list, instead of saying people, I'll say parents. So parents should . . . read to their kids. Parents should . . . talk to their kids. Parents should . . . teach their kids right from wrong." I jotted these down as I said them. "Did you see how I stayed on the topic I care about and thought about what people—or parents—should do to form a thesis? These might not all be so great, but the point is I'm going to keep pushing and pushing myself until I hit on a thesis that feels exactly like what I want to say.

> - People should not steel
> - Birthdays are the best
> - Friends should usually help eachother out.
> - It is important that family helps you out.
> - Some people think that you can only slick your hair back in special acasions, but I say, you can do any time.

> Friends should help eachother out for many reasons. There is one exception to that though, if its not a good thing your doing, your friends should not help you. But in most kases your friends should help you out. For example if you have to get somewere and your friend takes you there, that is helping eachother. As you can see, friends should help eachother out if it's ok.

FIG. 16–2   Andrew writing off of persuasive opinion sentence starters and then writing long about one

(continues)

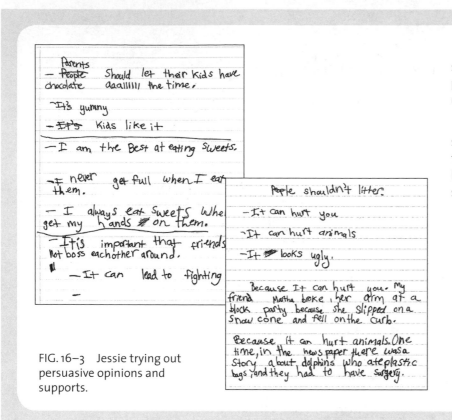

FIG. 16–3   Jessie trying out persuasive opinions and supports.

"Okay, quickly in your head, think of your topic—the territory of your writing—and say in your mind, 'People should . . . ,' and try to fill in that answer with whatever pops into your head first. Thumbs up when you have thought of a thesis." I waited until thumbs popped up.

"Okay, if you liked what popped into your head, jot it down. Otherwise try another strategy. Keep squeezing your brain to try out different theses on your topic until you feel, 'Yes! That's what I want to say about my topic!' Okay, you have a few minutes left to work on coming up with a persuasive thesis, and then we'll work on making sure you can support whatever persuasive thesis you choose. Get to it!"

Then you can get the writers to pull out their webs and look across these, thinking about what they want to say about the topic that they want all people to believe. You might offer a few suggestions and voiceovers to get them involved in studying their webs, giving comments such as, "So if you were thinking before that 'You Love Being an Only Child,' now maybe you could write about how 'Only Children are Lucky.' Or if you wrote before about how 'My Dog is My Best Friend,' maybe now you can write about how 'Pets are the Best Friends Kids Can Have.' Pushing writers toward these simpler theses may make you feel a little uneasy, but for writers who tend to have difficulty, working to support and gather evidence for a thesis is challenging work in and of itself. Providing the extra support of a less complicated thesis is likely to set the writer up for future success in developing a supportive essay.

On the other hand, there will also be writers for whom the work of developing a thesis feels comfortable and they can produce a relatively strong persuasive thesis fairly quickly. When you see this, you'll want to gather a group and ratchet up the level of the work. One way to raise the level of thesis writing is to push writers to use precise language. For example, you might say to the group, "These thesis statements show that you are grappling with hugely important ideas about the world and trying to wrap your arms around them. For those kinds of complicated thoughts it can help to speak in metaphor." After giving this tip, you might show an example of how to speak in metaphor, telling them that to you, loss is a thief, your best friend is like a warm blanket, and jealousy between friends is like a pair of scissors, cutting them apart. To support students even further, you can offer pictures of images and objects that are commonly used as symbols; a suitcase, for example, or a snake, or a knotted rope. You could charge students with finding their own metaphors that help them find the words to express their complicated feelings. Don't worry if you hear students start offering metaphors that seem terribly clichéd to you. Be prepared to welcome these approximations. This is likely their first entry into this work, and they need time and repeated practice to grasp the subtle nuances of doing it well. Encourage their efforts and keep offering examples and help them to transfer speaking in metaphors to the work they do in reading workshop and across the content areas. ("King George is a dark cloud over the colonies!" "The character Fox is a pair of scissors cutting Magpie and Dog apart!") Across the curriculum, you'll want to keep offering opportunities to think and talk and write metaphorically to all of your students. Before long you'll be astounded by your students' level of interpretive thinking.

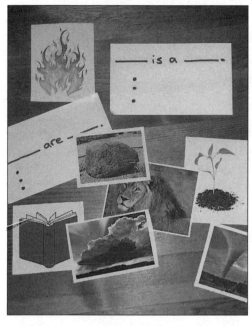

FIG. 16–4

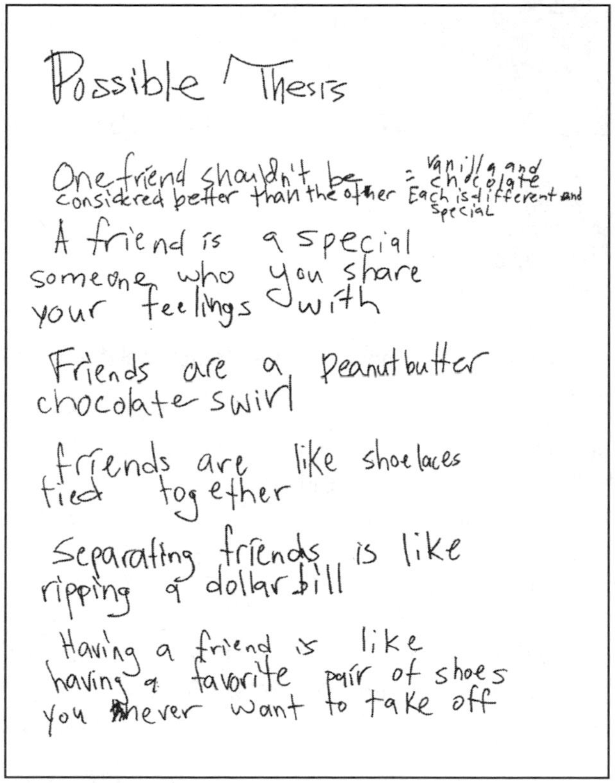

Possible Thesis

One friend shouldn't be = vanilla and chocolate
considered better than the other Each is different and special

A friend is a special
someone who you share
your feelings with

Friends are a peanutbutter
chocolate swirl

friends are like shoelaces
tied together

Separating friends is like
ripping a dollar bill

Having a friend is like
having a favorite pair of shoes
you never want to take off

FIG. 16–5   To push students to take on the challenge of trying out different metaphors to develop a thesis, I often show an older student's work to give them a vision of what this work can look like. This was done by Laura in fifth grade.

Crafting Reasons with Audience in Mind

Convene writers and compliment them on how they are already starting to think of reasons to support their theses as they develop them.

"Writers, can I have your eyes and attention? I know we are starting our share a little earlier than normal, but you have one more piece of important work to do before the end of today's workshop. I'm noticing something really important and exciting about your work today and it is this: you are thinking about whether you can come up with reasons as another way of checking to make sure that your persuasive thesis will work. This is so smart of you and actually, this is what people who are best at making arguments actually do.

"Researchers say that when you develop your thesis, it's almost like you are going through the process of creating the whole essay. You need to imagine how it might go to make sure it will work. So you need to ask yourself: Do I have reasons to support that? Do I have evidence? And if the answers are yes, then you know you are on the right track."

Let writers know that the best thesis statements and reasons work to convince a particular audience. Let them practice this work by involving them in looking over a set of reasons and deciding which of two possible audiences each reason is most likely to convince.

"But I want to give you one other tip that researchers have found leads to the best essays. Here it is: When you are selecting reasons to support your persuasive essay, you want to think about who your particular audience is and then select reasons that are designed especially to convince that particular audience. So let's try out some of that work for a bit. I'm going to show you a thesis statement and two different possible audiences for that piece."

School uniforms are terrible!

Parents

Kids

"So, if this writer was trying to convince kids that school uniforms are terrible, she would likely have very different reasons than if she were trying to convince parents. I'm going to show you a few of the reasons that the writer came up with to support this thesis. Would you work with a partner and figure out if that reason would be more convincing to kids or more convincing to parents? And could a couple of you come up here and work with me?"

Paul Deane, who heads the research department for ETS let us in on an interesting idea when we met with him during a joint project between the Teachers College Reading and Writing Project, ETS, and the Joint Council of the Chiefs of States. Paul asserted that the process of creating a thesis statement requires almost thinking out the entire essay, that you need to, in a sense, plan how your essay will go as you are developing your thesis to make sure it will work. And your thesis needs to anticipate and take into account the counterarguments others may make. Watch for how we lay the beginning steps for that work with the students.

School uniforms are terrible because they don't let you express yourself.

School uniforms are terrible because they are expensive.

School uniforms are terrible because they are not preparing kids for the real world.

School uniforms are terrible because they don't look good on every kid.

Highlight the work that one group of writers did as a way of sharing answers.

"So writers, here's what the group up here came up with. Take a look and see if you agree or not.

School uniforms are terrible.

Parents

School uniforms are terrible because they are expensive.

School uniforms are terrible because they are not preparing kids for the real world.

Kids

School uniforms are terrible because they don't let you express yourself.

School uniforms are terrible because they don't look good on every kid.

"Writers, the group up here was thinking that kids probably wouldn't care that much if uniforms were expensive but parents would care *a lot*. And let's say that parents thought uniforms were a good thing because it would be easier just to have your kids' clothes all ready to go without having to think about it.

"Well, then letting parents know that uniforms are expensive might make them less likely to want them. It's like the reason against uniforms would be even stronger than the parents' reasons for uniforms so they'd be more convinced to believe the writer! Were the rest of you thinking that as well?

"And the group up here was thinking that parents might not care as much as kids that uniforms might not let you express yourself. Do you agree?" Heads nodded.

Get writers starting to consider the particular audience for their piece and develop reasons to convince that particular audience.

"So writers, you know how to select reasons that support your thesis. You know how to make strong boxes-and-bullets plans. But now I want to raise the level of your work by telling you that you need to first think of what audience you are trying to convince and then think of reasons that would be convincing to that particular audience. This is not easy work. Help each other today. Check your reasons with a partner and see if your partner agrees that they will be convincing to your particular audience. You'll have more time to work on this tonight at home and you'll come in tomorrow and hand in your boxes-and-bullets plan to me first thing in the morning. Okay, you have a lot of work to do—Let's get going!"

Notice here that I'm subtly raising the notion of counterargument, working to plant the notion in kids' minds that others could object to their opinion and they can craft reasons that can already anticipate and meet these objections. Explicit discussion of counterargument will come a bit later in, but for now the seed is planted.

MOVING FROM PERSONAL TO PERSUASIVE

Writers, tonight you will work like the dickens on your plan for your essay until it is right. Come in tomorrow with your boxes and bullets written down because you'll hand in the paper first thing so I can check it. If I were going to create a solid plan for convincing my particular audience of my thesis, I would make a note to myself about who my audience might be. I'm going to actually write down in my notebook who I want my audience to be so I can remember that when I start working tonight. You might have more than one audience in mind right now. You might be thinking, "There are two possible audiences that I want to convince!" That's okay. Tonight you can try out two different boxes-and-bullets plans, one for each audience and you can see which feels better. Think about which one will lead to a stronger essay and for which one you think you will be able to gather the best evidence. It's like we're getting ready to start building again and tonight you're making the frames! Boxes-and-bullets plans for your persuasive essays due tomorrow!

Inquiry into Persuasive Essay

TOO OFTEN, STUDENTS CAN MISS the connection between next steps in learning and what has come before. They can tend to regard new learning as brand-new rather than see how it relates to what they already know. When this happens, they lose the chance to transfer and apply what they know to new work. It is our job as teachers to make sure that students see the connections from one day to the next, from one subject to another, and to make those connections explicit in ways that allow students to draw on all they know to help them with the learning at hand.

Today's work is designed to support just that sort of transference. At this point in the unit, students have gone through the process of creating personal essays, and they are poised to begin developing their persuasive essays. Rather than remind them of the process of creating essays, this session aims to raise the level of cognitive demand placed on students, laying the onus for heavy lifting on them.

So today you will involve your writers in an inquiry into a section of a persuasive essay, and students will notice what is similar to what they already have learned. If you are familiar with the third grade opinion-writing unit, *Changing the World*, you may remember the inquiry session that pushes students to notice how all they have learned in writing persuasive speeches can be applied when writing other kinds of opinion pieces, such as petitions. Students ultimately come to see that certain writing elements undergird any kind of opinion writing. This inquiry will help them to come to similar understandings, seeing that all essay writing is built on the same foundational elements.

By the end of today, your students will begin to develop their persuasive essays and start to take themselves through the process of creating an essay with even greater independence. You will provide the deadline—three days to construct a draft. (This means that your students will come into workshop with a complete draft that can be edited on the fourth day so you can be sure they will be getting to try out that work.) As your writers move off, galvanized to begin their work, you will want to support their independence. Rather than stopping to answer questions, be sure that you have laid out all materials they may possibly need in clearly accessible places. Have a pile of folders near a bucket

IN THIS SESSION, you'll teach students that writers transfer all they know about one genre of writing to another genre. Writers ask themselves, "What is similar about personal essay writing and persuasive essay writing?"

GETTING READY

✔ Section of persuasive text copied on chart paper (see *No Uniforms!* on the CD-ROM) 💿

✔ Student writing materials

✔ Chart paper with the title: "Moves Persuasive Essay Writers Make That Are Also Used in Personal Essay Writing"

✔ Construction paper and manila folders for students to use to create files (if desired) as they start to gather and organize the evidence for their persuasive essays

✔ Anchor chart: "Opinion Writers"

✔ Your work plan from writing a personal essay

✔ Students' work plans from writing personal essays

✔ Two pieces of persuasive writing for writers to use as mentors while doing homework

COMMON CORE STATE STANDARDS: W.4.1, W.4.4, W.4.5, W.4.10, RI.4.2, SL.4.1, L.4.1, L.4.2, L.4.3

of markers so students can set up their files. Make sure the loose-leaf paper tray is brimming. Post your own work plan so students can refer to it for guidance. And you might also give out copies of the mentor piece used in the inquiry so that students can use this piece as a guide as they write. Students will be fully enabled to develop their persuasive essays if the room environment is set up to support independence.

"At its heart, today's work is about trusting your students and raising the level of cognitive demand."

At its heart, today's work is about trusting your students and raising the level of cognitive demand. In the previous bend of the unit, you took the students through the process step by step so you could be sure they would understand each part. You were like a ski coach on a mountain asking students to watch as you skied from a rock to a tree and then let them try that step, guiding their progress. But there comes a time when the instructor takes the class back to the top of the mountain and says, "You're ready to try out all you know. Go for it!" Today you will bring your class back to the top of the mountain, the starting point, and watch as they use all they know to take themselves through the process. And like the ski instructor you can have every confidence in their ability to do so. In your every word and action you will convey the key message: Go for it!

Inquiry into Persuasive Essay

CONNECTION

Gather writers and let them know that while some have been questioning how persuasive essay writing is different than personal essay writing, it is also important to ask how it is the same.

"Writers, now that you have your thesis statements for your persuasive essays, you are ready to start developing them. Many of you have been asking me: How are persuasive essays different than personal essays? Now, this is an interesting question, but I think it is even more interesting to think about how they are the same."

Ask writers to remind themselves of what they have already learned about essay writing.

"You have learned so much over the course of writing your personal essays and now you can push yourself to think about how much of what you have learned can help you do this new work. So right now, think about what you know about writing essays.

"When you have thought of one thing that you've learned, put a thumb up." I watched as many of the writers put thumbs up. "Okay, turn and tell a partner!"

"You need to have reasons and give evidence," Alex said eagerly to his partner.

"Right, I thought of that, too. And you can give stories as evidence and lists," Hannah said.

"And also you need to write an introduction and conclusion that gets the reader to care," Alex added.

Let writers know that today the class will participate in an inquiry into what is similar between personal and persuasive essay writing.

After a minute, I convened the class. "Okay, writers. So you have learned a ton about writing personal essays. So now you are ready to ask yourselves, 'How much of what we have learned can help us write persuasive essays?' So today we'll do an inquiry."

Much of the research on expert vs. novice writers has found that expert writers are strategic and plan before writing while novice writers simply tell the content. Here we are working to strengthen the likelihood of the transference and application of previous work by getting the students to put that foremost in their minds.

✤ **Name the question that will guide the inquiry.**

"You'll study a section of persuasive writing and ask yourself, 'What do persuasive essay writers do that is similar to personal essay writers?' Keep that question in mind as you listen to the beginning of this piece."

TEACHING AND ACTIVE ENGAGEMENT

Read a section of persuasive text to students and let them look for what is similar to what they have already learned to do when writing their personal essays.

I uncovered a piece of chart paper on which I had copied a section of a persuasive essay, "No Uniforms!" and began to read.

No Uniforms!

Imagine everyone in the world looking exactly the same. Well, if you go to a school with school uniforms that is what you see! School uniforms are terrible! School uniforms are terrible because they make everyone look the same, they are expensive, and they do not allow you to express your-self. Everyone should try to stop school uniforms and get schools to go back to letting kids wear their own clothes!

The first reason why everyone should think school uniforms are terrible is because they make you look the same as everyone else. You will look the same as everyone else on picture day. You will look the same as everyone else on field trips. You will even look the same as everyone else on your birthday. You will never look special. Also, if everyone looks the same, people can get mixed up. For example, my friend Cassie told me that last week she was calling down the hallway to our other friend Emily. "Emily, Emily!" she kept calling, but the person didn't turn around. Then she did and it turns out it wasn't even Emily! This shows that wearing uniforms can make everyone look the same and that is a reason why they are bad.

"Writers, are you thinking about that question? What has the writer of this persuasive piece done that you have already learned to do in your personal essay? Think for a minute. When you see one thing you notice, put a thumb up." I gave the students a minute to think until most thumbs were up. "Okay, turn and talk."

"The writer has a thesis and gives reasons," Abby said to Emma.

"Where do you see that? Give evidence from the piece," I coached her, gesturing to the piece to indicate she should point to specific lines.

"Um . . . right where it says 'school uniforms are terrible!'" Abby pointed. "That's the thesis. And then the reasons come right after that."

"And the next part is about the first reason," Emma added, also pointing. "There's the transition phrase. We learned that."

"Keep going and see what else you notice. Remember to give specific evidence from the text," I encouraged them and moved away to listen in on another conversation.

Convene writers and elicit moves they have noticed that are similar to moves they have learned while writing personal essays. Chart these moves.

"Writers, can I stop you for a minute? I'm hearing about so many moves that you are noticing that are similar to ones that you noticed when writing personal essays. I'm thinking we should get some of those down on a chart. So, here's our chart with the title: 'Moves persuasive essay writers make that are also used in personal essay writing.' Who has something to add to that chart?"

Because of what I had heard her saying, I called on Abby. "The writer has a thesis!" Abby said. "Like right there, it says 'school uniforms are terrible.' That's what the whole piece is about." I gave her thumbs up for remembering to point to specific text evidence, and wrote down her observation.

Then I called on Ethan who said, "The writer has reasons. But also I think the reasons might be in an order because it says 'the first reason.'"

"Hmm, . . ." I said, nodding. "So it seems like the writer may have made some deliberate decisions about how to order reasons. Did you learn to do that?"

They all nodded. "Take a second to look carefully at what the reasons are for the writer's thesis," I coached them. "Where in the piece do you see the reasons? Make sure you give specific text evidence like Abby and Ethan did to back up what you are saying." I listened in quickly as the writers spoke then jotted fast what Ethan had said.

I continued calling on writers and before long we had constructed this chart:

LINK

Get writers ready to start developing their own persuasive pieces.

"So writers, here's what I'm thinking. You worked so hard on your personal essays and it seems like a lot of what you have learned can help you to write your persuasive essays. So right now, take a minute and look over your boxes-and-bullets plan for your persuasive essay." I watched while the writers did this. "Okay, writers, I am going to tell you right now that you will have three days—today, tomorrow, and the day after tomorrow—to develop your persuasive essays. After the third day you must have your piece in class totally drafted and ready to be edited.

You'll need to decide how best to balance listening in to writers with charting comments in a way that keeps the lesson moving along. Some teachers have used these turn-and-talk times as assessment opportunities and have listened in to student conversations, deciding to jot in front of the students when they turn back. Other teachers have used the turn-and-talks as a chance to jot quickly on the chart, deciding that the student work done today will be the best assessment of their understanding. Still, others have combined these approaches, charting at times, listening in during other times. We encourage you to find the balance that is best for the needs of your class.

Moves Persuasive Essay Writers
Make That Are Also Used in
Personal Essay Writing

- State a thesis

Moves persuasive essay writers make that are also used in personal essay writing

- State a thesis
- Give logically ordered reasons
- Support reasons with a variety of evidence
  - mini stories, lists
- Start off by letting the reader know that this topic is important
- Let reader know what is coming in the essay
- Use transition words and phrases to connect parts

FIG. 17–1

"So right now, if I were going to get started on making my persuasive essay, I would look back at my To-Do list that I made for my personal essay and I would also use everything I know about writing essays to help me. Will you take a minute and think in your heads of what you plan to do today when you leave the meeting area? How will you make sure your draft will be ready in three days? Maybe you will start by quickly jotting down a work plan for each day. Maybe you will start by setting up folders to help you gather evidence. Maybe you will start by making a flash-draft and then working to make it better and better. Give me a thumbs-up when you know your first step." I waited until I saw the writers with their thumbs up.

"Okay, we're going to get started. What you do today won't be perfect, but trust yourself to dive in and know what you will start working on tomorrow to make it better and better. I'll be watching and admiring how you are using all you know to do. Go for it!"

Notice the feeling that is conveyed to students in this link—that message of "Go for it!"—this is where we turn the kids loose and trust them. They may still make mistakes and produce work that is not perfect. That's fine and will let you know where your teaching needs to go next. Today is an assessment for you of your own progress as well as theirs. You can see how well you have pushed your writers to be independent and internalize the work they have learned over the past few lessons. Take a few minutes to observe students, taking note of your own teaching and how well it has transferred.

TO DO List!
• Find some one that disagres with you and convice them. (Robyn)!
• Find a expert that agrees with you.
• Rewrite, find or remeber examples.
• Write intro + clution P.

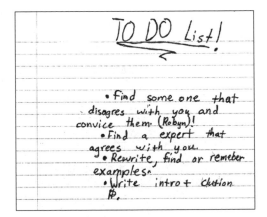

FIG. 17–2 Jonathan's To-Do list for his persuasive essay

TO DO LIST
•Make mini-stories
•Talk to kids who agree and disagree
•Make supporting paragraph
•Get details for supporting paragraphs
•Make conclusion paragraph
•Get details for conclusion paragraph

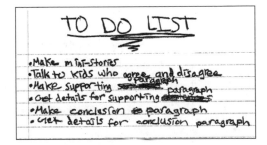

FIG. 17–3 Sam's To-Do list

Being an only child is great because
x You don't have to share your parents on vacation.
x You don't have to share your parents after-school
x You don't have to share your parents on holidays.
x You don't have to share your parents on your birthday
x You don't have to

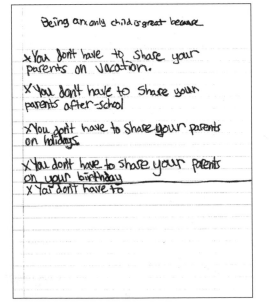

FIG. 17–4 Sam's thesis statement and supporting reasons

A fourth and fifth graders should be able to go out to lunch because it prepares them for when they get older. ~~and have to buy food~~ and other things

Possible lists
Kids that go out to lunch learn how to...
• buy food and other items,
cross the street,
not loss money and manage it.

It's not fair!
My friend Sam gos to Poly Prep and he can't go out to lunch. My friend Jimmy go's to PS 107 and he can't go out to lunch. My cousin who in high school can't evan go out to lunch.

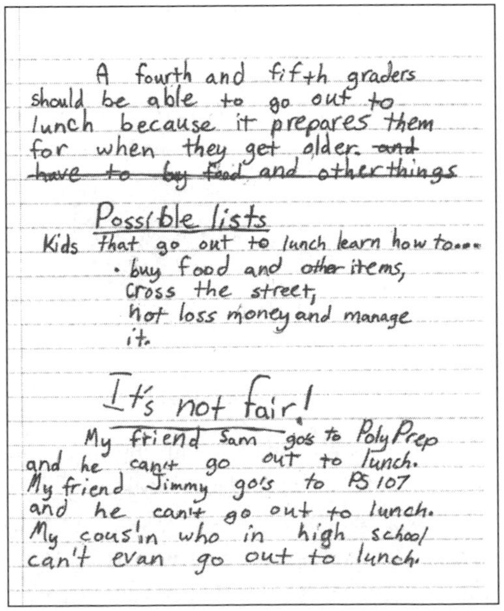

FIG. 17–5 Jonathan's collection of possible lists for his draft

Using Data to Guide Your Small-Group Instruction

THE VERY EXCITING THING about conferring and small-group work at this point in the unit is how much data you have to guide you. You know exactly what each of your writers needs. So as they get settled into working, plan ahead for some predictable small groups. You might reread their published pieces looking for patterns and trends and thinking to yourself, "If I see . . . then I can teach. . . ." Then you can round up a group of writers who would benefit from that work and involve them all. Some possibilities:

◆ **Students who are still having difficulty in creating boxes-and-bullets plans that are strong.** For these writers, you might look back at the kind of conferring you did in Session 6 to help students create bullets that feel supportive, not overlapping and parallel. You also might try to help this teaching transfer even more strongly for writers now through physicality. So for writers who still may be writing reasons that do not feel equally weighted, you might involve writers in becoming human scales with their arms out and show them how to "weigh" reasons. Give writers an example of two reasons that are not parallel. So you might say to them, "If I say parents are important teachers because they teach their children what they need to learn before they get to school and because they feed their kids dinner, are those reasons equal in importance? Are they equal in weight?" Then you can demonstrate becoming a scale yourself and showing writers how you weigh that evidence, tipping yourself over to show how unequal these reasons are. "Is feeding kids dinner as important as teaching them all they need to know before they get to school?" you can ask, showing them how one side of your human scale is all the way down and the other is up. "They're not equally weighted." Then you can give writers other examples and turn them to looking over and "weighing" their own reasons.

◆ **Students whose evidence is not angled to support their reasons.** For these writers, you might prepare two separate anecdotes and involve them in underlining what parts in the anecdote support the thesis and reason. Then you can ask the writers if you should cut this one or revise it. Have them try the work

---

MID-WORKSHOP TEACHING
Using an Anchor Chart to Guide Our Process

"Writers, can I stop you for a moment? I'm admiring all of you diving in and trying this work. Some of you are busy collecting stories and others have decided to just start at the top and try to write an introduction. This is brave, exciting work. I want to show you another tool that I use to take myself through the process of developing an essay independently that I think can help you. I listened to what you all said you had already learned

> **Opinion Writers:**
> 1. THINK about a topic to explore
> 2. PLAN how the writing might go
> 3. GATHER and ORGANIZE evidence
> 4. DRAFT
> 5. REVISE
>   ☐ Is evidence supportive?
>   ☐ Did I make my reader care?
>   ☐ Is the piece cohesive?
> 6. EDIT for audience

FIG. 17–6

about writing essays and turned it into an anchor chart that you can refer to in order to help yourselves. So why don't you take a look at it right now. Everything on it will seem very familiar to you. Ask yourself if you are taking yourself through the process in a way that is working for you or if maybe you missed an important step or want to start over in a new way."

---

again on the second anecdote and then involve them in helping you to revise it. You might push them to try this work on one of their own anecdotes with a partner right in front of you so you can watch how they do this work.

◆ **Students who are unsure how to take themselves through the process and seem "stuck."** You can group these writers and show them an anchor chart for this unit, letting them know that they can use this chart as a checklist if they wish.

Then you can get writers started on Step 1 and let them know you will come back in a few minutes to see how they have checked it off.

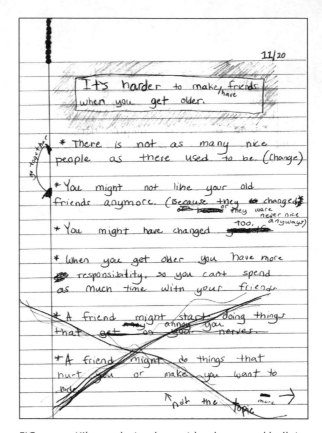

FIG. 17–7 Kika works to plan out her boxes and bullets for her friendship essay and notices overlapping reasons.

Considering What Is Unique to Persuasive Writing

Ask children to reread the persuasive essay, noticing how it is different from a personal essay, and then to discuss what they find.

"Writers, I want to compliment you on how well you are using all you know about essay writing to take yourselves through this process. Knowing how to write personal essays can definitely help you know how to write persuasive. But I want to take a minute and go back to that question that many of you were asking at the start of class, and that is: 'How are persuasive essays different than personal?' There definitely are some differences and it will raise the level of your work if you are very aware of them. So right now, you'll spend a few minutes rereading that persuasive piece we saw at the start of class and this time you'll read it asking yourself, 'How are persuasive essays different from personal essays?' I placed the chart paper with the section of the persuasive essay back up and let the students reread it.

No Uniforms!

Imagine everyone in the world looking exactly the same. Well, if you go to a school with school uniforms that is what you see! School uniforms are terrible! School uniforms are terrible because they make everyone look the same, they are expensive, and they do not allow you to express your-self. Everyone should try to stop school uniforms and get schools to go back to letting kids wear their own clothes!

The first reason why everyone should think school uniforms are terrible is because they make you look the same as everyone else. You will look the same as everyone else on picture day. You will look the same as everyone else on field trips. You will even look the same as everyone else on your birthday. You will never look special. Also, if everyone looks the same, people can get mixed up. For example, my friend Cassie told me that last week, she was calling down the hallway to our other friend Emily. "Emily, Emily!" she kept calling, but the person didn't turn around. Then she did and it turns out it wasn't even Emily! This shows that wearing uniforms can make every-one look the same and that is a reason why you should be against them!

"Okay, writers, what are you thinking? How are persuasive essays different from personal? Share your thoughts with someone at your table. Turn and talk!" The room erupted into conversation.

"Writers, let me share out a bit of what I heard and if you and someone at your table said something similar you can give me a nod or a thumbs-up.

"First of all, I heard you saying that the evidence in a persuasive piece doesn't only come from your own personal experience. You can tell other people's stories, as well, like this writer told her friend's story and some of you were thinking you might even do some research. Thumbs up if you said that."

"I also heard some people talking about the language the writer used. Like this writer talked to the audience and used words like 'everyone' and 'you.' So rather than just talking about yourself, you are talking about and to other people. Thumbs up if you noticed that."

"One last thing I heard you saying that I think is really important. This piece seems to be trying to get the reader to think or act in a certain way. Like this piece really wants you to feel a certain way about uniforms and maybe at the end will want you to act a certain way.

These seem very important to keep in mind, writers, and I'm betting there might be a few other things to notice too. Tonight you'll spend a bit more time looking at some persuasive essays for homework and then tomorrow you will come in prepared to talk about what you are noticing."

Rather than eliciting comments, I'm choosing to highlight what I've heard to make efficient use of time, as the inquiry lesson is typically a little longer than a traditional minilesson, and also so that I can word the observations about persuasive writing precisely.

SESSION 17 HOMEWORK

INQUIRY INTO PERSUASIVE ESSAY

Writers, to write persuasive essays really well, we need to be as immersed in them as we were in personal essays. So tonight I'm going to give you two different persuasive essays. I want you to read them and think about what makes them similar and different from personal essays. Mark up and write all over them and star places that you think might be especially important to talk about with a partner tomorrow. After you read and read and get filled up with persuasive writing, I want you try out writing a flash-draft essay. You've done this before. But now, instead of flash-drafting a personal essay, you'll flash-draft a persuasive one. Use all you know about writing essays to help you! Read these persuasive essays and fill yourself up with everything you see the writers of the persuasive pieces doing and then try it!

Broader Evidence

Dear Teachers,

Today is another day on which we are turning the reins over to you. As your students continue to take themselves through the process of creating essays independently, you can teach into raising the level of that work. Today then, you will help writers to see that when writing persuasive essays, they can gather evidence in order to substantiate what they are saying.

MINILESSON

You will want to give your writers a bit of time to discuss their homework from last night. You might give them a few quick minutes to again assess how well they are meeting their goals. You can invite writers to come to the meeting area and with their copy of the Opinion Writing Checklist, Grades 4 and 5, with their goals circled.

"Take a few minutes to look at your piece against the checklist and see how you've gotten stronger," you might start off. "You have goals marked on your checklist. How does your piece show you are working on those goals? What can you push yourself to do even better? Talk to a partner about what you are noticing!"

Then you can let writers know that these goals are the same when they are writing personal or persuasive essays. Remind writers that while there are key similarities between the two kinds of essays, they have noticed some important differences, and ask them to think over what they noticed about persuasive essays while reading through them last night. Ask them to quickly talk to a partner about these observations. You'll likely hear students offering comments such as, "Persuasive writing makes people want to take action," "Persuasive writers seem to have a more urgent tone," and, "Persuasive writers have a more and different kinds of evidence." You can use what your students are noticing to help you

COMMON CORE STATE STANDARDS: W.4.1.b,c, W.4.5, W.4.10, RI.4.2, RI.4.4, SL.4.1, SL.4.3, L.4.1, L.4.2, L.4.3, L.4.6

set up your teaching point. You might let your writers know that you hear them all discussing how persuasive writers use evidence from the world, not just their own experiences to support what they are saying.

Then you can give your writers the teaching point for today, framing it in a way that is ambitious and provides worthy work for them. You might say, "Today I want to teach you that persuasive writers draw on evidence from the world to convince others. One way to do this is to gather a variety of broad evidence that can apply to lots of people."

After this you might let your writers know that one way you try to gather a variety of broad evidence is to push yourself to gain different types of evidence, such as stories from other people, quotes from experts, and so on. You might show writers how you set up a chart with sections to gather different types of evidence. Then involve writers in watching how you start to fill in one of those sections, the one for other people's stories, with one of your reasons in mind. If, for example, you have a reason like "Parents teach children what they cannot learn in school," you can easily show how you can use stories of others to support this reason, filling in the box with a story like a time a friend of yours showed her children that all animals deserve a proper goodbye by involving her children in planning a funeral for their family bird. You will want to use specifics like your friend's name and show students that the more specific and concrete the facts and details are, the more persuasive they are.

FIG. 18–1   Malik's chart for collecting evidence

For your active involvement, you will want to involve students in taking one of their reasons and thinking about what kinds of broader evidence they might gather to support that reason. You can remind them that thinking about other people's stories is one way to gather evidence from the world and charge them with thinking of a story of something that happened to someone else—a friend, someone on the news—and jot that story down. You can have them turn and share this story with a partner, setting one partner up to tell the story and the other partner to say whether or not it supported the reason.

You can set writers up to go off and continue working, reminding them that creating a chart such as the one you showed them can help to collect a variety of broad evidence. You will also want to let them know that they have today's and tomorrow's writing workshops in which to work before their draft is due. Emphasize the deadline and let writers know that you are sure they will probably be starting to draft at least one of their sections by the end of today's workshop.

CONFERRING AND SMALL-GROUP WORK

For writers who seem ready to be even more deliberate in their selection of which evidence to include in their essay and how, you can work with them on the challenging task of weighing evidence. You might show writers three pieces of evidence that a student in another class gathered to support her persuasive essay thesis, "It's Hard to Be a Good Friend." You can let them know that today you will all work with the writer's first reason, "It's hard to be a good friend because you don't always want to do what your friend wants to do." "Not all evidence is equally powerful," you might tell students. "Some evidence is more powerful than other evidence. Let's say you were going to put this evidence on a big scale. Which of these pieces of evidence do you think would weigh a lot? Which would weigh only a little?"

Three Pieces of Evidence

✓ For example, last Thursday my friend Colin wanted to play checkers and I didn't really want to play. So we played checkers first and then Legos.

✓ Lots of kids in my class have told me about how they don't always want to do what their friends want them to do. Like Matthew didn't want to go outside to play football because he was in the middle of a really good book. But his friends kept asking him so finally he went.

✓ For example, over the summer my friend Colin came over. "Let's play video games!" he said. He was really excited about it and kept hopping up and down. But I didn't want to play video games. "Let's pretend we're spies," I said, but Colin got mad. "No, I want to play video games." "We can't," I lied to Colin. "The Xbox 360 is broken." I felt really bad I lied. I wasn't being a good friend.

Writers can read over the three pieces of evidence, star the evidence they find most powerful, and then explain their decision.

Your writers will likely find the second piece of evidence weighs more than the first, but the third weighs the most. So you might then ask them, "Let's say the writer could only include one of these pieces of evidence. Which would be the *best* to include? Why?"

You might find, as we did when we did this small-group work with students recently, that students see the third piece of evidence as the most powerful because it is more dramatic and gets the reader to feel a stronger emotion. Then you could ask them to look at the evidence they have for their first reason and pretend to weigh it on a scale. Which is the most powerful? Ask them to star that and talk about why they have chosen this evidence as the most powerful. Then you can get them started in making some tough choices. Maybe they will cut other pieces of evidence or need to revise pieces of evidence to bring them up to being as powerful as the starred piece.

MID-WORKSHOP TEACHING

For your mid-workshop, you might highlight some of the work that you did in your small group and conferring, sharing an example of a writer who has weighed evidence, for example. You might let your writers know that some evidence is more powerful than other evidence and explain how one writer ranked her evidence and decided what she would and would not include in her essay. Then you can involve all of your writers in starring pieces of evidence that seem particularly important and convincing, and considering how they will use these in their essays. Let writers know that particularly important pieces of evidence are like secret weapons and so the writers should think carefully about how best to use them. Will they put them right up front in a body paragraph? Will they save a powerful piece of evidence for the end of the essay to

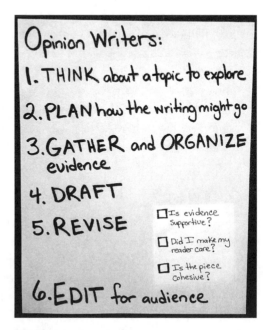

FIG. 18–2

leave the reader with a punch? Is there some evidence they are now thinking they might cut? Charge the writers with considering these questions as they continue taking themselves through the process. Remind them that their deadline is fast approaching and again show writers the anchor chart so they can look and see where in the process they are and where they need to be by the end of the workshop tomorrow.

SHARE

For your share, you might involve writers in checking to see how convincing a section of their writing is by letting a partner rank the section along a convincing continuum: Very Convincing—Somewhat Convincing—Not That Convincing. You can provide writers with index cards that list reasons explaining the choice. So you might give your students cards that say reasons such as: "You have a variety of convincing evidence," "You have some evidence but not all of it is related to your reason," "You don't have that much evidence." You can demonstrate how this might go by ranking a section of the school uniform piece, asking writers how they would rank it and why while you do the same.

> Another reason why you should hate uniforms is because you will not be able to express yourself. For example, all my friends like different colors and they never get to wear the colors they like. We all have to wear the same thing. Uniforms are terrible!

Give your writers time to think and then let them know that you were thinking of ranking this as "Not That Convincing" and ask them if they were thinking along the same lines. Ask your writers why they've made that choice and you'll probably hear that the writer doesn't have very much evidence. "So if this writer wanted to revise, he or she would have to go back and get a variety of extra evidence for this section," you can tell your writers.

Then you can set your writers up to go off and try out this work in partners, reminding them that when they listen to a partner explain why he or she has ranked a section a certain way, the writer should take notes about how to revise it to make it even more convincing.

HOMEWORK

For homework, you will want your students to make action plans and decide what evidence they might still need to gather. Remind writers that they have notes for how to revise the sections of their essay and many of them still need to gather more outside evidence. You can also remind writers that they probably want to have at least some of each kind of evidence on the chart. You can model looking at the chart with your own reasons in mind, considering that for a reason like "Parents teach children what they cannot learn in school," you will probably need quotes from child psychologists saying

FIG. 18–3 Cards used for ranking along a convincing continuum

that parents teach kids to deal with issues like divorce, death, health, and so on. You will want to tell kids that you use an online search engine at home, typing in a phrase like "Parents help kids deal with divorce." You will want to write down your plan showing students how you write "need quotes that parents teach kids to deal with divorce, death, etc.—look online."

You can have your writers jot down their overall action plan for the evening and how they will gather a variety of outside evidence. You will want students to leave their notebooks out at a later point today so that you can check these plans while they are at gym or music, making sure that students are gathering at least one or two types of outside evidence for each of their reasons.

Enjoy!

Lucy, Kelly, and Cory

Connecting Evidence, Reason, and Thesis

IN THIS SESSION, you'll teach students that writers link their evidence to their reasons and thesis statement so that there are no gaps in their logic or reasoning.

GETTING READY

✔ "Transition Phrases to Connect Evidence to Reasons" chart, prewritten (see Teaching)

✔ A body paragraph where all of your evidence is not fully linked back to your reasons and thesis so you can demonstrate how to make it more cohesive

✔ Students' essay drafts, to be brought to the meeting area

✔ Your body paragraph from your personal essay in Session 11 (e.g., "My Father Is My Most Important Teacher"). You will revise this essay during the share to better connect your evidence and reasons. See the CD-ROM for a revised version of this essay. 💿

✔ Students' personal essays from Bend II, to revise during the share

COMMON CORE STATE STANDARDS: W.4.1.b,c, W.4.5, W.4.10, W.5.1.b, RI.4.2, RI.4.5, SL.4.1, SL.4.3, L.4.1, L.4.2, L.4.3

GREAT PERSUASIVE WRITING IS ABOUT RELATIONSHIPS. When all parts of an argument are connected, the reader can clearly trace a line of argument running throughout a text. Evidence in the form of facts and details supports reasons. The reader must see this connection and grasp how the evidence given supports the reason and the opinion. The writer's job is to illuminate that relationship.

We have all witnessed great scenes in literature and film and life where an argument is made to pitch perfection by connecting all of the evidence to such a degree that not a chink shows through. Despite the fact that Atticus Finch lost the trial, I don't know a single reader who was not utterly convinced of Tom Robinson's innocence through Atticus's famous closing argument in *To Kill a Mockingbird*. "To begin with this case should never have come to trial. This case is as simple as black and white. The state has not produced one iota of medical evidence to the effect that the crime Tom Robinson is charged with ever took place," Atticus says at the start of his closing, giving an assertion and supporting it with a reason (Harper Lee 1960, 271). He goes on to shed doubt on the testimony of witnesses, helping the reader to see the connection between each of his assertions, the evidence, and his overall argument that Tom is innocent beyond a reasonable doubt.

Great arguments are made so solid that there is little to no room for doubt to squeeze through so that a reader could dismiss the evidence, or worse, the argument itself.

Today's session aims to give students the essential skill of writing arguments that are cohesive. You will teach students how to explain and unpack their evidence so that the reader clearly sees how it supports their opinion and, ultimately, is persuaded. The Common Core Standards expect that students will use linking words and phrases to connect opinions and reasons, and today you will help your students learn common ways writers connect their evidence to their reasons through transition phrases, helping to lay the foundational steps and helping your writers see that when writing to prove a point, cohesion is key.

Illuminating the Relationship between Evidence, Reason, and Thesis Statement

CONNECTION

Return to the building metaphor as a way to communicate to students that there can be cracks in both buildings and drafts of essays. Tell students that today they will learn to go back and seal up cracks by linking their evidence to their thesis statements.

"Writers, yesterday I passed that new building on the corner of my block, the one I watched being built for so long. This time when I walked by I saw something that I hadn't seen before. A crack. A small crack on one wall of the building. Maybe the builders didn't notice it. But I did. And as I stopped to stare at that crack, it reminded me of something hugely important in essay writing. Essays can have cracks, too.

"A crack in an essay is a place where the evidence is not as convincing as it could be. A crack in an essay is a place where someone can read it and say, 'I don't believe that part. That doesn't prove your opinion is true. It doesn't say why or how your opinion is true.' The same way no builder wants his final building to have even one crack, no essayist wants his final essay to have even one place where someone could doubt his opinion."

❖ **Name the teaching point.**

"So today I am going to teach you one of the greatest and most important responsibilities an essayist has: to leave no cracks. One way that essayists make sure that every part of their essay is sealed tightly together is to make sure to link every piece of evidence directly to their thesis statement."

TEACHING

Explain that you have noticed that there are some common transition phrases that essayists use to link their evidence to their reason and thesis statement.

"I have been reading a lot of essays to help me learn how to write my own, and I have noticed that there are some common ways that essayists link each piece of evidence to their reason and their thesis statement. I made a list of what I have noticed." I uncovered a chart of transition phrases.

Notice the memorable sentence: "Essays can have cracks, too." This short sentence is designed to stick in a reader's mind and highlight the crux of the work.

"I'm going to reread my body paragraph I wrote yesterday and check that I have linked each piece of evidence back to my reason and thesis statement. You read along with me and look for places where I haven't connected my evidence back to my thesis. Give me a polite little thumbs down if you see a crack. Then, in a minute you'll try this with your piece."

Demonstrate how you go back and add transition phrases after each piece of evidence to link it back to the reason and thesis statement. Deliberately make mistakes as you do this and model fixing them.

"I'm going to read the draft of my first body paragraph that I wrote yesterday. This is the body paragraph I wrote to support the reason that parents teach their children what they need to succeed before school starts. I am going to reread my body paragraph and stop after each piece of evidence. Then I will use one of the transition phrases to link that evidence back to my reason and thesis." I uncovered a piece of chart paper with my drafted body paragraph.

> Parents are their children's best teachers. One reason that parents are their children's best teachers is because they teach their children what they need to succeed before they get to school. For instance, in order to teach their kids manners, they teach children to say please and thank you. Joyce Lollar, from babycenter.com, says kids pick up good or bad habits by age two. In addition, parents teach kids other things—like their letters and numbers—before school. For instance, my friend Natalie used to play with magnetic letters with her sons and make the sounds of the letters for fun and her sons knew all of their letters by the time they were two. So parents teach children what they need to succeed before they get to school and that is one reason they are the best teachers for their kids.

"Let me start reading my draft paragraph. 'Parents are their children's best teachers. One reason that parents are their children's best teachers is because they teach their children what they need to succeed before they get to school. For instance, in order to teach their kids manners, they teach children to say please and thank you. Joyce Lollar, from baby-center.com, says kids pick up good or bad habits by age two.' Okay, so let me stop there. I need to link this piece of evidence back to my overall claim. Let me try using one of the phrases from the chart. I will try 'this shows that.' I have to write the phrase, then explain how this piece of evidence exactly supports my thesis statement that parents are their children's most important teachers. So, I could write, 'Joyce Lollar, from babycenter.com, says that kids pick up good or bad habits by age two. This shows that teaching kids to be polite is really important.'" The students looked puzzled and some had thumbs down.

I stopped. "Wait, that doesn't link the evidence back to my *reason*, right? I need to link back to the reason that parents teach kids what they need to succeed before they get to school. Let me try again. This time I will first think of the reason and keep it in my mind." I closed my eyes and muttered to myself, "Parents teach kids what they need to succeed before they get to school." I opened my eyes. "Okay, let me try linking my evidence to my reason again. 'Joyce Lollar, from babycenter.com, says that kids pick up good or bad habits by age two. This shows that long before school starts parents are doing important teaching and helping kids learn what they need to succeed in school and after.'"

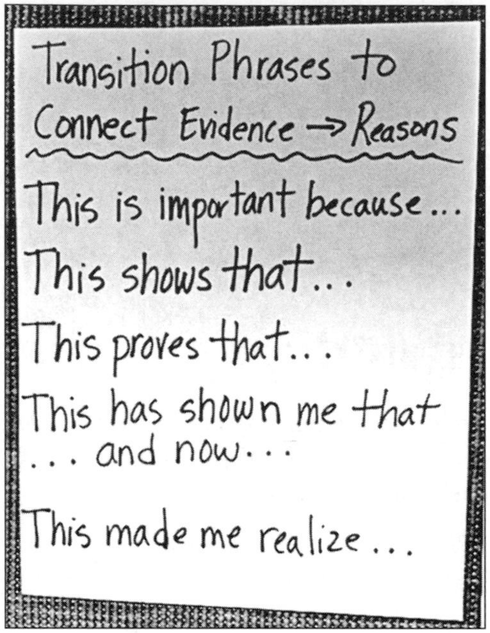

Transition Phrases to Connect Evidence → Reasons

This is important because...

This shows that...

This proves that...

This has shown me that ... and now...

This made me realize...

FIG. 19–1

Debrief quickly, pointing out the replicable steps you have followed that you want all writers to take.

"Writers, do you notice how I reread the section of my essay about one of my reasons and stopped after my first piece of evidence to link it to my reason and thesis statement? I have to keep the reason in mind and make sure that I directly refer back to that reason and the broader claim, too.'"

ACTIVE ENGAGEMENT

Set up writers to practice linking the evidence in their first body paragraph to their reasons and theses.

"Now you will try this. In a minute, you'll work with your first body paragraph to practice this. Just like I did, you will read through the paragraph and stop after each piece of evidence. You will look to make sure there is a link back to your reason and thesis after each piece of evidence. If there is not, you will make a link using one of the transition phrases that essayists use to link evidence to reasons. Right now, will you take out your first body paragraph? Will you reread your paragraph and stop when you come to the first piece of evidence and put your finger on that spot?" I waited until I saw fingers down on papers. "Okay, now you will look to see if you have made a link after that piece of evidence back to your reason and overall claim. Thumbs up if you *have* made a link." Very few thumbs popped up across the rug. "Okay, writers, that means you need to create a link. Look at the chart of transition phrases and decide what phrase you will use. Now bring your first reason into your mind. Close your eyes if it helps. Okay, reread the evidence and then say the phrase you have chosen in your head and link the evidence to your reason. Do that now." I gave them time to do this work.

Set writers up to share their revised paragraphs with a partner.

"Okay, writers, in a minute you'll have a chance to share your revised paragraphs with a partner. Partner 2, you will read your first body paragraph and say the link you made when you get to the end of your first piece of evidence. And Partner 1, you will give a thumbs up if the evidence connects back to the reason and claim and a thumbs down if it doesn't. Help Partner 2 to make the link, if needed. Go to it." The room erupted into conversation.

"So my thesis is that people shouldn't litter," Jessie was saying to her partner Hannah when I pulled up to listen. "And here's what I write: 'One reason people shouldn't litter is because it hurts animals. One example of that is when my mom read me an article about a dolphin who ate plastic and had to have surgery. So that proves it!'"

"Did Jessie connect her evidence back to her reason? Did she explain exactly *how* her evidence proved her reason?" I asked Hannah.

Hannah shook her head. "You didn't exactly say how it proved your reason."

"Maybe try one of the prompts," I coached Jessie.

"Okay, so this shows that . . . 'Animals can get really hurt from litter,'" Jessie said, and Hannah gave her a big thumbs up.

"Try the whole paragraph again, Jessie. Start by saying your thesis. Hannah, you listen to see if Jessie is convincing." I left them to move on to others.

Convene writers and highlight an example of what you heard.

"Writers, this work is far from easy. Jessie thought she had made a solid connection until Hannah pointed out that she hadn't *really* explained how her evidence proved her reason. So Jessie tried out a prompt from the chart and this time she tried to show exactly how the evidence proved her reason. We need to be very careful about this work. Sometimes you think you have made a solid connection, but there's still a crack. Help each other with this work. Use the convincing continuum or just ask a partner, 'Does this part convince you?'"

LINK

Send writers off to continue adding connections between their evidence, reasons, and theses.

"Writers, your drafts are due by the end of today. Use your time wisely." I eyed them seriously. "You need to use every second of your writing time well. So use the system that is best for you to meet the deadline. Get your To-Do lists out and make sure you are getting everything checked off. And remember your greatest responsibility as an essayist when you are drafting and revising your essay: Leave no cracks. Leave no spaces where someone could say, 'Oh that part doesn't prove your opinion.' Link all evidence to your reasons and thesis. I'm going to add this new work to our anchor chart and you can use the anchor chart to help you make sure you have gone through all of the parts of the process. Okay, go to work."

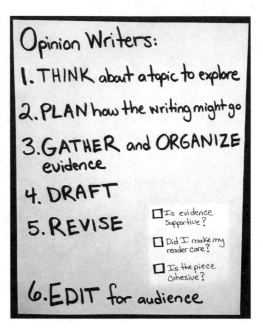

Opinion Writers:
1. THINK about a topic to explore
2. PLAN how the writing might go
3. GATHER and ORGANIZE evidence
4. DRAFT
5. REVISE
   ☐ Is evidence supportive?
   ☐ Did I make my reader care?
   ☐ Is the piece cohesive?
6. EDIT for audience

FIG. 19–2

Conveying Urgency in Meeting Deadlines

THE DEADLINE FOR COMPLETED DRAFTS IS FAST APPROACHING, and you want to make sure that every writer in your room produces an effective essay. You may need to convene the children who simply do not have enough done and help them make plans for how they will use today to be extra productive. Don't hesitate to make decisions for them based on what you see (or don't see) in their folders, notebooks, and/or drafts. Send them off with a clear sense of direction and a lot of urgency! If children really buckle down, they can produce a lot of work in a single day, but they often need us to add some pressure, raising their productivity a few notches. Sometimes it helps if these children all work alongside each other at a table reserved for the "we're racing to get a lot done" kids. Or it might help to give each of these kids a "private office"—a desk set far away from the maddening crowd. You decide.

You will also want to keep in mind critical opinion writing work with which your students may be having difficulty. Part of that work is cohesion. As mentioned previously, the Common Core Standards expect writers to use transition words to create a sense of cohesion in their pieces, and you might need to reinforce lessons you have previously taught related to using transition words. You might gather writers around the chart of transition words and remind them that these words are much like the signs you follow on highways that tell you where to go. In similar ways, these transition words help the reader know how to follow the writer's line of thinking. Then you might leave them with the chart in front of them to reivse their work.

You also might want to reinforce the lesson about "not any cracks behind" to writers who seem to need that work. So you might gather a small group of students who are having difficulty unpacking their evidence and demonstrate continuing to reread your body paragraph, linking your evidence to your reason and claim.

When I gathered Andrew, Jessie, and Christina, I showed them how I wanted to finish revising my body paragraph on "parents teach kids important things before they start school." I started reading from where I had left off. *(continues)*

MID-WORKSHOP TEACHING   **Every Part Must Connect: Thinking Backward Between the Piece and the Introduction**

"Writers, I know you are working like the dickens to get these drafts completed! You can almost smell the productivity in this room and that's a beautiful thing. As you're approaching the finish line, I want to give you one more tip to help you make all parts of your writing feel cohesive. And that's to think about how the introduction fits with the rest of the piece. So rather than just tacking one on that just seems to follow one of the strategies you have learned, you can really think about what ideas you are discussing and bringing out in this piece. Then you can think backward between the rest of your piece and how your introduction will fit with what comes later. One way to craft a piece that feels really connected to the rest is to tell another mini-story, one that you don't tell in the body of the piece that reveals its heart. This is not easy work. Let me show you what I mean.

"Let me try to think backward between the body of my essay on 'Parents Are the Most Important Teachers for Their Children' and how it should start. First, I'll think about what ideas I am trying to really bring out and why this piece matters. So if I think about why my essay on 'Parents Are the Most Important Teachers for Their Children' truly matters, I think one reason is about the enormous responsibility parents have. They literally have their children's lives in their hands. So I might tell a story about a time when I first realized that. If I don't remember all of the details of the moment, I can imagine some of them, but I want to try to find a moment when I really realized that parents have this enormous responsibility. For me it was when I brought my first child home from the hospital. Let me try to tell this story and angle it to show the great responsibility that parents have."

(continues)

I began voicing what I would write and jotting on a clipboard.

On the first night I brought my child home from the hospital, I remember I sat rocking him to sleep, and staring at him in disbelief. He was just a tiny little baby and somehow I had to raise him to be a person in the world. How would I ever do that? How would I teach him all he needed to know? I realized at that moment the huge responsibility that I had. It would be my job to guide him and steer him and help him to become all that he was meant to be. I realized that even though he was only a few days old, my life as his teacher had already begun, and I realized in a way that I had not realized before that parents are the most important teachers for their children. Parents are the most important teachers for their children because they teach them what they need to learn before they get to school, what they need to learn outside of school, and what they cannot learn in school.

"Writers, do you see how I have really angled this moment to be about how I realized some of the big ideas that are in this essay? You could try that as well. Other writers also try to do this backward thinking work and if they don't have an exact moment that they realized some of the big ideas in the essay, they help their reader imagine a moment that gets at the heart of the essay. Sometimes they start by saying, 'Imagine you are. . . .' So right now, as you round the final bend in this essay

writing, spend some time looking backward between the ideas in your piece and your introduction and make sure your piece is completely cohesive by letting the introduction bring out some of the ideas at the heart of your piece.

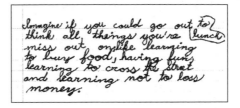

FIG. 19–3 Jonathan trying out an introduction by setting a scene for the reader to imagine

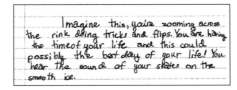

FIG. 19–4 Hannah trying out an introduction by starting out with a powerful image for the reader to envision

In addition, parents teach kids other things—like their letters and numbers—before school. For instance, my friend Natalie used to play with magnetic letters with her sons and make the sounds of the letters for fun and her sons knew all of their letters by the time they were two.

"Now I'm going to link that evidence back to the reason. Let me try another of the phrases, 'This is important because.'"

For instance, my friend Natalie used to play with magnetic letters with her sons and make the sounds of the letters for fun and her sons knew all of their letters by the time they were two. This is

important because Natalie got her sons ready to succeed in school before they got there.

"Okay, I have linked that piece of evidence to the reason that parents help kids learn what they need to succeed in school before they get there. And because I used 'this is important because. . . .' I've also linked this piece of evidence back to my overall claim that parents are their children's most important teachers. There is no other piece of evidence in that body paragraph, so I'm ready to check my next body paragraph and link the evidence."

I asked the students to get started on linking one of their pieces of evidence in front of me so I could watch and coach into what they needed as they worked.

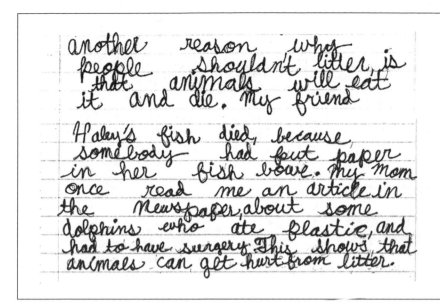

another reason why
people shouldn't litter, is
that animals will eat
it and die. My friend

Haley's fish died, because,
somebody had put paper
in her fish bowe. My Mom
once read me an article in
the Newspaper, about some
dolphins who ate plastic, and
had to have surgery. This shows that
animals can get hurt from litter.

FIG. 19–5   Jessie works to connect her evidence to her reason and thesis.

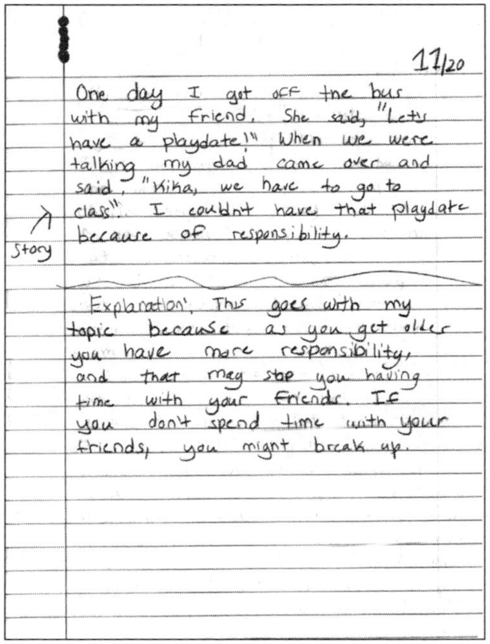

17/20

Story →

One day I got off the bus
with my friend. She said, "Let's
have a playdate!" When we were
talking my dad came over and
said, "Kika, we have to go to
class." I couldn't have that playdate
because of responsibility.

Explanation: This goes with my
topic because as you get older
you have more responsibility,
and that may stop you having
time with your friend. If
you don't spend time with your
friends, you might break up.

FIG. 19–6   Kika works to connect her mini-story to her reason and thesis.

Transferring New Learning to Previous Writing

Rally writers to transfer and apply their new learning to the essays they wrote earlier in the unit.

"Writers, can I have your eyes and attention? I want to remind you that when you learn something new, you can go back and use that learning to revise your previous writing, making it even stronger. I am definitely going to do that with my previous essays. Doing all this work to make my persuasive essay tight and focused made me start thinking back to my personal essay. I went back to reread it last night and I revised my body paragraphs to better connect my evidence to my reasons and thesis. I am going to put up my one of my paragraphs and show you the new and revised version. This is the part of the essay about how my father taught me to love work. Will you look at the old and revised versions and talk to a partner about all the ways I revised this and how it has gotten stronger? Underline and take notes in the margin as you talk to help you remember what you said."

I put up my first body paragraph from "My Father Is My Most Important Teacher" from Session 11 and a new revised version.

Original Version

<u>One reason my father is my most important teacher</u> is because he taught me to love work, <u>for example</u>, he took me sailing at the end of summer and told me he was happy vacation was ending. When I asked him why, he said, "I miss work." Seeing him so happy to go to work made me realize that work can be wonderful. <u>Another example that shows this is</u> every Christmas morning, my dad set off for the hospital carrying a waffle iron, ready to make waffles for all the doctors and patients. Dad wasn't sad to go. I asked him why he didn't send someone else and he admitted he liked going to work. "It's my hobby," he said. I wanted to grow up and find work that I loved as much as he loved his. My dad taught me to love work.

Revised Version

One reason that my father is my most important teacher is because he taught me to love work. He taught me to love work by telling me about how much he loved his work. For instance, one summer my father took me sailing and told me he was happy vacation was ending. When I asked him why, he said, "I miss work." I realized how happy work made him. I wanted to grow up and find work that made me as happy. Dad also taught me to love work by showing me how he was always excited to go. For instance, every Christmas, my dad set off for the hospital carrying a waffle iron, ready to make waffles for all the doctors and patients. Dad wasn't sad to go. I asked him why he didn't send someone else and he admitted he liked going to work. "It's my hobby," he said. By telling me about how much he loved his work and showing me how excited he was to go, Dad made me realize that I wanted to grow up and find a job that I loved the way he loved his. Now, as an adult, I love my work as much as Dad loves his. My dad taught me to love work and that is one reason why he is my most important teacher.

As the students talked, I circled the room, coaching into their conversations and giving instructive feedback as well as rephrasing their comments to help the writers better grasp the reasons behind the revisions I had made.

"Yes, that part was kind of connected to my reason but it didn't really prove that my father taught me to love work, right? But when I said 'by telling me . . . and showing me . . . ' I got the reader to see exactly *how* my father made me love work, right? It's like I took the reader's hand and led the reader to believe me.

"Right, one example is a transition but we've learned other, more sophisticated transition words so that was a place where I tried out new learning, right?

"Writers, I'm hearing you notice quite a few ways in which I revised to make sure I connected my evidence to my reasons and thesis more solidly and made this part more convincing. Tonight for homework, I'll give you a copy of my revised piece so you can use it and study it to help you revise yours. (On the CD-ROM, you can find a revised version of the "My Father Is My Most Important Teacher" essay.)

"But for right now, will you pull out your own personal essay and look at one of your body paragraphs? With a partner, will you read aloud a paragraph and decide together how to make it better? Think of all you have learned about essay writing."

Getting Ready to Put Our Opinions into the World

IN THIS SESSION, you'll teach students that writers get their essays ready for the world by carefully checking their spelling, punctuation, and other conventions.

GETTING READY

✔ Sample of your own essay with spelling errors

✔ Students' essay drafts, to be brought to the meeting area

✔ Students' editing checklists from Session 15

✔ Opinion Writing Checklist, Grades 4 and 5, on chart paper, and small copies for each student ✪

✔ Idea for where you would want to publish your persuasive essay based on the audience for your piece (see Share)

COMMON CORE STATE STANDARDS: W.4.1, W.4.5, W.4.6, RFS.4.3, RFS.4.4, SL.4.1, L.4.1, L.4.2, L.4.3

ONE OF THE GREATEST GIFTS you can give your writers is to imbue them with the sense that they should strive to produce work of the highest quality. Rather than need to have you, the teacher, pushing them to raise the level of their work and telling them how to do so, students who push themselves are more equipped to be independent and invested. Students have edited for years, for every piece they have produced across the curriculum. Today's session aims to take a different slant on the work of readying a piece for publication, helping students to see that their work will be more seriously regarded when it is readable. As we all know, the work of editing is painstaking, involving reading, rereading, and more rereading to ensure that a reader will not find a single error. Today you will support your students in feeling that sense, that need to reread one more time to make sure nothing was overlooked.

By the end of Grade 4, the Common Core State Standards expect students to "spell grade-appropriate words correctly, consulting references when needed" (L 4.2), so this lesson shines the spotlight on spelling, aiming to tackle work that is often very difficult for students (and adults), that of identifying misspellings in a piece they know well. In their book *Spelling K–8: Planning and Teaching*, Diane Snowball and Faye Bolton acknowledge this pitfall in proofreading, saying, "sometimes writers and editors become so familiar with the writing that they do not notice errors" (1999, 203). We've all had students who skip right by words that we know they could recognize if they read more carefully. Then too, you may have students who are not sure if a word is misspelled or not. Today you will place value on the need to reread carefully, puzzling over which words seem to look odd and circling even those of which you are the slightest bit unsure. In this age of computer spell-checking, locating spelling mistakes is quite a bit simpler but not without flaw. Spell-check programs miss words and wrongly identify other words as misspelled. Careful proofreading will never go out of style, and thus today's lesson is of critical importance.

Of course, you will not want students to only edit for spelling but, rather, to rely on all they have learned about conventions and transfer and apply that learning to proofread this draft. You will want to see them drawing upon the resources and tools they have used previously—the charts, the editing checklists, and so on. You will want to remind them that, as Snowball and Bolton suggest, working with a partner to proofread can also be a way to ensure that a piece is completed in as professional a manner as possible. Above all, you will want to stress that these pieces are going to be read by real readers and that ensuring they represent the students' best work *matters*. Putting value on that notion will help your students to regard it as important.

"Today's session aims to take a different slant on the work of readying a piece for publication, helping students to see that their work will be more seriously regarded when it is readable."

Then, too, getting ready to publish means reflecting on a piece with goals in mind, holding oneself accountable to checking whether or not a piece actually reflects that you worked to meet your goals. And getting ready to publish means deciding where in the world the piece will go and who will read it. Students will engage in all of that work today, pushing themselves constantly as they work to ready their pieces to go into the world.

Getting Ready to Put Our Opinions into the World

CONNECTION

Return to a metaphor from the world of baking as a way to communicate to students that professional-looking work is taken more seriously.

"Writers, I watched that cake contest show again last night. This time, on the episode, one of the bakers finished his cake and just shoved it on a plate. Then he brought the cake right into the judges without taking the time to clean up. There were drips of cake batter on the plate and a big spill of flour, and the icing on the cake was lumpy in places. When the baker put the cake in front of the judges, they all made faces like this." I indicated a very displeased look. "And no one looked excited to try it.

"Then there was this other baker who finished her cake and put it carefully on a plate and wiped all the edges of the plate, and then she picked up her spatula and smoothed down the icing on the cake again in a few places. When she brought her cake in to the judges, I noticed them all sitting up a little straighter and nodding. It was like they were taking her more seriously. They all smiled even before they started to eat. It was clear that cake had the advantage right from the start. By taking some time to make sure her cake looked professional, neat, and attractive, that baker got people to take her seriously and want to eat the cake she had made.

"And as I watched the episode, writers, I started to think about writing. Just as in baking, spending time making our writing look as professional as possible can make an audience take our writing more seriously.

"Today, you'll begin to get your essays ready to put out into the world. You have worked so hard to form brave opinions, and you want readers to consider your reasons and evidence seriously and thoughtfully and be convinced by them. You need to make sure that your work looks as professional as possible so readers will take your writing seriously right from the start."

❖ **Name the teaching point.**

"Today, I want to teach you that writers never let their work go out into the world unless it is their best. Having pride in your work means that you can stand behind any piece of writing you do and say, "I'm proud of this. This is my best work.""

Notice the return to the cake metaphor. This motif has served us well, threading through multiple sessions, and now we are drawing upon it again to help students grasp the notion that neat, professional-looking work is regarded more seriously. The image of a sloppy vs. neat cake is visual, accessible, and makes the point.

Note also the way we highlight the fact that readers will read these pieces. The notion of an audience is key, particularly in opinion writing where anticipating what an audience might say in response is work which strengthens argument building. We are slipping that concept of audience in whenever possible to make that concept foremost in students' minds.

TEACHING

Set students up to be researchers and watch while you check one of the sections of your essay for misspelled words.

"I am going to check one of the sections of my essay for misspelled words. I have lots of strategies for correcting the spelling of a word, but it is more difficult to recognize when a word is misspelled. Sometimes I have trouble recognizing whether a word is incorrect or not, so today I am going to devote a little bit of time to looking at each word and considering whether or not it looks like a word I have seen before. You be researchers and watch how I do this, and then in a minute, you'll get a chance to try this."

Demonstrate checking one of your body paragraphs for misspelled words. Deliberately model making mistakes and fixing them.

"So I am going to check the section of my essay about my reason: Parents teach kids what they cannot learn in school. Let me tell you what I am going to do to check the first sentence of this section. I'm going to read it carefully, word by word. I'll put my finger under each word and look at it and see if it looks like a word I have seen in print. If I have trouble reading it or it looks like a word I haven't seen in print or if I'm just not sure, I'll circle it. Then later I'll go back to all of my circled words and correct them. So here is the section of my essay on 'parents teach kids what they cannot learn in school.'"

> Another reason that parnts are there children's most impertent teachers is because they teach them what they can't lern in school. Parents teach there children to deal with issues. One issue that parnts teach their children to deal with is how to say goodbye. Parnts teach there children how to say goodbye to those they love whethr they are pets who have died or friends who have moved away. For example, my friend, Kim, showed her children how to say goodbye to their family bird. She dug a small grave and had her kids help her give Feathers a funnerel where they each said one thing they loved about Feathers and then said goodbye. This proves that parnts teach kids what they can't lern in school because there is no room in the school day to have funnerals or say goodbye. Parnts teach their kids what they cannot lern in school and that is another reason why they are their children's most impertent teachers.

"I'm going to check my first sentence. I'll read carefully, putting my finger under each word so I don't miss any misspelled words. If I have the slightest doubt, I'll circle the word to make sure I don't leave any misspelled words behind. You read along with me and if you see me come to a word you think is misspelled give me a polite little thumbs down." I put my finger under my first word, *another*. "Hmm, looks like a word I've seen many times. I'll keep going. 'Reason that parnts–'" I stopped and students stuck their thumbs down. "*Parnts.* Hmm, that word is supposed to be *parents*, but that word doesn't look quite right to me. It doesn't look like a word I've seen in print. Quick, let me circle it and keep going."

I put my finger back on my paper and kept reading. "'Are there–'" I stopped again. "Hmm, this word looks right, but I know that I can sometimes mix up *their*, *there*, *they're*, and other words that sound the same but are spelled differently.

Teachers, I have chosen to model proofreading my own work to place value on the importance of painstakingly reading and rereading one's own work. I understand that some may feel that showing students a sample of student work, perhaps from a previous student, might enable you to show students a piece with more authentic spelling errors, yet one of my goals is to give students the sense of caring intensely about the quality of one's own work, and thus, using a piece in which I am invested feels important. Likely, you will have noticed that I have chosen to place errors in my essay that are frequent misspellings in students' work. You will want to use your own observations of student work and assessment data to decide what kind of errors to "correct" in your own work.

So let me circle that word to be sure I can go back and give it a careful study." I circled quickly then put my finger back on the paper. "'Children's most impertent—' Hmm, that doesn't look right. I'll circle it."

Debrief quickly, pointing out the replicable steps you have taken that you want the students to follow.

"Writers, do you notice how I am checking my writing word by word, and if I'm even a little unsure, I circle the word so I can go back and check if it is correct later?"

ACTIVE ENGAGEMENT

"I'm hoping you'll help me to finish checking the rest of this part. Would you right now read the rest of this and be as hard as you can on the writing. Circle any words you are even a little unsure of. I'll do the same and then we can compare what we found."

Resume reading the piece in front of students to support those students who might need this.

I resumed reading and circled other misspelled words as I came to them.

"Another reason that (parnts) are (there) children's most (impertent) teachers is because they teach them what they can't (lern) in school. Parents teach (there) children to deal with issues. One issue that (parnts) teach their children to deal with is how to say goodbye. (Parnts) teach (there) children how to say goodbye to those they love (whethr) they are pets who have died or friends who have moved away. For example, my friend, Kim, showed her children how to say goodbye to their family bird. She dug a small grave and had her kids help her give Feathers a (funnerel) where they each said one thing they loved about Feathers and then said goodbye. This proves that (parnts) teach kids what they can't (lern) in school because there is no room in the school day to have (funnerals) or say goodbye. (Parnts) teach their kids what they cannot (lern) in school and that is another reason why they are their children's most (impertent) teachers.

Set writers up to discuss how they identified which words to circle.

"Writers, the important thing is to be able to notice when words are misspelled and to not let any words slip by you. In a minute, you will talk to a partner about how you identified the misspelled words. What strategies did you use? How did you know which words to circle? Turn and talk." The rug erupted with conversation.

"I noticed that some of the same words were misspelled a bunch of times so I kept looking for them," Christina said. "Like *parents* was wrong a lot."

"Yeah, and I circled words that were kind of hard to read in case maybe they were spelled wrong," Jessie said.

Set writers up to check the spelling in their own drafts, one word at a time.

"Writers, this is such a big deal that I want you to have a chance to check one of your essay sections for misspelled words. Right now, will you take out your draft and lay it down in front of you? Just to practice, go to your first paragraph and put your finger under the first word. Look at that word carefully. Ask yourself, 'Does this word look like a word I've seen in print?' If not, circle it. Be hard on yourself. If you are even a little unsure, circle it. Now go to the next word. Look at that word carefully. Ask yourself, 'Does this word look like a word I've seen in print?' If not, circle it. Remember to hold yourself accountable by looking carefully at each word and circling it even if you are a little unsure about it."

LINK

Send writers off to continue checking their drafts for spelling errors, in addition to the other conventions they know to check for during editing. Remind them to use their editing checklists to help them.

"Writers, you may not have finished checking your paragraph yet, but that's okay. You'll have more time to do that work today. I'm going to send you off today to get your drafts ready for publication. Before I do, I want to tell you a secret. I've seen adults look at a kid's writing, and if they see spelling mistakes, sentence fragments, or other errors, they sort of shrug and say, 'This needs a lot of help.' Even if the writing is powerful, the mistakes can interfere with how seriously readers take the piece. Let me tell you right now, that will *never* happen in this room. Readers will take your writing seriously because your essays are beautiful, powerful, *and* they will look professional. Spend every minute of today making sure your essay will be taken seriously by your readers. You don't just check for spelling when you get your piece ready to be read by others. Apply everything you know about editing and conventions to help you make your essay professional. Use your personal editing checklist, check your essay carefully for errors, and use every strategy you know to correct any mistakes you see. And today's definitely a day when you'll want to help each other. Use a partner to help you proofread and do a final read of your piece. Okay, writers, go to it!"

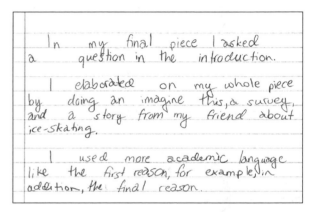

> In this essay I forgot to hook the reader in. I did write more and refer back to the main idea though.

FIG. 20–1   Andrew reflects on his final piece.

> In my final piece I asked a question in the introduction.
>
> I elaborated on my whole piece by doing an imagine this, a survey, and a story from my friend about ice-skating.
>
> I used more academic language like the first reason, for example, in addition, the final reason.

FIG. 20–2   Hannah reflects on her final essay.

Supporting Writers in Grammar and Spelling Work

AFTER YOU SEND YOUR WRITERS OFF to ready their pieces for publication, you can spend workshop time gathering groups of writers based on their grammar and spelling needs. You will want to help your writers continue to proceed along the trajectory of work in conventions that you have established. For example, you might continue the work of verbs with your students who need to learn command of various forms. For those students with whom you worked on the simple form of verbs (I walked, I walk, I will walk), you might next decide to show them progressive forms of verbs (I was walking, I am walking, I will be walking) and help students see the subtle differences in time between these. You might help students to notice that "I am walking" helps your reader to see what is happening right in the moment, as the events occurring in this verb tense are happening "now." You might demonstrate deciding a key place in your essay where you want the reader to see events occurring "now." You might model looking at your introduction and realizing that another way to pull your reader into your essay from the first line would be to tell a small anecdote relating to your opinion that shows the reader something happening in the moment. You might choose to model jotting a moment concerning you teaching your child something, showing your students that the reader is with you in this moment. "I am leaning over my son's shoulder, watching him do his math homework. He is five and this is his first time ever having to do homework," you might start a quick anecdote. Or "I am holding my newborn baby in my arms, watching him sleep. He is only five hours old, but my life as his teacher has already begun." You might coach your writers into trying their own anecdotes, encouraging them to jot a few possible moments, getting the feel for the verb tense as they do so. You can leave them to work and pull other groups, and when you return, teach into what they need, perhaps reminding them that they can transfer all of this work to other areas, like narrative writing and writing about history. Let your writers come up with their own application ideas.

For another group of writers, you may want to show them how to use the dictionary to look up words. Many students circle mistakes but have difficulty correcting these if they are not sure how the word starts and therefore are not sure how to look the word up. For these writers, you might decide you want to show them how to use computers to

MID-WORKSHOP TEACHING
Evaluate Essays against the Opinion Writing Checklist

"Writers, can I have your eyes and attention? As you are getting your piece ready for publication and making sure that readers will take it seriously, this is your final chance to make sure that your piece shows all that you have learned over the past weeks. I'm going to put our Opinion Writing Checklist back up." (This checklist can be found on the CD-ROM.) I taped the chart up next to me. "Writers, soon you will self-assess how well your essay has met these goals, and I will assess how well your essay has met these goals, but now is your chance to take a good, long hard look at these goals and raise the level of your piece so that it does meet and exceed them! Remember, you should not need to wonder whether or not your essay is good. You know what makes for effective opinion writing for fourth grade. And you know what makes for effective opinion writing in *fifth* grade. You can look at your essay and evaluate how well it meets each goal and then decide what you need to do to apply what you've learned to make your essay even better. You probably will find that you have already met the goals you have set for yourself and that you will need to set new goals. You should always be working to outgrow what you can already do and get even stronger. But we always need to make sure that your work shows all that you have learned and is your best work. I'm going to give you two minutes to talk with a partner about how you will make your essay the best essay it can be, and then I'll give you more time to work. Okay, talk to a friend."

look up the spellings of words. The ability to use a computer to find the correct spelling of a word is not a skill that should be avoided; rather, it is one that should be encouraged. I've found myself quickly typing a word into a blank document in Word and quickly getting its correct spelling, and I want to show students this work too. You might gather a group of students around a computer or a Smart Board, if you have one, and demonstrate doing just that: type a word on the screen and show students how to click on the word and look at the menu of spellings and decide on the one that looks the way you have seen that word look before. You will also want to show students, of course, how to use a print dictionary. You can show them a blown-up page from the dictionary or put a page on the document camera and get students to restate the purpose of the guide words and how to use these to look up words. You can support students in stretching out the beginning sounds of a word to jot down an educated guess for how the word might start so they have enough information to look it up in a reference tool.

You'll want to continue the work you started around conventions, checking to see that the students are applying your teaching. For any need you see, you can prepare a demonstration text that you can involve writers in helping correct, before giving them another section to try correcting (or rewriting with more independence). You might even talk to the other teachers in your grade and divvy up this work so you can all benefit. One of you writes some demonstration pieces that can help provide guided practice in correcting run-ons and sentence fragments, another can create a piece that

Opinion Writing Checklist

	Grade 4	NOT YET	STARTING TO	YES!	Grade 5	NOT YET	STARTING TO	YES!
	Structure				**Structure**			
Overall	I made a claim about a topic or a text and tried to support my reasons.	☐	☐	☐	I made a claim or thesis on a topic or text, supported it with reasons, and provided a variety of evidence for each reason.	☐	☐	☐
Lead	I wrote a few sentences to hook my readers, perhaps by asking a question, explaining why the topic mattered, telling a surprising fact, or giving background information.	☐	☐	☐	I wrote an introduction that led to a claim or thesis and got my readers to care about my opinion. I got my readers to care by not only including a cool fact or jazzy question, but also figuring out was significant in or around the topic and giving readers information about what was significant about the topic.	☐	☐	☐
	I stated my claim.				I worked to find the precise words to state my claim; I let readers know the reasons I would develop later.	☐	☐	☐
Transitions	I used words and phrases to glue parts of my piece together. I used phrases such as *for example*, *another example*, *one time*, and *for instance* to show when I was shifting from saying reasons to giving evidence and *in addition to*, *also*, and *another* to show when I wanted to make a new point.	☐	☐	☐	I used transition words and phrases to connect evidence back to my reasons using phrases such as *this shows that. . . .*	☐	☐	☐
					I helped readers follow my thinking with phrases such as *another reason* and *the most important reason*. I used phrases such as *consequently* and *because of* to show what happened.	☐	☐	☐
					I used words such as *specifically* and *in particular* in order to be more precise.	☐	☐	☐

writers can use to practice correcting for shifts in verb tense, and a third teacher might even create an inappropriately informal piece filled with plenty of phrases like: "Sit back and enjoy this essay" or "Hope you enjoyed this essay!" and involve students in rewriting a more formal version of a section. You can take all of these demonstration texts and compile them. What a valuable resource for everyone on the grade team!

Another way to conduct small-group work around proofreading is to gather a group around a partnership and have them fishbowl how they go about helping each other to locate and correct errors. Both students might be leaning over one student's draft, discussing what errors they are identifying and demonstrating how they are correcting the work. Or the students might have earlier proofread each other's drafts and they are now demonstrating how they discuss one of their pieces and correct found errors. Thus, for a few minutes you might fishbowl two writers debating over which form of *their/there/they're* one of them should use in a particular place. Or writers might

quickly help each other figure out which sentences are run-ons and correct those by reading aloud and placing ending punctuation when they pause. After watching the fishbowl, the members of the small group can break into partnerships and try out this work themselves. Again, this work would reinforce to your writers that these decisions matter, that taking the time to figure out when to use the appropriate word is important. Simply by allowing time for this and by placing value on it, you will be doing much to convey the importance of this work to students.

You can also lean on programs such as *Words Their Way* to assess the developmental spelling level of students and place them into groups that meet outside of writing workshop time. During the workshop, you can pull groups and remind them they should be using the patterns they have learned to help them spell words as they write in writing workshop. They should be holding themselves accountable for checking for and correcting the spelling of words they have learned.

Publishing Persuasive Essays

Rally writers to consider where in the world their essay belongs, choosing a place to publish their writing.

"Writers, can I have your eyes and attention? As you are wrapping up your final revisions, it is time to consider where you see this piece going in the world. This decision might actually cause you to make some more revisions, so it's important to consider this now. You're writing brave, bold opinions, and these deserve to go out into the world where the audience you have in mind will be able to read and see your work and be influenced by your thinking. The whole point of opinion writing is to persuade others, so you need to make sure that you're addressing the people who you want to take action. Remember last year you spent time thinking about the exact audience for your persuasive speech, your editorial, your letter. Remember how you asked yourself what you wanted to change and who could help you? And you spent some time at the start of this bend thinking about which audience you most wanted to convince. Now you will make sure to think about how you will reach that audience, where in the world your piece should go, and how your audience can best access your piece.

"So, I already have a sense of who I want my audience to be. I really want parents to read this and think about what an important role they play in their children's education and take that job seriously. So, I have my audience in mind.

"Hmm, okay, so the next question is 'Where in the world is the best place for this to go so that my audience can see it?' So I need to put this essay in a place where lots of parents will be able to read it. I'm going to list some places where I know lots of parents will see it and then decide if I should put my essay in one or more of those places. Let me see." I held up my fingers and listed across them. "Um, I know that lots of parents read the notices on the bulletin board by the front of the school. So, that's a possibility. But really, I want to reach parents of little, little kids, too, not just parents who already have kids in school. So, um, oh, I have an idea. I could put my essay up in a pediatrician's office. Lots of parents go there, and they have kids of all ages. Or on a parenting website or blog. Then lots of parents could read it there too. I think I'll do both of those. I'll put some essays in the pediatrician's office, and I'll also find an online blog for parents where I can publish my essay. I'll search for one tonight.

"Writers, do you see how I asked myself who my audience is for this essay and then where in the world is the best place to put this essay so my audience can see it? Now you'll try this. Right now, will you consider the audience for your piece and where in the world it belongs? Think in your mind of who you really want to read your piece and be persuaded to act or think differently." I gave them time to think. "Writers, this is something that you will probably want to talk over

Considering audience is a critical component of opinion writing and we are returning to that notion to reinforce the importance of that idea to students. In the third grade opinion writing unit, students spent multiple lessons thinking about audience and the effect their words would have and now we want to build on that work.

with a partner. You might come up with a few possibilities for audiences and a few possibilities for where your essay should go, and that's great, too. Talk to each other about your ideas and help each other.

"Each of you will need to consider who you want to read your piece and where in the world it belongs. Some of you may find that after you decide on your audience and where your essay belongs, you might need to make some changes to your essay. For example, I might decide I want to directly address my audience at times in my essay now that I know I'll be writing directly to parents. When I say, for example, 'You should realize how important you are,' I know that I'll be writing to parents. You might find you want to make some changes to consider your audience, as well. Spend the rest of the day getting your piece ready to go out into the world!"

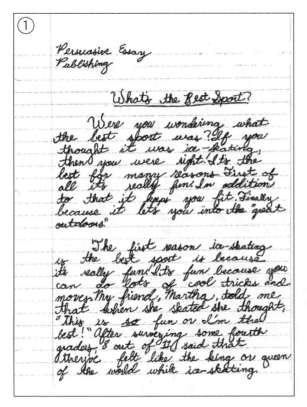

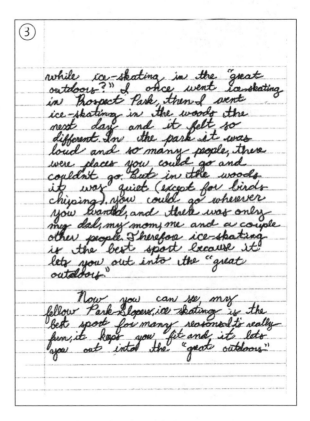

FIG. 20–3   Hannah's final draft

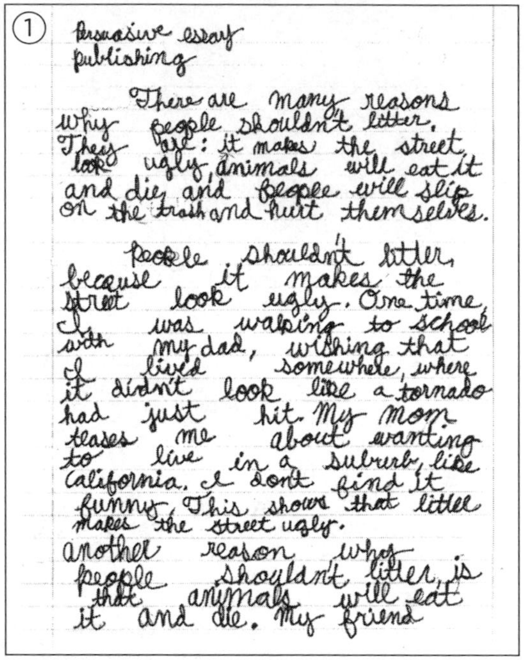

FIG. 20–4   Jessie's final piece

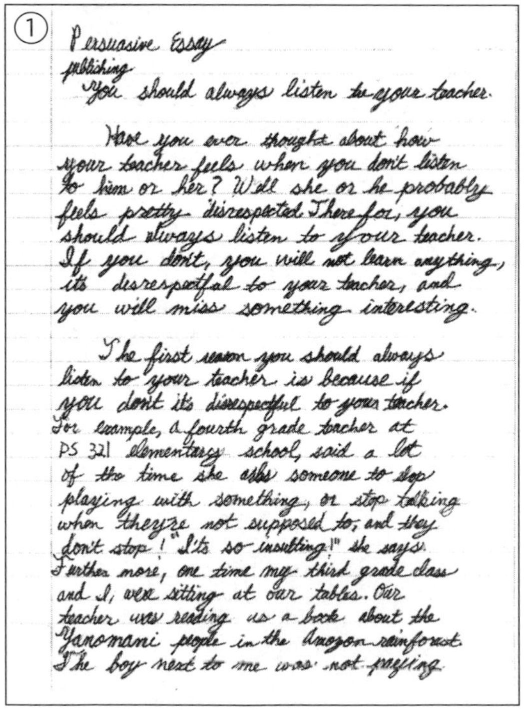

① Persuasive essay
publishing

    There are many reasons why people shouldn't litter. They are: it makes the street look ugly, animals will eat it and die, and people will slip on the trash and hurt themselves.

    People shouldn't litter, because it makes the street look ugly. One time I was walking to school with my dad, wishing that I lived somewhere, where it didn't look like a tornado had just hit. My mom teases me about wanting to live in a suburb, like California. I don't find it funny. This shows that litter makes the street ugly.

    Another reason why people shouldn't litter, is that animals will eat it and die. My friend

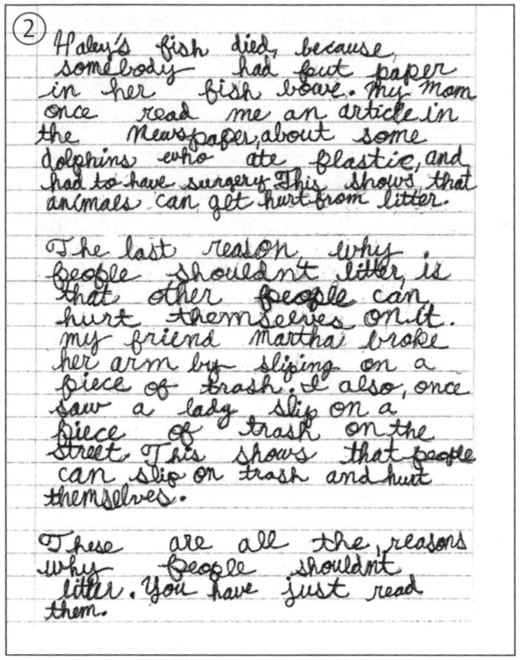

② Haley's fish died, because somebody had put paper in her fish bowl. My mom once read me an article in the Newspaper about some dolphins who ate plastic, and had to have surgery. This shows that animals can get hurt from litter.

    The last reason, why people shouldn't litter, is that other people can hurt themselves on it. My friend Martha broke her arm by sliping on a piece of trash. I also, once saw a lady slip on a piece of trash on the street. This shows that people can slip on trash and hurt themselves.

    These are all the reasons why people shouldn't litter. You have just read them.

① Persuasive Essay
publishing
You should always listen to your teacher.

    Have you ever thought about how your teacher feels when you don't listen to him or her? Well she or he probably feels pretty disrespected. Therefore, you should always listen to your teacher. If you don't, you will not learn anything, it's disrespectful to your teacher, and you will miss something interesting.

    The first reason you should always listen to your teacher is because if you don't it's disrespectful to your teacher. For example, a fourth grade teacher at PS 321 elementary school, said a lot of the time she asks someone to stop playing with something, or stop talking when they're not supposed to, and they don't stop! "It's so insulting!" she says. Furthermore, one time my third grade class and I were sitting at our tables. Our teacher was reading us a book about the Yanomani people in the Amazon rainforest. The boy next to me was not paying

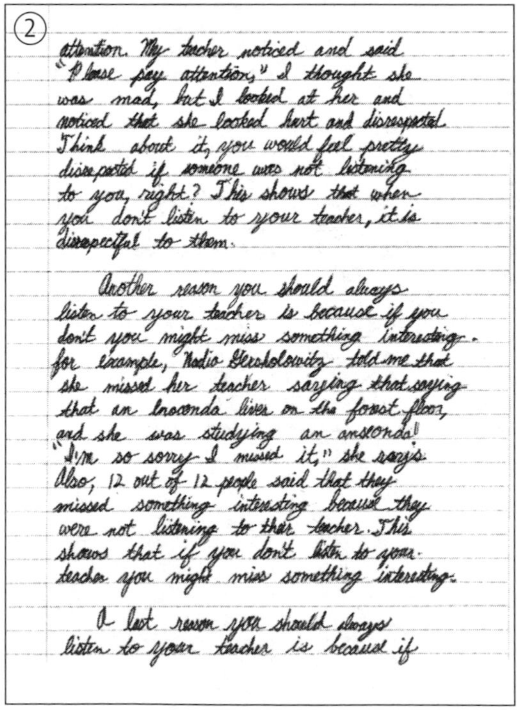

② attention. My teacher noticed and said "Please pay attention." I thought she was mad, but I looked at her and noticed that she looked hurt and disrespected. Think about it, you would feel pretty disrespected if someone was not listening to you, right? This shows that when you don't listen to your teacher, it is disrespectful to them.

    Another reason you should always listen to your teacher is because if you don't you might miss something interesting. For example, Nadia Glenholowitz told me that she missed her teacher saying that saying that an Iwaanda lives on the forest floor, and she was studying an ansonda! "I'm so sorry I missed it," she says. Also, 12 out of 12 people said that they missed something interesting because they were not listening to their teacher. This shows that if you don't listen to your teacher you might miss something interesting.

    A last reason you should always listen to your teacher is because if

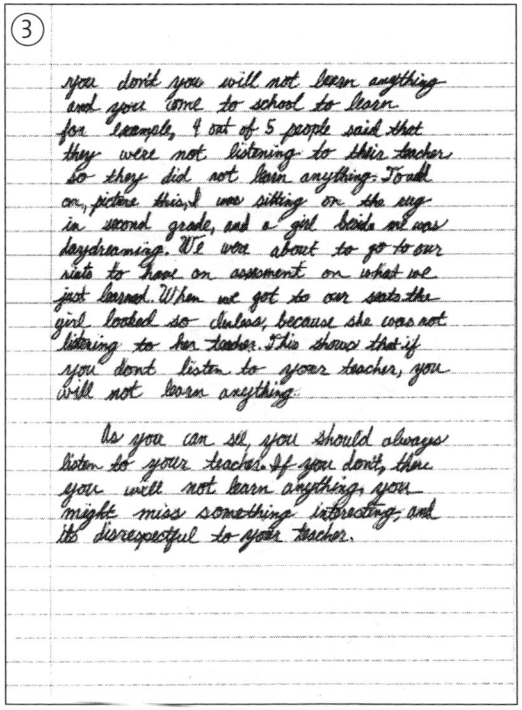

③ you don't you will not learn anything and you come to school to learn. For example, 4 out of 5 people said that they were not listening to their teacher so they did not learn anything. To add on, picture this, I was sitting on the rug in second grade, and a girl beside me was daydreaming. We were about to go to our seats to have an assessment on what we just learned. When we got to our seats the girl looked so clueless, because she was not listening to her teacher. This shows that if you don't listen to your teacher, you will not learn anything.

    As you can see, you should always listen to your teacher. If you don't, then you will not learn anything, you might miss something interesting, and it's disrespectful to your teacher.

FIG. 20–5   Emma's final piece

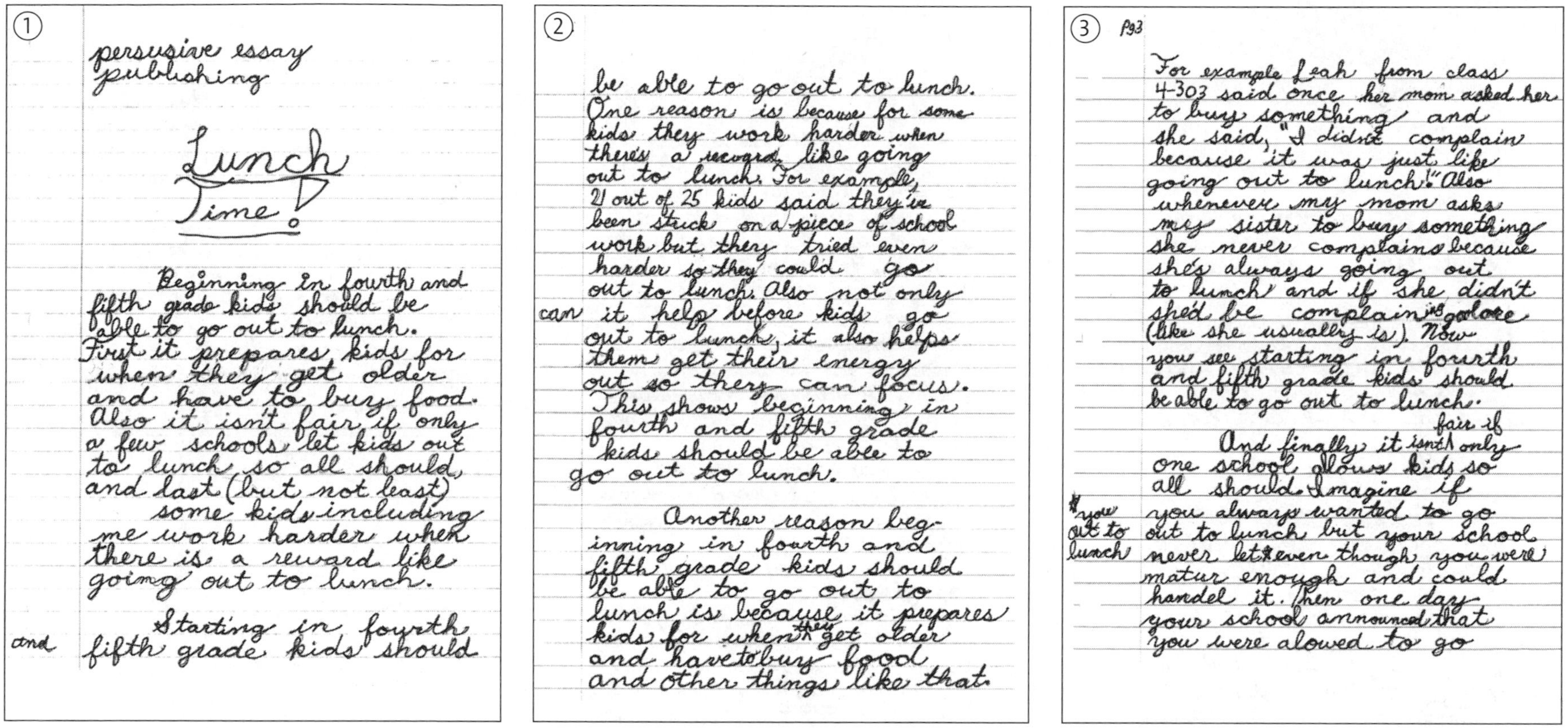

① persuasive essay
publishing

Lunch
Time!

Beginning in fourth and fifth grade kids should be able to go out to lunch. First it prepares kids for when they get older and have to buy food. Also it isn't fair if only a few schools let kids out to lunch so all should, and last (but not least) some kids including me work harder when there is a reward like going out to lunch.

Starting in fourth and fifth grade kids should

and

② be able to go out to lunch. One reason is because for some kids they work harder when there's a reward like going out to lunch. For example, 21 out of 25 kids said they've been stuck on a piece of school work but they tried even harder so they could go out to lunch. Also not only can it help before kids go out to lunch, it also helps them get their energy out so they can focus. This shows beginning in fourth and fifth grade kids should be able to go out to lunch.

Another reason beginning in fourth and fifth grade kids should be able to go out to lunch is because it prepares kids for when they get older and have to buy food and other things like that.

③ p93

For example Leah from class 4-303 said once her mom asked her to buy something and she said, "I didn't complain because it was just like going out to lunch." Also whenever my mom asks my sister to buy something she never complains because she's always going out to lunch and if she didn't she'd be complaining galore (like she usually is). Now you see starting in fourth and fifth grade kids should be able to go out to lunch.

And finally it isn't fair if only one school allows kids so all should. Imagine if you always wanted to go out to lunch but your school never let even though you were matur enough and could handel it. Then one day your school announced that you were alowed to go

you
out to
lunch

FIG. 20–6   Jonathan's final piece (The full draft can be found on the CD-ROM.)

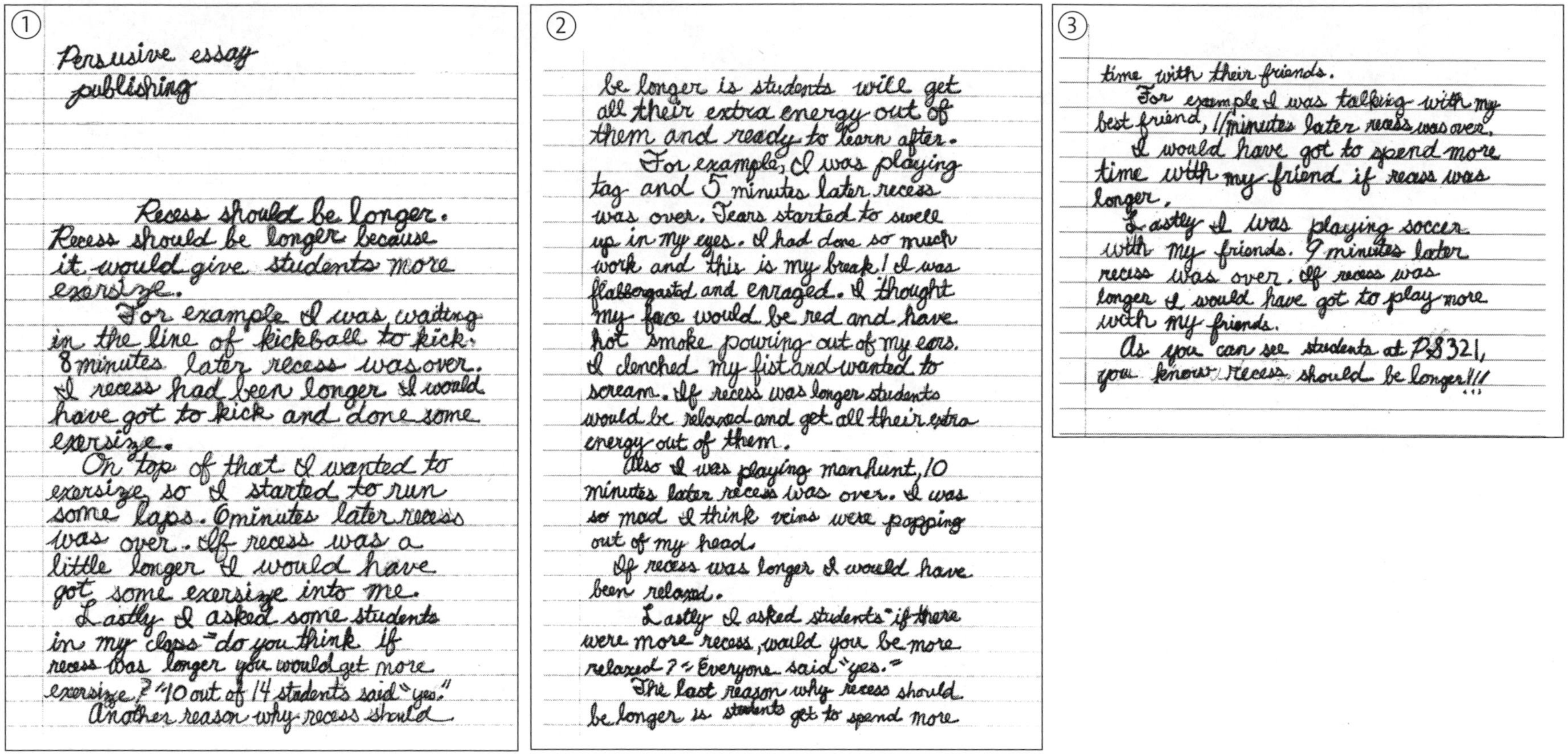

①

Persusive essay
publishing

      Recess should be longer.
Recess should be longer because
it would give students more
exersize.
      For example I was waiting
in the line of kickball to kick.
8 minutes later recess was over.
If recess had been longer I would
have got to kick and done some
exersize.
      On top of that I wanted to
exersize so I started to run
some laps. 6 minutes later recess
was over. If recess was a
little longer I would have
got some exersize into me.
      Lastly I asked some students
in my class "do you think if
recess was longer you would get more
exersize?" "10 out of 14 students said "yes."
      Another reason why recess should

②

be longer is students will get
all their extra energy out of
them and ready to learn after.
      For example, I was playing
tag and 5 minutes later recess
was over. Tears started to swell
up in my eyes. I had done so much
work and this is my break! I was
flabbergasted and enraged. I thought
my face would be red and have
hot smoke powring out of my ears.
I clenched my fist and wanted to
scream. If recess was longer students
would be relaxed and get all their extra
energy out of them.
      Also I was playing manhunt, 10
minutes later recess was over. I was
so mad I think veins were popping
out of my head.
      If recess was longer I would have
been relaxed.
      Lastly I asked students "if there
were more recess, would you be more
relaxed?" "Everyone said "yes."
      The last reason why recess should
be longer is students get to spend more

③

time with their friends.
      For example I was talking with my
best friend, 11 minutes later reass was over.
      I would have got to spend more
time with my friend if reass was
longer.
      Lastly I was playing soccer
with my friends. 9 minutes later
recess was over. If recess was
longer I would have got to play more
with my friends.
      As you can see students at PS321,
you know recess should be longer!!!

FIG. 20–7 Andrew's final piece

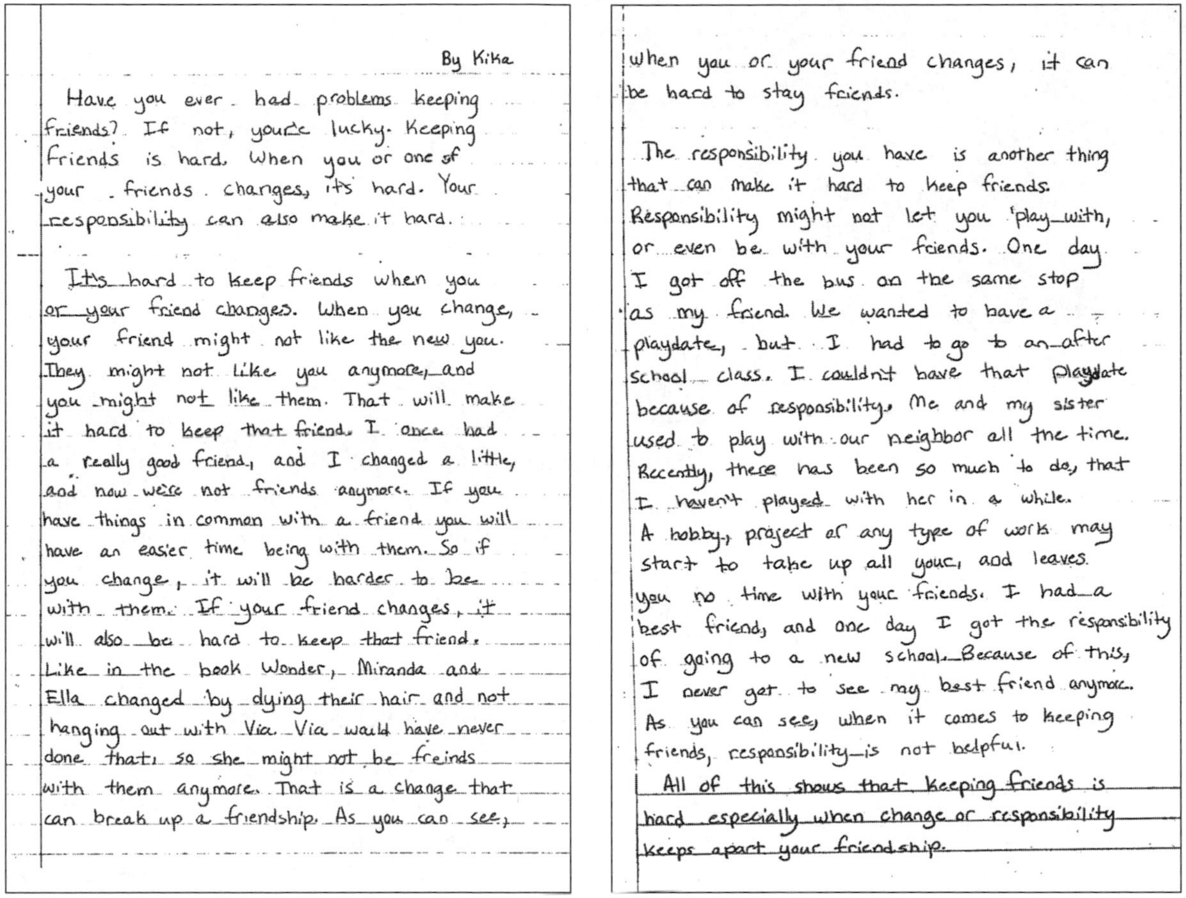

By Kika

Have you ever had problems keeping friends? If not, you're lucky. Keeping friends is hard. When you or one of your friends changes, it's hard. Your responsibility can also make it hard.

It's hard to keep friends when you or your friend changes. When you change, your friend might not like the new you. They might not like you anymore, and you might not like them. That will make it hard to keep that friend. I once had a really good friend, and I changed a little, and now we're not friends anymore. If you have things in common with a friend you will have an easier time being with them. So if you change, it will be harder to be with them. If your friend changes, it will also be hard to keep that friend. Like in the book Wonder, Miranda and Ella changed by dying their hair and not hanging out with Via. Via would have never done that, so she might not be freinds with them anymore. That is a change that can break up a friendship. As you can see,

when you or your friend changes, it can be hard to stay friends.

The responsibility you have is another thing that can make it hard to keep friends. Responsibility might not let you play with, or even be with your friends. One day I got off the bus on the same stop as my friend. We wanted to have a playdate, but I had to go to an after school class. I couldn't have that playdate because of responsibility. Me and my sister used to play with our neighbor all the time. Recently, there has been so much to do, that I haven't played with her in a while. A hobby, project or any type of work may start to take up all your, and leaves you no time with your friends. I had a best friend, and one day I got the responsibility of going to a new school. Because of this, I never get to see my best friend anymore. As you can see, when it comes to keeping friends, responsibility is not helpful.

All of this shows that keeping friends is hard especially when change or responsibility keeps apart your friendship.

FIG. 20–8   Kika's final piece

Hey World, Listen Up!

Sharing Our Opinions Loudly and Proudly

Dear Teachers,

Today is the day for which your students have been waiting for weeks, and in this letter we will offer suggestions for how to celebrate! Today is the day that the students find that their words do not fall on deaf ears but become like rain, watering soil that in turn supports new growth. Today is the day that students come to see that persuasive writing can matter and that they can ask the world to Listen Up!

PREPARING FOR THE CELEBRATION

As each child has chosen where to publish in the world, you could support children putting their essays where their chosen audience can view them (e.g., an essay on recycling posted on the wall in each classroom above the recycling bin, an essay against bullying read to the cafeteria for all lunch shifts one day, an essay on parents as their children's most important teachers posted on the wall in a pediatrician's office, and so on).

In addition to this, as the students have been writing persuasively and considering how best to put their ideas into the world, we are suggesting that the celebration incorporate digital media. There are many forms of digital media available to help your students reach a wider audience. Henry Jenkins et al. assert that the world is changing into a "participatory culture" (*Confronting the Challenges of Participatory Culture*, 2006), and to help students understand how to navigate that culture, we need to teach them about the tools.

Blogging is one such form. You could choose to register at a blog creation website and create a class blog where you post each child's essay and send a letter (or email) home, inviting others to comment. You might even extend that initial setup and connect the work students have posted in the physical world with their digitally posted work by taking photos of where each student's piece has gone in the world and posting these pictures along with the essays on the blog.

Each class in the school, for a few days, might be given time to read the work of your students and comment on their posts. In only a few day's time, a large number of responses can be gathered. Some of those who comment will respond not just to the essays but also to previous comments and thus, each essay can inspire the start of a conversation, one that lives and breathes and continues to evolve.

Yet the work of the unit will extend far beyond this one day's celebration. Your writers can take all they have learned about developing and crafting essays and transfer and apply that work across the curriculum. So, for example, they might flash-draft quick essays about the class read-aloud or in their book clubs. And they might use methods for developing thesis statements in the content areas. This unit has been a journey of thought and your writers can use everything they know to think, to explore, and to defend ideas in all areas of their learning.

CELEBRATION

Today's celebration, then, might take place in a computer room where parents can scroll down screens and join in the conversations around their children's work. Or the start of the celebration might take place on a Smart Board, where the entire gathering can view and read full-screen versions of a few of the posts while their authors read these aloud. You will want to honor not just the final published piece, but also the entire journey. So you might help each writer set up a display of his or her progress across the units, from on-demand to persuasive essay. You can set writers up to talk about their journeys, pointing out to visitors how they have grown. Writers can lay out the display of their work to show their growth and use Post-its and index cards to note ways they have gotten stronger between the pieces.

When all are gathered, you might begin by saying, "There is a quote that I love by a writer named Ursula LeGuin, and it goes like this, 'It is good to have an end to journey toward; but it is the journey that matters, in the end.' Writers, I tell you this because journeys matter. They create memories . . . they take us to far-away places. And the journeys that matter most may not be the ones that take us to far-away places, but instead the ones that take us to new understandings. They are journeys of thought, journeys that help us understand our own lives—and the world—in a new way."

Then you can let writers know that you are saying this because all of the writers in the classroom, along with you, their teacher, have been on a journey together and alone—and it has taken you inside your notebooks and drafts. Today is an end of sorts, and you have reached where you were headed. But like LeGuin says, we must always remember that it is the journey that matters most, as today's celebration will show all who have come on this journey.

Then you can set writers up behind all of their work, ready to talk through their journeys and read snippets of their work to everyone who stops by. Have half the class ready to share first, while the other half tours, and then switch halfway through. Provide comment sheets for visitors to record thoughts on this incredible process.

Here's to celebrating opinions!

Lucy, Cory, and Kelly

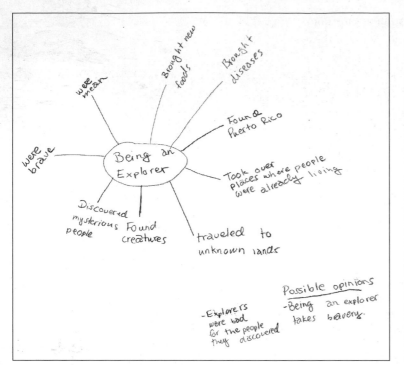

Picture this, a buzy town full of people. Everyone is living their own lives. Then strange people show up and everything changes! Now people are sick from the visitors diseases. The visitors are bossing everyone around and taking things. People who don't listen to the visitors are punished. Explorers were bad for the people they discovered.

FIG. 21–1   Hannah prepares for a content-area essay by using the strategies she learned in personal/persuasive essay writing.

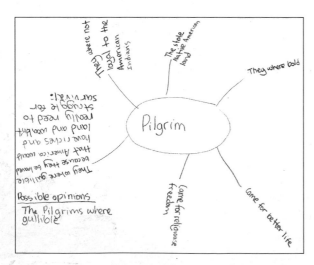

FIG. 21–2   Andrew's mosaic for his content-area essay